WRITING A
DRAMA

CW00802242

Tim Crook

Routledge
Taylor & Francis Group

LONDON AND NEW YORK

Cover image: © Getty Images/JuShoot

First published 2023
by Routledge
4 Park Square, Milton Park, Abingdon, Oxon OX14 4RN

and by Routledge
605 Third Avenue, New York, NY 10158

Routledge is an imprint of the Taylor & Francis Group, an informa business

© 2023 Tim Crook

British Library Cataloguing-in-Publication Data
A catalogue record for this book is available from the British Library

ISBN: 978-0-415-57075-6 (hbk)
ISBN: 978-0-415-57077-0 (pbk)
ISBN: 978-0-203-83818-1 (ebk)

DOI: 10.4324/9780203838181

Typeset in Bembo
by SPi Technologies India Pvt Ltd (Straive)

Access the Support Material: https://kulturapress.com/writing-audio-drama/

CONTENTS

ABOUT THE AUTHOR

Professor Tim Crook PhD is an author, playwright, journalist, and academic who pioneered British independent production in audio drama in the 1980s and 1990s with UK co-productions with NPR in the USA, and new writing festivals and competitions. He has secured multiple national and international awards for his writing, direction, production, and sound design. He originated audio drama teaching at Goldsmiths, University of London, and taught the specialist sound storytelling course for 30 years. He has written influential books and chapters on radio drama history and practice. These include Radio Drama Theory & Practice (1999), The Sound Handbook (2013), and Audio Drama Modernism: The Missing Link between Descriptive Phonograph Sketches and Microphone Plays on the Radio (2020). He investigates the past to discover and create new insights informing the present art of audio drama on the radio and in online podcasting.

PREFACE

This book is the result of a passion and commitment to the art of audio/radio drama which I have had since I was able to start listening to the radio as a child. I have had the privilege of working professionally in radio and indeed in the audio/radio drama field and the further privilege of teaching sound drama writing at Goldsmiths, University of London, for 30 years.

I would like to pay a special tribute to my longstanding friend Richard Shannon with whom I embarked on the wonderful journey into professional radio drama; my wife and partner Marja Giejgo who joined that journey and pioneered online and digital innovation; producers and editors at LBC in London who gave us the green light to produce and broadcast that innovation to radio listeners; to the BBC for inspiration and unrivalled contribution and development of the art of sound drama; Professor Julian Henriques who supported the formalising of my Sound Storytelling course at Goldsmiths, University of London; and, of course, to all the brilliant writers, actors, sound designers, students, and fellow directors and producers I have truly cherished working with and learning from. There is also a special dedication to National Public Radio and the American people who recognised, commissioned, and rewarded us so generously and enthusiastically.

Such privileges need to be earned or at least repaid. So in this text I have tried to draw on decades of studying, writing, making, and listening to sound drama in as many forms, formats, places, languages, and situations as I have been able to and to offer ideas, analysis, and summarise concepts of good practice in the art of writing sound drama.

I am not sure I am saying anything that has not been said before. But I am certainly reporting and interpreting the rich legacy of thinking, talking, and writing about the art and craft. The experimentalists and explorers created beautifully in the 1920s and 1930s in Great Britain and the USA and elsewhere and wrote about it. They carried on doing so throughout the 20th century and in the 21st century they have continued to do so and are now riding the crest of a new wave of prosperous and diverse sources of funding, huge new global online audiences through podcasting, and the blossoming of new generations of creative writers and producers who are originating and finding new imaginative ways of telling stories in sound. They used to call the 1940s and 1950s 'the golden age of radio drama'. Perhaps at the time of writing we are now experiencing the platinum age of audio drama with so many of the possibilities and potential of online origination, monetisation, and distribution being realised. The writer and sound drama producer Ella Watts produced a significant research report in late 2018 for BBC Sounds identifying what audio-dramatist and author on podcast writing Barry M. Putt, Jr. has described as the new frontier. Many of my former students at Goldsmiths, including Lance Dann, Ella Watts, Andy Goddard, and John Wakefield are among the pioneers creating in this new frontier with exceptional talent, innovation, and achievement.

Sound drama scholarship and teaching is also thriving. In recent years I have been fortunate enough to examine PhD researchers who have been ground-breaking and magisterial in the depth, quality, and approach to the critical appreciation of this unique dramatic artform. The leading academic publishers have been bringing out new titles with Neil Verma's *Theater of the Mind: Imagination, Aesthetics, and American Radio Drama* (2012), Leslie McMurtry's *Revolution in the echo chamber: Audio drama's past, present, and future* (2019), Hugh Chignell's *British Radio Drama, 1945–63* (2019), and the edited volume by Lars Bernaerts and Jarmila Mildorf *Audionarratology: Lessons from Radio Drama* (2021) being just a few notable examples. The online academic journal *RadioDoc Review* now has a radio drama section with McMurtry in its inaugural publication declaring:

> We make a case for the necessity, the pleasure, and the provocation of radio drama by arguing that it is important for its accessibility, the way it uses imagination, and its sense of intimacy. We note the current state of academic study on radio drama and provide the reasons and history behind the founding of the Echo Salon Audio Drama Listening Group.
>
> *(McMurtry, 2021)*

I apologise if some degree of immodesty permits me to mention the publication of my monograph by Palgrave Macmillan in 2020 *Audio Drama Modernism The Missing Link between Descriptive Phonograph Sketches and Microphone Plays on the Radio* which was the result of 30 years of research into the work of sound dramatists in the pre-radio age, perhaps what can be properly described as the first recorded audio drama age, and the links with developing the radio play in early sound broadcasting. New research published for the companion website page on the BBC's first original radio playwright, Phyllis M. Twigg, reveals that the characters, world and style of her Christmas Eve 1922 play *The Truth About Father Christmas As Told By The Fairy Dustman* had been produced with six sketches and songs for the London Gramophone Company and released on three 78 rpm phonograph records in the same year. Perhaps it can be said the early sound podcasting informed and influenced the creation of Britain's first broadcast original radio drama.

It is good to connect the present with the past. We can read what the pioneers said and imagine how what they wrote sounded, and indeed for those whose productions survive through archiving to hear again what they did, and to talk about it. My text is biased towards the English speaking tradition of audio/radio drama because I am not fluent and expert enough in other languages and cultures.

The philosophy of this book, as is my 'teaching' of the subject, is that I would not presume to tell, pontificate, and lecture any writer on how to write in one particular way or another. It would not be a good idea to be prescriptive, or even worse proscriptive. That is something writers know themselves because in the end they can only learn how to do it themselves and that's always the hard way.

The creative discipline of writing is demanding, exhausting, sometimes lonely, and most of the time a marathon of imaginative effort and emotional application. Those that do it know it is an extremely hard and sometimes isolated calling.

Writers do their best to pick up some good ideas along the way. And at the same time they learn what to reject, ignore, and partly use for their benefit and purpose. It is something the writer Alan Plater explained to me when sitting in the control room of a radio studio when I was directing new plays by new writers; something he enjoyed encouraging.

I think writers are entitled to be insecure, selfish, thieving as Robin Hoods in terms of taking the good to give back to the deserving, plagiaristic in a creative way in terms of using with respect what has worked so well in the past and to give their own spin, and I describe these tendencies with affection rather than moral condemnation.

As a result 'dramaturgists', the rather grand-sounding name for script experts who guide and encourage authors/writers to develop their scripts for production in the dramatic arts are inevitably heroic and long-suffering. They may get little thanks. Some of their 'students', who then go on to greater success, may be loath to say they owed their 'tutors' anything. Others are generous enough to acknowledge and remember. Perhaps the best thing that could be said for writing 'teachers' or 'dramaturgists' is that they did not get in the way of genius. Little ripples can turn into waves. A little spark of inspiration can ignite a furnace of talent.

Podcasting has become a big part of what is being described as the revolution, renaissance, and revival of sound drama and 'audio fiction'. Drama at the BBC is not simply a matter of being part of the schedule of BBC Radio 4, 3, or 4 Extra national radio networks. It is 'BBC Sounds' travelling out in exponential arenas of reception in the digital and online media sphere. It could be argued that Amazon's Audible, the world's largest producer of digital audiobooks, has become the sound equivalent of Hollywood for investment and production of sound storytelling.

The new generations of sound story tellers are awe-inspiring in the quality, ingenuity, and originality of their work and as a result there are newer and younger audiences and wider and different economic models and opportunities to fund new production. Many of these developments are now being reviewed, reported on, and discussed in the BBC Radio 4 Extra programme *Podcast Radio Hour*. Chris Pearson, Ella Watts, and Amanda Litherland have presented special editions focusing on

'Sci-Fi Audio Drama', 'Myths, Legends and Fairy Tales in Audio Drama', 'Audio Drama spin-offs', 'Podcasts that go bump in the night', 'Neil Gaiman and Audio Fiction', and 'British Audio Fiction'.

Radio drama started with a lot of improvisation and very quick learning. The first BBC practitioners had to create and produce without any blueprints or models on how to do these things in front of microphones and to reach the ears and minds of listeners. And it had to be good from the beginning. What followed later was enhancement, improvement, development in a socially and culturally evolving context, and somewhat amusingly repeating the mistakes of the past and false-consciously recognising as original what was originated in the past. The art also changes for technological reasons. There are new horizons and opportunities. Media forms morph, merge, bifurcate, retreat, and complement or substitute each other.

In the research for this book, I have been assisted enormously with past publication of audio drama scripts and the availability of historical radio drama scripts broadcast by the BBC and retained by the BBC Written Archives. It may be the case that fewer scripts are being published. The BBC sponsored annual publication of the Giles Cooper award-winning plays between 1978 and 1992. BBC support for audio script publications most probably rises and falls with the fortunes of funding support for public sector broadcasting. These have been an invaluable reference point enabling me to study Caryl Phillips' first play for radio *The Wasted Years* (1984), Nigel D. Moffatt's *Lifetime* (1987), and, of course, Anthony Minghella's *Cigarettes and Chocolate* (1988). The US publication in 1945 edited by Erik Barnouw *Radio Drama in Action: 25 plays of a changing World* provided an invaluable access to scripts challenging genocide, racism and discrimination all over the world, including *The Battle of the Warsaw Ghetto* by Morton Wishengrad, *Open Letter On Race Hatred* by William N. Robson, *Japanese-Americans* by Harry Kleiner, *The Negro Domestic* by Roi Ottley, and *Booker T. Washington In Atlanta* by Langston Hughes. These are plays which enlighten, give voice to the voiceless, educate and remain testaments to the fact that audio drama is as impactful and culturally significant as any other dramatic medium of expression. Langston Hughes' script was commissioned, but racism in the USA meant it was never produced. BBC producer D.G. Bridson did, however, commission and co-write with Langston Hughes the play *The Man Who Went to War* which was broadcast from New York to Britain by shortwave only in 1945 to an audience of 10 million listeners (Bridson, 1971, pp. 109–11). It was not heard in America. Wishengrad's play on the heroic resistance to Hitler's Final Solution in Poland was produced and widely discussed in the USA, but never broadcast in Britain.

But BBC Radio was the first mainstream broadcast media platform to tell the appalling story of the discrimination and degradation directed towards Nigerian immigrant David Oluwale who was hounded to his death in the River Aire in 1969 after arriving in Britain 20 years before. Jeremy Sandford's play *Oluwale* was specially commissioned by BBC Radio Brighton in association with the 1972 Brighton Festival and broadcast by BBC Radio 3 in 1972 and 1973. The BBC published the winning scripts in its 1988 Young Playwrights' Festival, and these included

Hurricane Dub by Benjamin Zephaniah and *Ragamuffin* by Ann Ogidi. Much more can be done to publish audio drama scripts. Perhaps greater engagement with audio drama at all levels of the education system could enhance demand. I have certainly been encouraged to discover that the elegant radio playwright Stephen Wyatt has been making some of his scripts, including the award-winning *Memorials to the Missing* (2007–8), available through Amazon publication.

I make references to and analysis of existing models and iconic representations of successful and 'award-winning' texts for the purposes of educational criticism and review. The companion website assists with links and sources where these texts may still be found and any existing sound archive of their productions. Where necessary I have connected the how to approach with historical enquiry and research into sound drama, but I have also done my best to avoid too much wearing of the academic jacket.

The online companion resources are not specifically integrative to the book text. They are there to enhance and take the reader on further journeys of discovery and reflection.

The bibliography has focused on published texts, and the companion website also tries to be an 'audiography' of sound play listening.

Links on the Internet are notoriously ephemeral and major publishers, broadcasters, and corporations tend to delete and change online addresses. I have tried to place as much of the universal and permanent into the printed text and leave the more unstable material and subjects requiring regular updating online.

Audio/radio drama was not and has never been a Cinderella dimension of the dramatic arts/professions. Some early practitioners only said that through self-deprecation, modesty, and the understandable fear and apprehension of those who have to invent a new art form and make it work. Everything that follows has been written to foster creating in this wonderful medium. Write well and have fun.

Companion Website Resources

Radio and Audio Drama Academic studies https://kulturapress.com/2022/08/29/radio-and-audio-drama-academic-studies/

Podcasting and Audio Drama https://kulturapress.com/2022/08/30/podcast-and-audio-drama/

BBC Radio Drama History https://kulturapress.com/2022/08/30/bbc-radio-drama-history/

1

RADIO DRAMA IS BORN AND IS IN ITS CRADLE

The Medium of Almost Unlimited Possibilities

The BBC's Radio Drama Department used to send out a photocopied eight-page guide 'Writing Plays For Radio' and explained with so much enthusiasm that 'Radio is an extraordinary medium' because it works on the principle that 'anything which can be described can be imagined'. They were trying to get across the idea that a radio play can traverse centuries in time and continents in geography. Film producers with limited budgets would have to think twice about the merits of running the story in terms of aeroplanes, ships, and exotic locations, but in radio since all this takes place in the confines of a single mind, the possibilities are indeed unlimited.

The word imagination is repeated over and over again in audio drama teaching. It is why Angela Carter said:

> [A]s with all forms of storytelling that are composed in words, not in visual images, radio always leaves that magical and enigmatic margin, that space of the invisible, which must be filled in by the imagination of the listener.
> *(Carter, 1985, p. 7)*

She also talked about sound drama's mythological and spiritual qualities rooted in oral cultures going back thousands of years: 'Indeed, radio retains the atavistic lure, the atavistic power, of voices in the dark, and the writer who gives the words to those voices retains some of the authority of the most antique tellers of tales' (Carter, 1985, p. 13).

My starting point is that unequivocally audio/radio drama is a beautiful and poetic medium. It is hugely creative with the limitless imaginative horizons talked about by the BBC in times gone past. It is deeply psychological and intimate, has

DOI: 10.4324/9780203838181-1

huge logistical advantages in being economical and realisable with modest resources, and gives the writer the power to fashion stories that are emotional, truthful, and thought-provoking. Radio and sound is an enduring medium, and rumours of its decline, eventual death, and replacement have always been wrong. I will use the terms radio drama and audio drama interchangeably and randomly throughout. Obviously some sound dramas are distributed in podcast form and online only. Others are produced for broadcast by radio stations. There is also another term in use – audio fiction – and it is argued that this encompasses the multiple dimensionalities of storytelling techniques, style, and genres that arise from the boom in Internet and online sound storytelling cultures.

I have decided to give the book the title 'audio drama' because it will be discussing how to write dramatic stories in the sound medium. My book *Audio Drama Modernism: The Missing Link between Descriptive Phonograph Sketches and Microphone Plays on the Radio*, published in 2020, sought to demonstrate that recorded storytelling in the sound medium clearly predated radio broadcasting, and there was certainly a mutually beneficial synergy between the practices in making sound plays for the phonograph and producing microphone plays in the early years of radio.

The first book ever to be published on the craft of radio drama writing was published in 1926 and written by a regional director of plays for the BBC at Newcastle upon Tyne. Gordon Lea produced a landmark and early chapters and the companion website resource reference much of the detail. To begin with I wanted to draw out and emphasise almost six key luminescent points he made. He explained that writing sound drama was very much about regulating and playing with human consciousness. He said writing and creating a radio play was about orchestrating the human voices of the players coming out of a canvas of silence. He said they were like jewels against a background of black velvet. He talked about the medium of the human voice as a mental pageantry of colour and delight which no artist in the world can emulate. He devoted an entire chapter to the listener's part, indeed participation in creating and being inside the world of the play. Listeners are in direct touch with the players inside this imaginative spectacle of human consciousness. There is no intervening convention – no barrier. Soul speaks to soul. He explained that there were two fundamental styles of structure to audio-dramatic writing. One was to deploy the narrator method and the other he described as the 'self-contained method'. This could be explained as the difference between telling and showing; a mantra so regularly articulated by creative writing teachers. Gordon Lea was so excited and even poetic about what can be achieved as a radio drama writer. He said if writers wish to set their plays in the heart of a buttercup, the imagination of the listener will provide the setting.

The BBC did not miss a trick with the poetic resonances in selection and production of radio plays. 'The Butterfly That Stamped' rings like the title of a drama specially written for the sound medium, but it is in fact an adaptation of the Rudyard Kipling story 'Just-So' adapted and produced by Maurice Brown for Boxing Day 1939. The then head of BBC Radio Drama Val Gielgud performed the role of the narrator storyteller.

The Problem with Stereotypes

The history of broadcasting and radio drama has uncomfortable and racist resonances in the past for on the very same page of the *Radio Times* promoting the butterfly play; there is a huge illustration of blacked-up minstrelling white men dancing and singing. This was advertising the Christmas Party of the BBC's then long-running vaudeville programme 'The Kentucky Minstrels' which ran for over 100 episodes between 1933 and 1950. At least four *Radio Times* entries for the series in 1933 used the deeply offensive 'n' word in the promotional blurb openly describing it as 'A N.***** Minstrel Show' (Anon, 1933, p. 852). At the time Dr. Harold Moody and the League for Coloured Peoples in London along with the League's magazine *Link* had been campaigning against the use of such demeaning and abusive language in the public sphere, and they played a key role in ending the use of the word in BBC continuity, presentation and content (Fryer, 1984, pp. 331–332). The most frequent comic entertainers appearing in the series were the African-Americans Harry Clifford Scott and Edward Peter Whaley who performed the characters Pussyfoot and Cuthbert. This compares with the racial-cultural trope of the most successful sitcom in US radio drama history being 'Amos "n" Andy' created and performed by two white Southern Americans, Freeman Gosden and Charles Correll. Their writing and acting of the minstrel style African-American protagonists Amos Jones (Gosden) and Andrew Hogg Brown (Correll) would make them millionaires and provoke a powerful campaign by Black American civil rights organisations to challenge the perpetuation of the tradition of derogatory racial stereotyping. The series ran from 1928 to 1960. Live short-wave relays of 'Amos "n" Andy' episodes were broadcast by NBC USA to the BBC from New Year's Eve in 1930 and through the early 1930s.

The *Radio Times* described the broadcast as 'something of an event. These pretended negroes, who broadcast daily in the interests of a powerful toothpaste corporation, are the single most popular item in the American programmes' (Anon, 1930, p. 655). The article suggested hearing it 'will be a step nearer to solving the great riddle of those United States' (Anon, 1930). It even revealed that plans were being discussed to produce a British equivalent through the impersonation of a Jewish family. Anti-Semitic language and characterisation have persisted in all forms of broadcasting and drama and even the progressive *Royal Court* theatre in London had to apologise and reflect on this in recent years. Morton Wishengrad's *The Battle of the Warsaw Ghetto* was first broadcast by the US NBC network on the eve of the Day of Atonement in 1943, barely a few months after the German Nazi regime's Final Solution had liquidated the Warsaw Ghetto and murdered millions in death camps such as Treblinka and Auschwitz. Three productions and broadcasts of Wishengrad's dramatisation of the heroic defence by young Jewish fighters drew over 12,000 letters of appreciation to the Network. The US War Department sent transcriptions overseas to be played on troop stations in all war theatres. The script was performed in hundreds of schools and colleges across the USA (Barnouw, 1945, p. 33). Yet it was never heard on the BBC and has never been fully broadcast in Britain. Close scrutiny of the BBC's archives reveals that senior executives deliberately suppressed programming about the developing Holocaust against European Jewry. One scribbled on a document: 'If you give Jewish broadcasters an inch, they come clamouring for a mile' (Crook, 1997, p. 199). The racism against African-Americans in the USA means Langston Hughes' commissioned radio play *Booker T Washington in Atlanta* was published as a script in 1945 but never produced for broadcast transmission.

Contemporary dramatists in any medium need to be sensitive and cautious about the risk of derogatory and stereotypical words and concepts slipping into characterisation and language through unconscious bias and cultural conditioning. It can certainly be argued that the repeated use of the 'n' word in Lawrence du Garde Peach's 1929 radio play *Ingredient X* could have been considered problematic even for its time (du Garde Peach, 1931, pp. 180–217). The humiliating and dehumanising depiction of Africans when given to the language of racist European colonialists means that this text is not appropriate for workshop teaching. This is despite being a progressive model for using long-form audio drama storytelling in the self-contained method of short scenes switching between dramatic action in storm at sea, plotting in the capitalist world of a City of London boardroom, and rebellion and conflict in an African colony.

The television version of 'Amos "n" Andy', though this time performed by African-American actors, was broadcast by the BBC during the 1950s. It was at the end of this decade in 1958 that BBC Television inaugurated the 'Black and White Minstrel Show' which ran for 20 years until 1978 and like 'Amos "n" Andy' in the USA faced criticism and campaigning for its cancellation by the Campaign Against Racial Discrimination. In an echo of the ambiguity experience for Scott and Whaley's participation in the Kentucky Minstrels, the teenage Sir Lenny Henry became the first black performer to appear in the show in 1975. His regret in being contractually obliged to appear caused him a 'wormhole of depression'. This book recognises his later achievements as a significant radio playwright in a subsequent award-winning career scriptwriting and performing in serious and classical drama.

Audio Drama Is Spoken Word – for the Ear and Not the Eye

One of the basic and foremost tricks I have always advised writers to deploy when writing audio drama is to create with the voice. What I mean by this is to speak the script – perhaps even before it is written down, and then speak it over and over again. For radio and sound has always been the spoken word medium. This is the reason it has connected culturally so well with the oral tradition in poetry and storytelling. General education has trained most people to write and read silently in literate English and good style values often relate to how the script looks on a page. Radio and broadcast journalists are always trained to rehearse their scripts through presentation and a silent broadcast newsroom full of journalists is often not a very good one. It should be possible to hear people talking their stories. Some highly experienced broadcasters do not even write their scripts before recording their links. They think them first and then speak them, and from an early time in their careers develop a very precise instinct for time. They acquire the ability to adlib into specific linear time frames. Some televisual journalists present/link the voice-over directly onto the sound track of their film sequences.

I would argue that audio dramatists should develop the same skills. In this way, the dramatic writing will have the necessary impact and form to connect with the listener's imagination. It can also be a lot of fun. Dramatising characters and the interaction between them will often spark and catalyse new ideas and thoughts as well as inform the writer about the layers of subtext that can be allowed to breathe in communication in developing scenes without overwriting. It is true that podcasting no longer binds sound play creators for the online platform to specific time frames, but the discipline of writing and performing to time will always be demanded by the broadcasting world.

In the days when most sound plays were performed live, the writing to time skill was even more essential. Rehearsals needed to take into account the pace of performance and potential variation in production of sound effects. Even the mood of a character as interpreted by an actor could vary the length of a speech or line by a few seconds. There was the celebrated occasion when the *Mercury Theatre on the Air* company directed by Orson Welles catastrophically mistimed their live production largely through the last-minute practices in writing and rehearsal. Orson Welles had to go to the CBS library during a passage when his character was not performing to find some books to bring back into the live studio so that he and his actors could present extracts from adaptations that they would be doing in future weeks.

Having the chance to try out sound drama scripts in a performing group of fellow writers and actors is always an advantage. The interpretation and performance of scripts by others offers writers the chance to be more objective about their work. Precious lines and ideas originally cherished might turn out to be not so successful when vocalised. The failure to establish the unique identity of a character through the cadence and specificity of their speaking persona will become obvious through performance whether by writers themselves or an ensemble group working together on each other's scripts.

The Theatre Workshop doctrine of going out into communities to interview and document human experiences is a fine example of the significance of listening to people talking about their lives, hopes, fears, and memories and then bringing them back to the drama workshop space and through transcription, interpretation, and improvisation producing refined dramatic expression of truths inspired by real life and real people. The dramatic language is not purely a recreation of the exact words of people speaking but crafted into dramatic narration and dialogue.

David Pownall – 'Sound Theatre Is a Performance Art of Special Purity'

When David Pownall's collection of award-winning radio plays was published in 1998, he was described by the Director Eoin O'Callaghan as 'one of this country's most talented and prolific writers for the medium' (Pownall, 1998). In 2010,

Oberon Books published his elegant memoir 'Sound Theatre: Thoughts on the Radio Play'. Pownall reminds us that one of the many advantages of radio drama is that there is no need for sequins on the microphone, make-up, stunning frocks, knowing winks, gurning, and certainly no nudity or 'cavorting eye-candy' (Pownall, 2010, p. 17). His gentle surmising is very much in the tradition of Gordon Lea's tribute to a medium which 'is suspended in a universe of its own, a cloud of starry verbal vapour' (Pownall, 2010, p. 19). The Goon Show when listened to without canned laughter or a studio audience as though cast into the silent air 'has a strange, floating pureness' (Pownall, 2010). The playwright has the simplest advice to his compatriots: 'Word, noise, silence, followable though – that's all there is to work with. Artists of sound theatre can make it mean anything and everything' (Pownall, 2010, p. 17). He also points out that there have been more original plays written for radio in Britain over the last 100 years than for the stage over the last 400 years. Between 30,000 and 40,000 plays have sparked and electrified the human imagination. Pownall's love and passion for the medium is witty and self-deferential. He was fascinated by the BBC's listener log for one of his plays broadcast in 2000. One phoned in saying: 'This is the most boring play I have ever listened to'. Another said: 'Thought it was marvelous' (Pownall, 2010, p. 61). Pownall observes that in the huge stream of swirling sound that is modern digital and online and analogue life, 'Bobbing along, in danger of being sucked down, is the radio play, needing a moment when the loop stops and the whirlpool ceases in which to be heard to advantage' (Pownall, 2010, p. 66).

Shakespeare as Radio Drama

David Pownall's most enduring achievement in writing a radio play which explored the spirit of discovering how they should be made is 'An Epiphanous Use of The Microphone' (1998). Not only did he make an art out of linking present understanding with past and early discovery, he conjured two worlds: 1923 and the BBC's decision to produce William Shakespeare's Twelfth Night from Savoy Hill as the first full-length radio play to be broadcast by the BBC's London station 2LO and Twelfth Night's earliest public performance which took place at Middle Temple Hall, one of the Inns of Court, on 2 February (Candlemas night) in 1602.

Shakespeare was first broadcast by the BBC with a scene from *Julius Caesar* on 16th February 1923 performed by Shayle Gardner and Hubert Carter 100 years ago. This was the famous quarrel scene, the argument between Brutus and Cassius. The BBC celebrated this in 2013 by producing for radio performance by Harriet Walter and Jenny Jules from Phyllida Lloyd's all-female Donmar Warehouse production.

It was artistically and historically astute for the producer Jeremy Mortimer to cast an all-female production because the complex cross-gender ambiguities and performance traditions in Shakespeare work so well in the sound medium. The British Empire Shakespeare Society had staged an all-female cast matinée reading performance of Hamlet during the 1920s. In 1923, the *Times* newspaper had reported on their reductive and minimalist word-based style of Shakespeare presentations:

In the periodical readings arranged in London by the British Empire Shakespeare Society we are presented with Shakespeare 'as he is wrote'. We are given the traditional text and the traditional arrangement of scenes; there is no scenery and there are no costumes. The artists sit round in a circle in their everyday clothes, the scenes and stage direction are indicated by a lady who is described on the programme as 'stage directions', and the action is carried through from beginning to end without pause. It is an ordeal from which the works only of the greatest dramatists could emerge with any measure of success...

(Anon, 20 March 1923, p. 10)

Alan Beck argues that it was their track-record in presenting no costume near equivalent radio studio style performances which led to their booking, most likely by Cecil Lewis to produce the first four full-length radio Shakespeare plays by the BBC in 1923: *Twelfth Night* (28th May), *The Merchant of Venice* (15th June), *Romeo and Juliet* (5th July), and *A Midsummer Night's Dream* (25th July 1923). Dr. Andrea Smith has brilliantly analysed the successful adaptations by Cathleen Nesbitt and reception of these broadcasts by newspapers and radio periodicals. Dr. Smith is effectively elevating Nesbitt's creative and professional contribution to radio drama's first successful impact on large-scale broadcast audiences in Britain. Nesbitt did not mention her BBC achievements in her 1975 autobiography *A Little Love and Good Company*. Her value and contribution to British culture is much more than the footnote of having been in love with the romantic Great War poet Rupert Brooke who died from fever on his way to the Gallipoli campaign in 1915. She references the Director and Producer Nigel Playfair in respect of stage and theatre productions. The BBC's Cecil Lewis and Playfair's important connections and work with the BBC are invisible as is the British Empire Shakespeare Society.

Some of the Royal Shakespeare Company actors I was fortunate enough to direct – Mike Shannon, Don Henderson, and Gerard Murphy – always emphasised how they thought Shakespeare had been writing for the radio age. There are many arguments why his plays are so suited for sound production and listening. The poetic nomenclature of verse speech is rooted in the oral tradition and in the Renaissance age for audiences with a high proportion of people who could not read. Shakespeare's plays were originally presented in contemporary dress. As a writer Shakespeare was an outstanding artist in writing for the imagination. His ability as a dramatist to bring emotional intensity to his plots and characters covered the vast range of human feelings. His words were invested with powerful psychology. The emotional imagination of his audience is drawn into participating with the world of his plays.

David Pownall characterises and dramatises Cathleen Nesbitt's role in *An Epiphanous Use of The Microphone* 'commissioned by the BBC for the 75th anniversary of the first play ever broadcast'. The history of the first 8–10 years of BBC Radio drama between 1922 and 1930 has been researched and written in three academic studies completed between 1988 and 2008 by Tina Pepler 'Discovering The Art

Of Wireless; A Critical History Of Radio Drama At The BBC 1922–1928' (a PhD with the University of Bristol), Alan Beck 'The Invisible Play' – History of Radio Drama in the UK, Radio Drama 1922–1928' (academic staff research project for Kent University), and Roger Wood, 'Radio Drama at the Crossroads: The history and contemporary context of radio drama at the BBC' (a PhD with De Montfort University, Leicester). Wood's research and writing covers the period until the completion and submission of this thesis in 2008. Andrea Smith's 2022 PhD thesis '"Look with thine ears": A Century of Shakespeare's Plays on BBC Radio' for the University of East Anglia is the most comprehensive study of Shakespearean production and broadcasting in BBC Radio spanning the corporation's first 100 years (Smith, 2022).

The nearest we can get to hearing what the sound drama of this period was actually like would be some focus on what was canonised as the first play specifically written for the microphone – 'Danger' by Richard Hughes. However, Tina Pepler's thesis identifies the radio drama script written for *Children's Hour* titled: 'The Truth About Father Christmas (as told by the "Fairy Dustman")' by Mrs. Phyllis M. Twigg as being the first sound play script commissioned, produced, and transmitted by the BBC on their first London 2LO station Christmas Eve, 23rd December 1922. It seems neither the script nor the play has survived in print or sound production, although three 'Fairy Dustman' 78 rpm records were produced by the London Gramophone Company (HMV) during the early 1920s. This fact had been hiding in plain sight since 1924 being clearly published in Arthur Burrows' book *A Story Of Broadcasting* (Burrows, 1924, p. 71). He mentions Mrs. Twigg originated the series of stories *Tales of a Fairy Dustman* broadcast throughout 1923. Mrs. Twigg wrote under the pseudonym of Moira Meighn. One of the most prolific original women dramatists for BBC radio in the 1920s, Kathleen Baker, wrote and published under the nom-de-plume John Overton.

As we know, the BBC decided that radio drama's 90th anniversary should fall on 16th February 2013 to commemorate the transmission from Marconi House of scenes from Shakespeare's *Julius Caesar* and *Othello*. Burrows clearly credits Cathleen Nesbitt for the 1923 BBC Shakespeare season: 'In this Miss Kathleen (sic) Nesbitt collaborated with Captain Lewis and took a prominent part' (Burrows, 1924, p. 81). Burrows identifies the next landmark development as the production by Milton Rosmer on 29th November 1923 of Gertrude Jennings' one act 'farce, *Five Birds in a Cage*, which is built on the situation following a breakdown in a tube lift' (Burrows, 1924). The stage script of Jennings' play and a detailed review by Archibald Haddon of its radio drama presentation have survived, and we can give this as much critical attention and evaluation as Richard Hughes's *Danger*, which Burrows describes as successful:

> *Grand Guignol*, depicting the plight of two lovers who find themselves in a mine disaster. I think all who heard this first attempt at building up a really dramatic situation entirely by sound effects will admit that it was very thrilling, and opened up a wide range of possibilities.
>
> *(Burrows, 1924)*

This success in developing sound drama directed to the imagination and the vicarious fears of listeners being trapped or enveloped by darkness and claustrophobia is a fully understandable epiphany on the potential of microphone drama.

David Pownall's Laser Test – *An Epiphanous Use of the Microphone*

By the time David Pownall had his collection of six plays published by Oberon in 1998, he had written 45 plays for the BBC over 27 years. He explained that 'Radio provides a laser test. If a piece succeeds in sound only it has the inner strength to survive the clumsier, cruder forms' (Pownall, 1998, p. 12). He explained that a play 'is essentially one thing standing in its own time, controlled by a defining action or movement of character. Its edges are its truth' (Pownall, 1998, p. 12). The radio play has to succeed in the totality of successful fictional writing as well as the frame and matrix of its intrinsic strengths as a sound-only medium. Pownall recognised that radio drama is 'the closest art to story-telling we have so its roots are very ancient' (Pownall, 1998, p. 10).

Why is *The Epiphanous Use of the Microphone* so successful? To begin with Pownall creates art out of the functional commission to fashion entertainment in the commemoration of Corporation history. The adjective 'Epiphanous' implies that playing with the microphone in the dramatic arts for the first time is going to reveal some important truths. There is going to be an almost spiritual awakening and birth of a new art form. The characters will be changed by the experience. The struggle and challenge is to produce the first full-length radio play, Shakespeare's Twelfth Night in May 1923. It is going to be 2 hours long and this has never been done before. Everyone is a novice in the radio medium. Cathleen Nesbitt and fellow actors have more professional experience of adapting and performing Shakespeare, but will they understand how to dramatise and perform for sound only? So much is at stake. For the BBC's Managing Director John Reith, who in real life fully understood radio drama's special characteristics, did not have the right to fail. The pressure on his very young producer Cecil Lewis is as great if not greater.

Pownall showed in unfolding scenes how Reith was under the cosh of political surveillance and censorship by the Conservative government's minister for broadcasting, the Postmaster-General, who just happened to be Neville Chamberlain. When Chamberlain warns Reith that the government will be listening very carefully to everything they are doing with an emphasis on the word 'very', Pownall dramatises how the two men are squaring up to each other. Reith is compliant but at the same time stating that the BBC is hoping everyone and not just government ministers will be listening to their new service.

Chamberlain makes it very clear that Whitehall is anxious something so powerful is not infiltrated and subverted by people with the wrong kind of politics. The skill in Pownall's writing here is to use entertaining dialogue to reference the actual fact that the Security Service MI5 would eventually closely work with the BBC to vet new appointments and exclude people, mainly communists, judged to be politically suspect (Pownall, 1998, p. 24).

Pownall wrote a parallel challenge for William Shakespeare and his company trying to put together the first public performance of *Twelfth Night* in the Middle Temple Dining Room in 1602. He had equally anxious censorship worries. His jealous rival Francis Bacon was spreading rumours that the play mocks Queen Elizabeth the First's personal tragedy in being forced to execute the Earl of Essex, a younger man she had been deeply in love with. She was being urged to see the performance to find out for herself. There are touches of what will later be explained as ironic transposition and resonance. In 1602, Shakespeare answered to the Queen's state censor of theatre the Lord Chamberlain. In 1923, Reith answered to a government minister in control of broadcasting called Chamberlain. The punning in names continues with the parallel of the 1923 BBC producer Cecil Lewis chiming with Queen Elizabeth's Chief Advisor being one Lord Cecil.

Pownall's play is a play with two inner plays, time present, time past 1923, and time past 1602. The struggles are paralleled. Reith's BBC needs to make Shakespeare succeed over 2 hours in virtual darkness. There is the sound they are creating in Savoy Hill's first and heavily draped studio directed to the ear, the mind, and the consciousness of the listener. In the switchback to 1602, when the Queen complains of being too hot and Middle Temple's windows are thrown open, a gust of wind rushes in to blow out all the candles and *Twelfth Night* 1602 is also performed in darkness. The wind metaphor is extended with wit to 1923 with Reith insisting that the BBC production begins with a storm.

Pownall's characterisation of Reith is clever and multidimensional. He does not reduce him to the reputation of a single-minded arrogant tyrant and dictator of broadcasting. He gives Reith flourishing and evangelistic language to describe how he sees on air drama. This is in accordance with the content of Reith's book *Broadcast over Britain* published in 1924. Reith did in fact have a poetic understanding of the power of radio and his writing about it was lyrical. So when Pownall has Reith enthusiastically exhorting Cathleen Nesbitt to begin the play with sound as a brushstroke, he builds his speech with multisyllabic words and at the very high point that he has Nesbitt charmed reveals that the play has to be cut by an hour. Nesbitt's replies to him are amusingly juxtaposed between the 'I do' of catching his drift on using sound artistically, and then consternation at the idea of an hour's amputation of the play's length being both a question and an exclamation (Pownall, 1998, p. 41).

Pownall's Sir John Reith performs the wind himself; almost as a bridging time warp of energy to release the power of the BBC's *Twelfth Night* upon the consciousness of the nation. Although Pownall characterises the Platonic and dictatorial Reith with the schoolboy charm of a player in the classroom of radio drama learning, there is all the tension of live cuing in broadcasting, with the studio manager positioning Reith properly in front of the microphone and even a joke from the managing director himself when he asks rhetorically how a storm can tread softly when he is asked to do so after finishing his brief performance. And after the countdown to the beginning of *Twelfth Night* by William Shakespeare, Reith makes wind, a quite brilliant expression of character through vocalising non-verbal sound; much more than any equivalent half hour or one hour formal speech (Pownall, 1998, p. 58).

Pownall's play is a magnificent example of how the multiplicity of conflicts between characters and the effects of the various crises and disequilibriums develop, reveal, and change the characters. The listener also joins the characters in their respective worlds of 1602 and 1923 to share what they are discovering by their experiences of producing *Twelfth Night* in the face of truly existential threats of censorship.

Cathleen Nesbitt is struggling to cope with Reith's diktat on slashing the sacred text. Understandably she is highly resistant, coming up with the solution of reading it faster to which Reith has an opportunity to explain the lessons they have been learning in producing radio; namely listeners are easily distracted, and class, education, and devotion to Shakespeare is not going to keep them listening. Nesbitt is given the magnificent quip that the play should be retitled *Sixth Night* (Pownall, 1998, p. 41).

Cathleen Nesbitt has to negotiate Reith's domineering and seemingly impossible demands and all the insecurities and anxieties of grumbling and disgruntled actors struggling to make sense of performing in a silent and sound-absorbing ambience to an imaginary audience. Pownall dramatises how the tensions ignite to the point of near rebellion. In a scene between Reith and actor Olivia Rose, he has Reith getting his own way when confronted by recalcitrance. He is insisting that she imagines him as the microphone in rehearsal and then universalises her thinking. The actress eventually concedes that the managing director has become the equivalent of both the microphone and the universe (Pownall, 1998, p. 39).

Pownall parallels the respective productions' fortunes in overcoming the problem of Act Three, Scene Four; specifically how can Malvolio make his important entrance in yellow hose and cross-garters if the audience is blind (Pownall, 1998, p. 55). For Reith, Nesbitt, and Lewis it is something that needs to be anticipated, translated, and transposed into the sound medium. There are only seconds before the red lights go on and 2LO's *Twelfth Night* is to fill the London ether.

Reith pontificates to the actor playing Malvolio that all the arts are afflicted by curses; namely music is too vague, painting lacks depth, statues have no body temperature, and the radio drama they are doing has an issue with yellow hose and cross-garters (Pownall, 1998, p. 58). Malvolio informs the Major (Reith's army rank in the Great War) that he will have to grin and bear it. He is not wearing a costume and just holding a script. But then 'he gets it' to use modern parlance when Reith has encouraged him to think about the actor's inner eye conveying the spirit and subtext of the scene (Pownall, 1998). It doesn't matter he is not wearing cross-garters.

This is great writing. Behold the subtlety engaged here and the genius in building up the anticipation of how they would actually present and perform this scene in the 1923 *Twelfth Night* production. Reith's wife Muriel is dramatised listening to the outcome in the radio drama version of a scene so tethered originally to visual cues, costume, business, and meaning (Pownall, 1998, p. 59). The only evidence of how this issue was negotiated in the original production and broadcast can be found in a review by Dame May Witty for *Popular Wireless* on 23rd June 1923 when she explained: 'I should commend the Malvolio. One realized the pomposity and fatu-ousness of the character, and one saw that painful smile and the yellow stockings cross gartered' (Witty, 1923, p. 688). Pownall the radio dramatist, 65 years later, has either imagined what actually happened or done research worthy of a university professor.

Pownall switches back to 1602 where William Shakespeare's production prob-lems have been no less troublesome. The sly machinations of Bacon, the complexity of Queen Elizabeth's grieving over Essex meeting the play's depiction of a play within the play about love's suffering, and the ego of his star actor Burbage having to be contained.

Pownall skilfully characterises both Shakespeare and Burbage by showing how he assuages artistic sensitivity and hubris with the necessary authority of a director. Burbage might want to be able to improvise for another 5 minutes by short-sight-edly pretending to find a letter his character reads, have this reading doubled and upgraded to a soliloquy, and have the interjecting lines of characters interrupting his reading cancelled, but Shakespeare insists he determines the stride of his actors, including the great and brilliant Burbage (Pownall, 1998, p. 30).

For William Shakespeare, the yellow hose and cross-garters problem is an unplanned emergency where improvisation needs to be the master of the apparent chaos of what has become a visual stage play now performing in the sound medium only in some kind of early 17th century black box theatre in the dark when all the candles have been snuffed out after the Queen insisted the windows be opened. Shakespeare hears his actors cut three lines and delights in appreciating the laughter and applause when Burbage says: 'Sad, lady! I could be sad: this does make some obstruction in the blood, this cross-gartering ...' (Pownall, 1998, p. 59).

Pownall adds further powerful punches of ironical resonance. Burbage thought the audience, including the Queen, would have all walked out but is amazed that they stayed, liked it, and could not see a thing (Pownall, 1998, p. 60). The most skilful twist of irony is when Burbage reveals that during the interval he heard two courtiers gossiping that the 70-year-old Queen would make the half her age young Essex put on yellow hose and cross-garters and dance about for her. The intensity of the irony in all the jeopardies and risks confronting Shakespeare continues during his private audience with her after the performance.

When the Queen asks how he knew about the yellow hose and cross-garters, he perhaps feigns that he cannot remember. Whether that is true or not, it is the right answer in an exchange and experience that could have cost him his life. The Queen indicates that if she had actually seen the scene as dramatised and representing something so intimate, her reaction would have been painful and much different to the laughter that ensued. She also observes Burbage lacks the good looks of her Robert, though he does share his vanity (Pownall, 1998, p. 61).

BBC Advice and Guidance: Past and Present

Throughout its history, the BBC has been doing its best to encourage new writing for radio as well as providing guidance on how to do it well and suitably for the sound medium. I would argue that this has been a narrative of continuous progress where the amount of logistical/clerical and instrumental information has gradually been replaced with more detailed and specific advice on the art and aesthetics of audio drama writing. Certainly, by 1929 when the BBC Drama Department had read more than 6,000 plays, there was a clear idea on what to emphasise and encourage. For example, the 1929 BBC Yearbook devoted three pages to an article 'Writing Plays for Broadcasting'. The tone was direct and realistic:

> The way of the broadcast playwright is hard, for the microphone is a merciless instrument. Every unnatural phrase or sentence uttered by a wireless play is magnified into something approaching burlesque. The microphone demands an even more natural style than stage dialogue usually possesses.
>
> *(BBC, 1929, p. 187)*

There was an open invitation 'for original minds to add other lines to the bold strokes already drawn on the canvas which will at last show the form of the new "drama of the ether"' (BBC, 1929, p. 187). All rather quaint and romantic. However, few contemporary writers for sound drama would disagree with this observation on the psychological relationship between writer and listener:

> It is a mistake to think that, as the wireless is a medium chiefly relying on words, words themselves are the material which authors of this new art must depend on for their effect. The words are only the means to an end. The mental reactions caused by the dialogue are far more important than the dialogue itself.
>
> An even greater knowledge of human psychology than that possessed by the stage playwright is necessary to the author who will write a brilliant broadcast play. At present, the only criterion of success is the listener's reaction...
>
> *(BBC, 1929, p. 189)*

The BBC offered the following hints with key points italicised for emphasis:

1. *Don't confuse the listener* by too many characters not differentiated, or not essential to your plot.
2. *Don't tire the listener* by unnecessary detail or long, pointless speeches.
3. Don't submit a play because you *like it*, but because you think, after careful consideration of your wide audience, that it will please and stimulate thousands.
4. *Don't meander*; let the plot be direct and clear to the average thinking man or woman.
5. *Don't introduce characters without due warning of their coming*, and don't make them talk for five minutes before we know who they are.
6. *Don't give any 'business'* to characters which is not indicated by dialogue.
7. *Don't use offensive plots*. The B.B.C. knows it cannot please everybody at once, but it does *try* to offend nobody at any time.

8.   *Don't be hampered* by the stage limitations of presentation and change.
9.   Finally, *listen to broadcast plays*, and hear what methods are used by writers and
     what the producers are able to do by use of devices for 'fading' one scene into
     another, superimposition of voices and sounds, noise effects, etc.

(BBC, 1929, p. 190)

The BBC thought these homilies would 'prove informative' (BBC, 1929). By
the 1980s what had changed? There was certainly more inspiration and an almost
spiritual and evangelistic proverbial attitude in the eight page photocopied handout
titled 'Writing Plays For Radio, BBC Radio Drama' with quotations from the former BBC Radio Drama Department Editor Martin Esslin 'The almost telepathic
transference of images from mind to mind is the beauty and the glory of the radio
play' (BBC, 1989, p. 1) and writer Sue Townsend 'Radio gives you terrific scope.
You can be anywhere, in any century, in any place' (BBC, 1989, p. 2) though the
quotation from producer Donald McWhinnie might be considered rather enigmatic
'The writer's business is to make excessive demands of his interpreters' (BBC, 1989).
Certainly the BBC was pointing out that good radio is very difficult to write:

1.   The audience has to be attracted and its attention held by means of sound
     alone, without the assistance of visual stimuli on which other media can rely.
2.   Deprived of light, colour, movement, and all the devices which will support a
     play for the screen or theatre, the radio writer must conceive a rich variety of
     sound in order to stimulate the listener's imagination.
3.   Much of this must, of course, depend on the quality of the dialogue itself. If
     what is said is interesting and exciting, it will carry a play a long way.
4.   In addition, the writer needs to think of the other aural elements of sounds,
     music and, most important, silence. Pauses help the listeners to assimilate what
     they have heard and prepare for what happens next.
5.   Speech will normally be the dominant element. Radio dialogue must often be
     more explicit than that written for the visual medium, but not actually sound
     explicit or it won't seem natural. It follows that the art of dialogue on radio is,
     at its best, extremely sophisticated.
6.   A variety of sound is essential for holding the listener's attention and engag-
     ing their imagination. This variety can be achieved by altering the lengths of
     sequences, number of people speaking, space of dialogue, volume of sound,
     background acoustics and location of action.
7.   Don't send scripts written for any other medium.
8.   As radio plays have to conform to a precise length, there is no way of meas-
     uring this by the number of words or pages. Reading aloud against the clock,
     making allowance for effects, music, and pauses, is the only reliable method.
9.   Obviously, the best way to become familiar with the possibilities of the medium
     is to listen to radio plays as often as possible and decide what works well and
     what doesn't.

(BBC, 1989, pp. 1–8)

When the BBC World Service last ran a radio playwriting competition in 2020, it had boiled down ten recommendations that are fleshed out and further explained behind the online links in bibliography:

1. Grab the audience from the start.
2. Write about something that is personal to you.
3. Vary the pace and length of your scenes.
4. Make sure the structure keeps them listening.
5. Get under the skin of your characters.
6. Express your characters between dialogue and interaction.
7. Use the four building blocks – speech, sound effects, music, and silence.
8. Express the visual elements in a subtle way.
9. Concentrate on your presentation.
10. Enjoy writing your play.

(BBC World Service Online, 2020)

The BBC World Service covers the ground on essential aspects of radio play writing, particularly on the importance of the beginning by drawing in or even accelerating the listener's attention and varying the pace and length of scenes. It also cites key aspects of fiction writing in respect of characterisation: 'get under the skin' and characterisation through dialogue and interaction. Principle seven is clearly based on a regular maxim of former BBC World Service drama editor Gordon House and was very well expressed in an interview recorded for the Spotlight programme in November 1996:

> Think of good characters, get them speaking in the way that we speak in a naturalistic way. Real characters talking in a way that is recognisable in your own culture. Conflict and story told through building blocks of radio drama – words, music, sound effects and silence. Then you can write a radio play.
>
> *(BBC World Service, 1996)*

Radio Drama guidance at the time of writing is contextualised by a multimedia approach to scriptwriting and with a much more clearly framed educational and workshopping policy provided by the BBC Writers Room website. The BBC identifies eight essentials generic to any form of scriptwriting, and the thinking behind this is presumably to know how to write dramatic stories well first and then explore the intrinsic characteristics and needs of audio drama. The eight essentials are: (1) Developing your idea; (2) Know what you want to write; (3) Beginnings (and Endings); (4) The muddle in the middle; (5) Characters bring your words to life; (6) Scenes; (7) Dialogue; and (8) Writing is rewriting (BBC Writers' Room Online, 2022). The explanations and more detailed guidance are accessible via the links in bibliography. All the points focus on the dramatic purpose of what can be seen as the engineering or building blocks of the scriptwriting process. There can be no muddle in the middle without scenes and the scene by scene structure can be determined by answering four questions: (1) What effect does this scene have on the character within the moment?; (2) What effect does it have on the subsequent events of the story?; (3) What impact does it have on the world of the story?; and (4) What else is going on below the surface and beyond the text? (BBC Writers' Room Online, 2022). Writer and dramaturg Paul Ashton produced ten online blogs to cover his recommended perfect framework for successful scriptwriting: (1) Medium, Form, and Format; (2) Get your story going!; (3) Coherence; (4) Character is Everything; (5) Emotion; (6) Surprise!; (7) Structure; (8) Exposition and Expression; (9) Passion; (10) Be Yourself (Ashton BBC, 2008–2009). In many respects, the short titles are self-explanatory, though it is certainly recommended to read the detail behind each one. The importance of surprising the listener as a way of maintaining the storytelling drive and imperatives within a play is well worth elevating as a key hope and expectation on the part of any audience to drama. The unexpected not only charges the listener with interest but also demands a reaction and response from the play's characters. How and why do they respond and critically how they are changed by what has happened.

This is very much a checklist way of disciplining the writing process. It is fashionable and widespread in contemporary creative writing teaching. John Yorke's top ten questions to unlock and refine stores are highlighted by the BBC Writers' Room: (1) Whose story is it?; (2) What does the character need? (What is their flaw?; What do they need to learn?); (3) What is the inciting incident?; (4) What does the character want?; (5) What obstacles are in the character's way?; (6) What's at stake?; (7) Why should we care?; (8) What do they learn?; (9) How and why?; and (10) How does it end? (Yorke BBC, 2022) This might be viewed as boiler-room style learning, but the questions set offer an effective template to judging dramatic purpose in any form of fictional writing.

The Writing Radio Drama section of the BBC Writers' Room resources in 2022 takes on a much more philosophical and poetic tone than the BBC's previous generations of 'bish bash' and 'do this' and 'don't do that' bullet-point prescriptions on writing for sound. My effort here to summarise the page in list form is somewhat unravelled by the elegant precision of inspiration and instruction in the original content:

1. **Pictures**. They are better on the radio. There's nothing you can't do, nowhere you can't go … The true 'budget' is that spent between you and the listener – the cost of two imaginations combined.
2. **Sounds**. Radio is not about sound – it's about significant, meaningful sound… The intimacy of a speaker with the listener can be immensely powerful… Use background sound to create an atmosphere that will help the listener's imagination create an entire world. Choose a setting with a distinct aural environment and use those sounds to underscore the story. Use sound to cut between places and times.
3. **Listeners**. Radio has the fastest turn-off rate of all drama so make the audience want to stay. Try to hit the ground running… Everything must earn its keep… emotionally tie the audience down. Simple often works best.

4. **Emotions**. No drama works without emotionally engaging characters. The audience must want to spend time with them and want to know what will happen to them. Each must be there for a reason… remember, a character who never speaks/appears can still be a strong absent-presence in radio.

5. **Endings**. Know your ending and leave us satisfied… Finish with a strong resolution (one way or another) to the issues raised. Don't be afraid to move at pace, like TV or film, if the story or genre demands it.

6. **Drama not prose on the radio**. Don't over-explain – keep it lean and dramatic… Boil it down to the minimum, the essential. The silence, the pause, the space between the words is important… Think too about inarticulacy… Every character needs their own 'grammar'.

7. **Sensitivities**. Language is more naked and potent on the radio, so less is definitely more. Audiences can be as sensitive to religious oaths as to bad language. Gratuitousness of any kind won't work – though something contentious put in meaningful context might.

8. **Liberating medium**. Radio drama is liberating, not restrictive – it can mean more variety, more locations, more action, more imagination, and more originality… use it to its full potential.

(BBC Radio Drama, 2022)

Special Characteristics and Early 'Secrets of the Radio Drama': Reith and Shaw

I have outlined how radio drama began to be systematically written and produced in Britain at the BBC during the 1920s when it was a private company controlled by radio manufacturers and operating in a broadcasting monopoly; in other words having no competition. It was clear that its first Managing Director John C. W. Reith was an enthusiast. This is evident from Chapter 5, Part 3 of his book *Broadcast Over Britain* which was published in 1924. Reith described 'radio drama' as 'a separate art in itself' (Reith, 1924, p. 165). He said very few theatrical plays were suitable for the new medium because 'so much depends on the eye, the acting positions' (Reith, 1924), although musical theatre such as opera was an exception.

Reith recognised, as did others, that radio drama requires its own techniques in writing and acting and to the term 'radio drama', he added 'radio-dramatist' and 'radio-actor' (Reith, 1924, p. 166). As he was responsible for hiring his programme makers and he listened to the output of his London station, 2LO, and many of the other local and regional BBC stations around the country when he went touring to visit the staff and station managers, Reith came to a quick understanding of what worked in terms of the radio play:

> The appeal is to the ear first, and thence to the other senses as well. In order to avoid unnecessary explanations, the dialogue must portray the setting. Brief references must be made by the characters to the scene, and the entrances and exits similarly revealed. Other aids to the imagination, such

as music, incidental sounds contingent to the situation, pauses and various dramatic devices are introduced wherever possible. Most plays written for the stage require specific adaptation for wireless presentation. With radio plays there must be a sharp contrast between all the voices of the players, and the characters should be as few in number as possible'.

(Reith, 1924)

Reith argued that if illusion and imagination were restricted to simulation by sound and hearing only, plays rooted in realism meant that the listener's concentration was less tested since 'we perceive the scenes as vividly as in a theatre, and can, in spirit, participate in that which is being portrayed. The background of sound is of immense effect' (Reith, 1924). He realised that the familiarity of the contemporary world meant that realist drama could transport the listener into true regions where the effect is 'tenfold. In this respect there is a distinct advantage over the theatre' (Reith, 1924, p. 167).

Reith realised that the distractions to the listener and the challenge in concentration had to be respected in the writing and making of the radio play. Unlike in theatre, the lights are not lowered, other people present are not ritually intent and silent and there is not a direct money contract of paying for your ticket. He thought the radio play simply has no chance with other people moving about the room, or the telephone ringing. Reith thought a radio play would have more success in being contained in less than 45 minutes. He thought it unlikely listeners could stay mentally tuned into an entire Shakespeare play (Reith, 1924, p. 168).

Reith fostered a creative hothouse of experimentation, innovation, and pioneering discoveries of the radio drama form during the 1920s. They ranged from R.E. Jeffrey, whom he recruited from the BBC station in Aberdeen to head drama productions, to young men who had survived the Great War of 1914–1918 as flyers in the Royal Flying Corps and Royal Naval Service such as Cecil Lewis and Lance Sieveking who wrote, adapted, and directed in the new studios situated in Savoy House by the River Thames embankment. A continuing debate about the new art form endured in the pages of the BBC's listings magazine *The Radio Times*, which was first published at the end of 1923, and in 1926 the first book on writing radio drama was published. It was written by Gordon Lea, with a foreword by Jeffrey as the BBC's productions director:

It is my hope that Radio Drama in its *real* form – not a bastard cultivation from the stage – will become a source of inspiration to its heterogeneous broadcast audience. A little has been done; much remains to do. Public-spirited playwrights especially are required; the broadcast has no nightly box-office. A new form of drama cannot be developed without a new form of play as its vehicle.

In this book we have something which will help to realize the high aim which the BBC has set before it in this most difficult branch of radio art.

(Lea, 1926, p. 12)

A popular writer of thrillers and respected radio writer of this period, Frank H. Shaw, whose reputation has not endured in either prose literature or drama, set out in a short article what he described as the 'Secrets of the Radio Drama'. He overlapped much of what Reith had reflected on 2 years before. Radio plays should be short on the basis that in the social environment as opposed to the proscenium arch theatre with dimmed lights and a difficult to negotiate exit, life is not an unbroken stretch. The performance cannot be paused while taking a call, answering the door, or even a call to nature. So 'brevity is the soul of wit' (Shaw, 1926).

Shaw said the radio play should, like any other dimension of drama, contain a 'definite story, a good plot, characters that introduce themselves smartly, an overwhelming climax, and no suggestion of anti-climax'. Climax once reached is the point when the play needs to end 'as if clean-cut with a knife' (Shaw, 1926). He argued that the sound play cannot work without a strong and convincing plot, characters delineated clearly, brisk action throughout, moving remorselessly forward to middle-climax, a slight suggestion of anti-climax can be permitted but only 'as a taking-off place for the final and ultimate climax' (Shaw, 1926).

Shaw confirmed the advice and conventions given out and followed by professional audio drama directors the world over. A small cast is the best. The listener dependent on hearing and imagination is 'apt to grow confused by many voices, unless they differ very considerably one from another' (Shaw, 1926). He advised on the construction of divergent and contrasting personalities even to the extent of exaggeration. He advised against the declamatory in style. He also realised that 'radio drama must depend for its success on its audible atmosphere, at least as much as on its story and dialogue' (Shaw, 1926). In 1926, he was alluding to the technique of modernist realism that would be the vogue form from the middle late 20th century to the present:

> [It] should carry throughout an excellent stamp of restraint. Long orations are out of place; dialogue should be eminently crisp and telling, with – as in the case of the legitimate stage-play – no single unnecessary word. The brain of the listener must not be confused and be clouded by verbal torrents leading nowhere. Dialogues must be 'snappy', conveying definite meaning. Furthermore, the situations must arise so naturally that the credulity of the listener is not strained.
>
> *(Shaw, 1926)*

Shaw wrote with confidence and determination. His faith in the new medium was such that the criticism that a listener can always turn off the loud speaker or remove the ear-phones and wait for something more to his liking was met with the intriguing riposte: 'Therein he scores over the stall-holder in the West-end theatre – the management in the theatre does not offer a substitute performance' (Shaw, 1926).

Seeing with the Mind's Eye, Studio Production, Perceptions of the Future, Art and Excelsior: Archer, Drinkwater, Jeffrey, Smythe, and Thorndike

On 29th August 1924, William Archer, described as 'the Distinguished Dramatic Critic' was already fulminating about 'The Future of Wireless Drama'. He listened to a live performance of BBC 2LO's production of Richard Brinsley Sheridan's 'The School for Scandal' from its Savoy Hill headquarters – the location of the earliest and most rudimentary of studios soundproofed by multiple drapes of curtains and picked up by what were nicknamed as 'meat-safe' microphones mounted in boxes on wooden chair-legs. He roamed around the production areas, sitting with the performers during two of the acts, sampling the output on headphones and then through an early valve powered loudspeaker.

Archer immediately appreciated the concentration on the word through speech. He could hear everything and see no one. Archer expressed his frustration that contemporary theatre was blighted by the loveliest actress and ugliest, most magnetic actor ceasing to please when he had been left straining his ears to catch whispered remarks and feeling envious of those members of the audience close to the stage who could be seen laughing heartily to lines he had missed.

Archer realised that wireless drama was fostering an enhancement of the art of using the voice to express character and perform the plotting of stories. The need to cast voice to character and not face or physique was apparent. He immediately realised the problem of same voice casting so that he felt: 'the Sir Peter and the Joseph Surface (both very good) had voices of such similar timbre that in their long duologue before the Screen Scene it was sometimes not easy to tell which was speaking' (Archer, 1924).

He observed the need to carefully rehearse wireless drama scripts with the skilled producer/director in the room to judge with critically listening ears. In particular, the volume of a performers' voice needed to be modified in order to achieve expression. He quite rightly predicted that radio drama acting would become a highly developed vocal art with suitability of appearance, age usually being disregarded: 'Old actors and actresses may renew the triumphs of their youth and a large class of people who have no "stage appearance," or who are even debarred from the stage by some deformity' had a future in the new medium (Archer, 1924).

On the subject of writing, Archer concluded that traditional stage classics such as *The School for Scandal* were imperfect with the script so reliant on physical movement, facial expression and theatrical business. What was missing from listening could be supplied by the repository of his own familiarity with the memory of stage performance. A listener who did not know the play would make very little of it. In conclusion, the new wireless drama had to depend upon its writing to exploit the emotional interplay of vocally contrasted characters. And in the context of comedy, he suggested the presence of a reaction of a live audience to it would prevent a sense of flatness being experienced by isolated small groups of wireless audience scattered all over the country.

The Radio Times had earlier in 1924 (29 February) given a director/producer's perspective of radio drama's strengths and weaknesses. Victor Smythe convened a regional repertory of radio drama production in Manchester which was part of a pattern of local station early BBC development in the 1920s. He saw the need to achieve voice balance and atmosphere in what was clearly a studio-based art. Smythe advanced the concept of 'seeing through the sense of hearing' (Smythe, 1924) a longstanding debate in the perception of listening that is with us today. But the director/producer had realised the nature of radio drama's blind medium status by accompanying a blind man to the theatre during a play which heavily depended on action, and he was intrigued to learn that the gentleman's blindness was not the handicap he thought it was; 'little had been lost' in his friend's appreciation of the action (Smythe, 1924). Smythe extended his research by enquiring of a doctor friend about the status of hearing as a sense in the psychological matrix of perception, and he was assured that hearing as a sense can be intensified by the focus on listening to broadcast performances. Smythe's curiosity would be followed up by broad, systematic, empirical, and academic research on the part of Professor T. H. Pear of Manchester University in the late 1920s culminating in the publication of *Voice And Personality* by Chapman and Hall in 1931.

Smythe outlined observations that began to acquire a consensus throughout the 1920s: Radio plays needed a coherent story; strong dialogue based on the word in action was important; avoid farce because of its reliance on action; consider voice balance when casting particularly in relation to volume; music is a useful device in filling up the gaps of a plot overlooked by dialogue and as imaginative suggestion; establish an atmosphere for the world of the play through direction in the studio and if necessary set the studio with props.

Smythe realised that actors in radio are supported by a physical realism within the sound studio that can support the psychology of their performance as much as the quality of spot effects:

> If a telephone is a "property" in the play, use it. If a meal is supposed to take place, a few cups, saucers and plates, knives and forks used judiciously are sufficient for the microphone to pick up a very effective impression of the scene.
>
> *(Smythe, 1924)*

In September 1924, the dramatist John Drinkwater discussed his reflections on radio as an art form in a front cover article for *The Radio Times*. He saw how radio widened the sound horizon from the gramophone to an 'infinitely larger and more varied scale' (Drinkwater, 1924) and saw it having altogether greater promise than cinema; although it needs to be appreciated, his article was a few years away from cinema's fusion with sound. Drinkwater realised that communicating through the ear 'is the most delicate and subtle of all approaches to man's comprehension' (Drinkwater, 1924). Drinkwater was certainly Reithian in his wish for wireless to embrace the broadcasting of poetry and music and avoid 'pandering to the lowest common denominator of mob intelligence' (Drinkwater, 1924). The commercial necessity that 'makes a large section of our Press and much of our public entertainment a daily disgrace and revolting to the common decencies of life' (Drinkwater, 1924) clearly marked Drinkwater out as a writer who did not think radio drama should serve a popular fare.

Drinkwater's rather superior elitism let rip on the idea that hearing 'banal ballads', 'drivelling patter', and 'imbecile melodies' is not proper listening (Drinkwater, 1924). He invited George Bernard Shaw and John Galsworthy (two of the greatest living playwrights of the time) to turn their gifts to radio.

Dame Sybil Thorndike discussed 'Where Radio Drama Excels' on the front cover of *The Radio Times* in July 1925 and after having performed *Medea of Euripides* from the BBC's new studios at Savoy Hill. She realised that the task needed an artistic interplay of imagination and personality. Radio was about 'kindling that imagination by word-pictures and poetry that are as fresh and as thought-compelling as they were' (Thorndike, 1925) in Shakespeare's distant day. Radio drama did not deny imagination but revivified and inspired it. Thorndike believed that the kinds of plays best suited to sound broadcasting were those with mystic or divine characters: Mysticism is a quality in the drama that is in every case better conveyed to the mind by the ear than by the eye; it should be felt, rather than interpreted, by the medium of sight' (Thorndike, 1925). Thorndike defines what became the time-honoured memory of sound drama that the colours were always better on the radio: 'Each member of a wireless audience is required [...] to bring his own individual imagination into play, devising his own settings and conjuring up images of the situation based on his own emotional experience' (Thorndike, 1925).

The BBC's first Director of Productions R.E. Jeffrey wrote a number of articles for *The Radio Times* discussing what he wanted to achieve in terms of 'The Need for a Radio Drama'. On 17th July 1925 he started to define the playwriting technique needed to overcome the many obstacles and turn to advantage the medium's limitations. Jeffrey decided that an early solution was educating the listener to turn the lights out and listen to radio plays in darkness so that the play of scenery in their own imaginations was given its full potential. He was worried about the psychological and mental antagonism of the world around the listener: 'we have to endeavour to present situations and emotions that will penetrate deeply into the human consciousness' (Jeffrey, 1925).

Jeffrey believed thrilling melodramatic situations were more effective than subtle ones – an idea that has certainly not been decided in radio drama's history. He talked about the need for writing to stimulate the power of imagination of listeners. He thought that publication of 'radio players in modern dress, sitting with manuscripts in their hands and postured in nonchalant fashion around the microphone' (Jeffrey, 1925) combined with 'the extraordinary objects in the background for producing noises incidental to the play' 'baulked', stifled, and distorted the imagination (Jeffrey, 1925). In production, Jeffrey introduced the projection of radio drama scripts onto screens so that the actor had greater physical freedom to perform without any constriction of the throat – a methodology that neither endured nor lasted.

Like Drinkwater before him, he was preoccupied with lowering standards of public taste and decency 'they will not follow the trend of the present stage play, with its predominating sex, or, rather, sexual, interest' (Jeffrey, 1925). He reminded his readers: 'It must be remembered that radio plays are presented at the family fireside. Their ethics must be unquestionable' (Jeffrey, 1925). By the time this article was written and published, he was struggling to make clear that radio drama writing was not going to be lucrative, but he was able to report that leading writers of the time such as Richard Hughes, Reginald Berkeley, and Edgar Wallace had 'written for broadcasting, have amused or thrilled hundreds of thousands of listeners' (Jeffrey, 1925).

We need to move on to 5th November 1926 and 28th September 1928 to find any clear framework of advice from R.E. Jeffrey for aspiring radio drama playwrights. By then the BBC had mounted national writing competitions, and he felt he had a clear idea of technique for the sound dramatist. In 'Seeing with the Mind's Eye' Jeffrey had decided that 'it has now been established beyond all doubt that every listener who really and truly listens is able to see with his mind's eye every movement and scene of a broadcast play' (Jeffrey, 1926b). He argued that after 4 years of 'careful experiment and study' (Jeffrey, 1926b) he was able to confidently assert 'we know now that mere dialogue, if unattended by considerable action becomes tiresome to even the most attentive listener' (Jeffrey, 1926b). Scripts needed to be filleted with lines 'inessential to the action of character or plot' (Jeffrey, 1926b) cut ruthlessly. Writers and producers of radio plays were 'now thinking in forms, not words. We know now that words when heard are instantaneously translated into forms by the subconscious, and it is thus that we see them' (Jeffrey, 1926b). Jeffrey for all his prejudices and mistakes, for which he is somewhat castigated by radio historians, had settled upon the essential knowledge that sound drama was a thinking and emotional dramatic medium. It was truly cinema of the mind particularly when he was talking about presenting to 'the mind of the listener a continuous and ever-changing series of pictures' (Jeffrey, 1926b). As Jeffrey emphasised 'true drama is emotion, and emotion stimulates its own picture, not through the eye, but through the sub-conscious – the mind's eye' (Jeffrey, 1926b).

Jeffrey advised that 'Good radio plays must possess the quality of reality. They must bear some relation to life as we each and all understand it' (Jeffrey, 1926b), and this certainly did not rule out the appeal of the fantastic or the strange. Jeffrey was an eloquent and poetic theorist when he spoke about striking 'chords which we, too, in our imaginative moments have vibrated' (Jeffrey, 1926b). Jeffrey sought the attuning of minds to the listening experience and he was certainly idealistic in his ambition: 'It gives to those who listen mind pictures painted by sound and imagination only, pictures which will live longer in the memory than those seen by the eyes and painted by the brush of the artist' (Jeffrey, 1926b).

Companion Website Resources

Additions and Updates for Chapter 1 Radio Drama is Born and in its Cradle https://kulturapress.com/2022/08/12/updates-for-chapter-1-radio-drama-is-born-and-in-its-cradle/

David Pownall and Radio Plays https://kulturapress.com/2022/08/09/david-pownall-radio-drama-laureate/

BBC Audio Drama Teaching and Learning https://kulturapress.com/2022/08/10/bbc-audio-drama-teaching-and-learning/

Glossary of Audio and Radio Drama Terms and Vocabulary https://kulturapress.com/2022/08/30/glossary-of-audio-and-radio-drama-terms-and-vocabulary/

Phyllis M Twigg – the BBC's First Original Radio Dramatist https://kulturapress.com/2022/09/24/phyllis-m-twigg-the-bbcs-first-original-radio-dramatist/

Kathleen Baker aka John Overton – a prolific BBC radio playwright lost to history https://kulturapress.com/2022/12/28/kathleen-baker-aka-john-overton-a-prolific-bbc-radio-playwright-lost-to-history/

2

THE PSYCHOLOGY OF WRITING AND LISTENING

At this stage, it is intriguing to compare what is regarded as needed and workable now in the digital age of multi-track digital production for legacy radio, online podcast, and audio fiction audiences with R.E. Jeffrey's thoughts on the psychology of listening in a draft article titled 'Wireless Drama' that has been retained in the BBC Drama Department's archives. It states that it was published in the *Radio Times* with 'slight exertions'. It is the 'exertions' or actual excisions from this primary draft that generate the most interest in terms of defining his sophisticated grasp of the imaginative mutuality in storytelling between sound dramatist and listener.

It is my belief that Jeffrey has had a somewhat negative press from broadcasting historians and academics, and I suspect this was initiated by the character assassination instigated by his successor Val Gielgud with fake letters of criticism to the *Radio Times*. It is also possible there were others who disagreed with Jeffrey's leadership of drama productions and wanted him out. Certainly, he became the scapegoat and lightning rod for blame and responsibility when Reginald Berkeley challenged and embarrassed the BBC over the censorship of his plays. He was publicly humiliated by the appointment of a young Val Gielgud to his job when he had no experience at all of having ever produced a radio programme. Jeffrey's leaving of the BBC in 1929 was bitter and acrimonious.

Consequently, I do not think the depth and sensitivity of his understanding of the psychology of writing audio drama and listening to it has been appreciated. There is a document in BBC Written Archives which appears to be the copy he submitted for a *Radio Times* article while he was drama directions director.

He said there was something amazing about being able to listen without sight to words arranged to conjure emotionally compelling situations. This is because every person places the emotion in a setting specific to their knowledge and the emotion is also a power interacting with their personal experience. This dispenses with artificiality, and combined with high-quality acting this emotion can be universally

DOI: 10.4324/9780203838181-2

accepted. He talked about the personal picture in the mentality of the individual listener assuming a reality which is far more effectual than anything currently offered by stage theatre. He recognised this was a development of Shakespeare's belief that background curtains in theatre should be of unostentatious appearance. This intuitive understanding of the psychology of the imagination of the audience clearly had its parallel with radio drama (BBC Written Archives Centre, Jeffrey, 1924a, p. 2).

Jeffrey certainly indicates that he read psychology and was familiar with the theories of Sigmund Freud. He purposefully applies psychological theory to the practice of writing sound drama. He argues that everyone has a strong conscious and subconscious which is dramatic. Our life histories are made up of dramatic events that are usually suffused with a wide range of emotions, including hate, love, joy, fear, agony, passion, anger, and inspiration. Even if we have never encountered disaster at sea, subconsciousness can supply the analogies needed to construct the imaginative scene with fear of death, steadfast courage, or anything else engaged (BBC Written Archives Centre, Jeffrey, 1924b, pp. 1–2).

It is presumed that Jeffrey compiled the internal briefing on 'Notes on Technique Playwriting for Wireless Broadcast' shortly after his appointment as head of BBC drama productions in July 1924. The document is undated, but the suggested methods for building and sustaining the mental picture seem to draw from the lessons learned through 1923 and early 1924, in particular, the successful series of full-length Shakespeare broadcasts and *Five Birds in a Cage* by Gertrude E. Jennings and *Danger* by Richard Hughes. Jeffrey emphasised the need to avoid confusion of characters, the importance of creating the mental pictures of scenes and appearance of characters, and creating anticipatory atmosphere for the action in the play through dialogue and sound ambience and effects. This is effectively the aural *mise en scène* of the radio play.

He decided there were three types of plays best suited for broadcasting: plays with action set in one scene; plays with action set in one scene but introducing imaginative pictures; and plays with action which move from place to place following the characters' adventures. *Five Birds in a Cage* and *Danger* belong to category one. Jeffrey explained that the second category was the stage equivalent of dream scenes where an illuminated gauze cloth allows another scene to be shown and played while the foreground scene remains (BBC Written Archives Centre, Jeffrey, 1924b, p. 3). He was describing a play with sound cross-fading of times past, present and future, flashbacks, and flashforwards, or more particularly the playing of exterior and interior characterisation. He said this was the equivalent of the cinema play, where the thoughts of a character are reproduced on the screen in picture form to illustrate what is passing in his mind. Essentially, he is explaining how a dramatic character's interior voice and thinking becomes part of the showing self-contained method of dramatic exposition rather than operating merely as a 'voice of god' narrative telling method. It could be argued that Tyrone Guthrie's 1930 radio play *The Flowers Are Not for You to Pick* is a sophisticated example of this genre. The play has effectively one all-enveloping scene where a young clergyman Edward has fallen overboard from a ship bound for China. As he struggles for life in the water, the sounds, images, and emotions of his past life play through his inner consciousness and the listener is part of this spiritual experience. The action play moving from place to place would grow in sophistication through the 1920s and some attention is given in Chapter 4 to L. du Garde Peach's dramatisation of *The 'Mary Celeste'* mystery as an example as well as Tyrone Guthrie's additional experimental plays such as *Squirrel's Cage* and *Matrimonial News*.

Darkness Epiphany Plays of 1923 and 1924

During the first 2 years of BBC radio drama writing and production, writers and producers were certainly preoccupied with exploring the idea that if the main characters in action could be dramatised in darkness, then their effectively blind-fold listeners could vicariously participate. What Gertrude E Jennings achieved in *Five Birds in a Cage* and Richard Hughes with *Danger*, Reginald Berkeley would do with his first BBC radio play *Dweller in the Darkness*. Fast forward 75 years and David Pownall appreciated the culture with his imagining how *Twelfth Night* was produced.

In some respects, Milton Rosmer's direction and production of *Five Birds in a Cage* on 29th November 1923 had many of the characteristics of a contemporary independent production. The play was written by the country's leading exponent of one-act stage comedies and 'specially produced' for the BBC, as the *Radio Times* put it by an experienced theatrical polymath with a developing reputation for act-ing in all media, as well as directing and screenwriting in Britain's developing cin-ema industry. Rosmer would also play the lead role of Professor Ludwig Gerbach in the searingly visceral presentation of anti-Semitism and the Nazi persecution of Jews in Germany in the BBC production and broadcast of *I Am a Jew* in March 1940. The internal history of the BBC Radio Drama Department completed in 1948 identified *Five Birds in a Cage* as the first non-Shakespeare play to be broadcast from a BBC studio. It was hailed by the *Radio Times* in 1934 as:

> This brilliant one-act play, featuring five people trapped in a lift, … possibly the best ever written by the best known writer of one-act plays of modern times. It sparkles with wit and draws character with a deft hand. It was orig-inally produced at the Haymarket Theatre, London, for a special matinée in 1915, and went into the evening bill, where it remained for 284 consecutive performances … and it was one of Martyn C. Webster's most popular pro-ductions last winter.

Five Birds in a Cage and *Danger* were replete with comedic and satirical observations about class context and conflict. The risks and dangers of getting stuck in modern lifts and large-scale mining disasters killing people in trapped circumstances were also abiding global news stories of the time. Packing into London Underground lifts such as those at Goodge Street and Elephant and Castle stations to get to the deep-tunnelled Bakerloo and Northern Lines was a familiar daily commuter experience. In 1909, four men were killed and three seriously injured when a hydraulic lift failed at St Katherine's Dock. Fourteen years previously 'a gentleman' was killed at Lloyds of London in the city when the cage of a lift he was travelling in plunged into the basement from a higher floor. Only a few months after the broadcast of the play, seven people would die when the lift cable in the Zonnebeke church tower in Belgium snapped with the cage crashing more than 100 ft to the ground. The loss of life in mining explosions and shaft cave-ins was much worse. In 1913, 439 miners perished in the gas explosion at the Senghenydd Colliery Disaster in Glamorgan. The haunting sound in *Danger* of Welsh miners singing to console themselves in the darkness of the pit was powerfully resonant. Three years earlier, 344 men died in the Pretoria Pit disaster in Lancashire when there had been an underground explosion at the Hulton Colliery near Bolton.

Five Birds in a Cage ran for about 35 minutes. Jennings' early broadcast scripts have not been archived at the BBC. Fortunately, they were all adapted from her one-act stage plays which were published by Samuel French in the 'French Acting Editions' serving the world-wide demand from English speaking amateur dramatic societies. Every amateur presentation would earn the playwright a fee of one Guinea (1 pound and 1 shilling in old currency or 1 pound and 5 pence in new). They were perfect scripts for regional and touring repertory companies.

The play was first presented in a matinée performance at the Haymarket Theatre in London's West End on Friday 19th March 1915 in the first year of the Great War, when soldiers arriving home on leave at Charing Cross station could pop in for high-quality escapism and entertainment. As celebrated in the *Radio Times* billing, it went into the evening bill 20th April and then ran for 284 consecutive performances. Its beginning could be described as the perfect opening of a radio play and both Alan Beck and Roger Wood would later argue this structure, setting, theme, and production would be the inspiration and template for *Danger* by Richard Hughes in February 1924.

We do not know how Milton Rosmer adapted the play for broadcasting. The stage script seems ready-made for almost immediate performance in front of the microphone. The opening direction does not need any narrator method of setting the scene. It begins sharply with the sound of an ascending lift which suddenly stops. Then we hear the voice of Susan, the Duchess of Wiltshire, complaining that they have stopped, the lights have gone out and asking why. The cockney liftman has no idea. Perhaps somebody could strike a match. Susan hates being in the dark and she warns her male companion Leonard to stop being helpless and strike a light, but he doesn't have any. In the darkness as soon as Susan asks if anyone else can oblige we realise there are other passengers (Jennings, 1915, p. 7).

Had the BBC opened with an edited version of the stage direction, listeners would have missed the anticipation of waiting for the answer to the question of where is the lift and what kind of building or journey has it been halted in? The description is obviously overwritten because the detail is set out primarily for the set designer. As Jeffrey had indicated in his notes for playwriting, the listener's own memory or imagination of London Underground tube lifts would have been sufficient.

The French acting edition describes a stage set showing a tube lift broadside on and the wall covered with framed advertisements. A bench traverses gates at each end which are set at an angle and illumination comes from an electric light in the ceiling and two oil-lamps hanging on nails near each gate. Everything is precise for the purposes of stage management and design. The characters perform within a lift 8 ft deep by 17 ft wide. The left-hand gate needs to be made to open with two backings outside the gates representing the funnel of the tube in a neutral colour. When the curtain rises the scene is in total darkness. The lighting design and operation is also directed: First cue is a good light thrown on the scene from behind the left-hand gate and the second cue light is thrown from the right-hand gate and then the third cue light from an electric bulb at the top, or if not practicable, full lights (Jennings, 1915, p. 7). All of this is, of course, redundant in sound drama. The sound of the lift running, the stopping, rattling of the metal gates, and the voices of the actors are all that is needed to set the scene for the listener's individual imagination.

Alan Beck describes the play as 'an exuberant social satire...The hierarchy of class is temporarily turned upside-down...witty and urbane entertainment' (Beck, 2000:4.1) It is instructive to identify why it succeeds as sound drama. There are five characters who are delineated successfully in gender, class, age, and personality. The play fulfils a golden rule of drama with characters speaking as individuals. A line from each in language, tone, and rhythm will be different and specific to their character. The cast of five are: Susan, the Duchess of Wiltshire; Leonard, Lord Porth; Nelly, a millener's assistant; Bert, a workman (bricklayer); and Horace, the liftman ('Orace' Erbert Evans).

We continue with its intense and suspenseful beginning. The lift has stopped and the lights have gone out. Questions: Is there anyone who can find a light? What is going to happen next? Who are the people in this anxious situation? So far we have heard the voices of Susan, Liftman, and Leonard. While the stage and visual version will proceed with Bert striking a match and revealing his presence for the first time along with Nelly in addition to Susan, Leonard, and the liftman, the radio production would have to achieve this by voices.

The radio script has not been retained in the BBC archives, so we can only surmise how the play would have been adapted. When Susan receives another 'Dunno, lady' in reply to her demand of the liftman to explain what is going on, she turns graciously to Bert and changes the demeanour of her language to include polite hesitation when asking him. He is unable to answer though his cockney voice and class is revealed when calling the Duchess of Wiltshire 'mum'. Susan continues to berate Leonard whom she groups with the liftman as the men who never know anything.

Again the development of this play at the beginning for radio is exquisite. People find themselves trapped in a lift, the lights go out, somebody strikes a match but is told to put it out because there's no smoking in underground lifts, the Liftman has a lamp and switches it on, the dominant character and play's protagonist, Susan, asks him to get the lift moving, but he explains it's nothing to do with him and he can't. The tension between Susan and Leonard, who she identifies in anger as a Peer of the realm, Lord Porth, is palpable particularly when he patronises her by stating the obvious and telling her not to be frightened. They shouldn't be there together at all. We want to know why and if and how they will be released. Up until now Nelly has been described in stage direction notes but not said a word. It could be argued that the way Liftman, Bert, Susan, and Leonard speak with their dialogue effectively gives them the costume for the mind's eye (Jennings, 1915, pp. 8–9). The stage direction to Susan to express her anger towards Leonard by 'lowering her voice' can be heard in its radio version as close microphone and less volume – the expression of human anger in voice with so much more effect than shouting. How did this play actually sound to the BBC's audience at the end of November 1923?

We are fortunate that Gertrude Jennings' play was subject to the first detailed attempt at radio drama criticism. Archibald Haddon was Dramatic Critic to the BBC and only a week later broadcast his talk 'Growth of National Drama' on 5th December 1923 on 2LO. His famous catchphrase was 'Hullo Playgoers'! At the end of his review of theatre across Britain he turned his attention to *Five Birds in a Cage*. In this he was helping to coin the wireless drama vocabulary with phrases such as 'radioplay'. Haddon was impressed by the technical and creative quality of the listening experience:

> Now a word about the radioplay – Gertrude Jennings' 'Five Birds in a Cage' – which was wirelessed from the room where I am speaking. I heard this in a town thirty-five miles from London, and was more than satisfied – indeed, I was delighted. I could almost hear the performers breathing. Not a syllable was slurred; the vocal tones were as clear as the proverbial bell; and the various enunciations of the players, all strikingly contrasted according to character and accent, were every bit as distinct as they were when I saw the play in its original form at the Haymarket Theatre.
>
> It was astonishing to find how easily and naturally the missing visual effects were realised by the imagination without the least expenditure of mental effort. The scene of the piece is a London tube lift which has stuck half-way down. One of the characters, a workman, descends the lift-shaft to reconnoitre. Thirty-five miles from London, I heard the workman's voice receding and fading as he made the descent, and I could hear the women in the lift above him giving tiny little exclamations of apprehension lest he should slip and fall. I could hear the soft drawing of a match over a match-box when an agitated male passenger in the lift sought to relieve his feelings with a cigarette, and the Cockney liftman ordering 'No smoking in the lift'! I could hear the lift gates rattling when the lift arrived at the bottom, and I did not miss the smallest stutter of the dude (sic) [tube] passenger who wanted to know 'What are they d-d-d-doing'?
>
> *(Haddon, 1924, p. 123)*

Milton Rosmer has created a sound design in the BBC Savoy Hill studio that has worked. There are spot effects such as lift sounds and match striking, which in film production are called Foley, operating live and close to the microphone. The properties for the stage script are Fire-extinguisher, two oil lamps, matches (Liftman), Matches (Bert), lighter, and cigarettes (Leonard), large dress box (Nelly), pamphlet, purse, cardcase, and parasol (Jennings, 1915, p. 27). What are the equivalent sound properties for the radio production? This is the transmedia journey taking place in the winter of 1923. Some of the physical props will work as sound props. Others not. This is before the introduction of the Dramatic Control Panel, the grand name for a sound mixing panel. So it was not possible to fade in and out and balance sound from other studios. The Director Rosmer has positioned, blocked, and rehearsed the cast to perform in front of the single microphone radiophonically. *Five Birds in a Cage* ignited Haddon's enthusiasm and hopes for the 'radioplay':

> All this is marvellous, yet it is only the beginning, the inception of the radio play. The producer and announcer, Mr. Milton Rosmer, did the thing perfectly, and Miss Athene Seyler, Mr. Hugh Wakefield, and Mr. Fred Grove were excellent. The radioplay, when it is in full blast, will be a profitable new medium of expression for the actor.
>
> *(Haddon, 1924, pp. 123–124)*

The play then develops with twists and turns and conflict between some of the characters and the emotional tensions that arise from their different needs frustrated by the lift's breakdown. Susan is in conflict with Lord Porth because it appears their car had broken down on the way to or from a 'beastly night club' (Jennings, 1915, p. 9). That's why they used public transport at his behest when she wanted to hail a taxi. It's his fault. Though he gives as good as he gets in the face of Susan's barracking: 'Don't be down on me, Susan' (Jennings, 1915).

We hear from Nelly for the first time who because of their commonality in class first addresses Bert:

> Are we likely to be kept waiting long, do you know? ... Oh, I'm not frightened, in that way. It's only of being late ... it's important. I've got to take the dress, you see. It's due there at half-past seven. Promised. And it's for some one very grand, who'll be very angry if I'm late.
>
> *(ibid 9-10)*

The play in terms of its writing must move forward with dramatic impetus and purpose.

Jennings invests the comedy with substantial layers of political observation. But the BBC was a newly formed private monopoly being listened to closely by government which was determined that it should avoid politically controversial programming. Despite this, the comedy writing cleverly weaves in political satire.

Susan declares that she is a socialist with a capital 'S' because despite being an aristocrat she has been happy to travel third class, take buses, and even on occasion go in a tram. She claims to be the same as Nelly, the working class servant now sharing her space in the lift, and that class distinctions should not exist as they are. She then insults Leonard by saying the only difference between him and the other men in the lift is that they can light lamps and he cannot (Jennings, 1915, p. 11).

The conflict between the upper class couple, Susan and Leonard, intensifies and with the Duchess getting the upper hand over the Lord; largely through mocking and verbal emasculation. There is something rather Suffragettish about Susan. However, respect, sympathy, and affection develops between the working class couple Bert and Nelly.

There are a number of dramatic imperatives now to develop and resolve. Where is the conflict between Susan and Leonard heading? How will the five people in the lift who would never usually choose each other's company escape their confinement? Who will be the saviour and hero or heroine securing their release? What will happen to Nelly if she does not deliver the dress she is carrying on time? Will Bert and Nelly discover a romantic future together as a result of meeting each other in this crisis? How will the class and power relationships between all five characters change or solidify in this experience? Soldiers on leave from the Western Front watching the play in 1915 and 1916 may well have identified how war made classes closely live with one another and fight together in situations of great danger. Certainly listeners will be wondering whether the Liftman moves from his rather morose 'not my fault or job governor' obtuseness and get the lift he is in charge of actually moving.

This is actually a micro-society of a Duchess, a Lord, two workmen, and a servant/seamstress who can cope and work together in a crisis which threatens them all. They are equal in the danger and frustration of their predicament, but they are unequal in different ways in the skills they have which can help them and in their socio-economic standing. If released, Duchess and Lord can return to their privileged lives. Servant/seamstress Nelly may lose her job because she has been unable to deliver the dress on time. Bert still has to strive to earn his living to survive. The liftman will continue working machinery that might get stuck on its way down or up from time to time.

In her persistent belittling of Leonard the Lord, Susan reveals that her challenging personality has dispensed with at least one husband and there is some comedy to be had in the hypocrisy of her condemnation of him as a potential husband, when it is clear that her success as a wife is somewhat in doubt. It is also the case that her nickname is 'Bubbles' and some listeners must surely want to know how she acquired that. Susan remains frustrated that even though Leonard looks intelligent, he remains very, said two times and with emphasis, useless. He is nothing but a shop window. She says that she would have been ashamed to marry him as she is in no doubt he would be much more of a failure as a husband than her first (Jennings, 1915, pp. 10–11).

Susan is what is known as a primary protagonist character. She has the agency in the play in terms of precipitating action and reactions; although, she is as helpless and hopeless as everyone else in the lift due to its malfunction.

Gertrude Jennings has written a political comedy. She satirises the tensions and upturning of social class roles. It is fascinating that on the platform of a private monopoly broadcasting platform being closely monitored for anything remotely bristling with politically controversial content, she gets away with a lot of dramatic cheek. Jennings' credentials as a political activist playwright would surely have been known by anyone making some persistent enquiries. In 1912, she wrote *A Woman's Influence* commissioned by Inez Bensusan as a suffrage play for the Actresses' Franchise League. It was never produced for the BBC, perhaps for obvious reasons. Dale Spender described it as 'biting...and one of its most salient features is the portrayal of men as fools' (Spender & Hayman, 1985, p. 127). One of the main characters, Margaret Lawrence (wife), is described by Carole Hayman 'as a formidable woman, kind, intelligent and moral. Herbert (her husband) probably finds her terrifying' (Spender & Hayman, 1985, p. 128).

The same could be said of the Duchess Susan who takes an interest in the foreman bricklayer Bert for his frequenting of Socialist meetings. Bert's objective in the play is to primarily court Nelly who poignantly describes her consternation of always being at the beck and call of demanding ladies such as Susan: 'I shall be very late with the dress. It's to be worn to-night at a big party and the lady is very particular. She'll be annoyed if the dress isn't there in time' (Jennings, 1915, p. 13). Leonard seems intent on being polite, kind, and apparently dim. Susan clearly realises Bert is the only man in the lift capable of achieving some kind of salvation for all of them and persuades him to ignore the Liftman 'Orace "Erbert Evans" direction that such actions breach all "regilations"'. Nelly fears for Bert's safety and makes her feelings towards Susan very clear by asking why her ladyship does not do the climbing out the lift to get help herself. Nelly asks why she cannot send her young man while gesturing towards Leonard. The row intensifies. Susan is insulted that Nelly should even think of Leonard as her young man. Nelly accuses her of vanity and Leonard agrees with her by declaring that the lady does what she pleases with all of them. Nelly rages that she is confronted by selfishness, cruelty, and that she hates ladies and has no wish to ever become one as long as she lives. Her speech is rounded off with an exclaiming 'never'! (Jennings, 1915, p. 20).

As none of the radio scripts of *Five Birds in a Cage* have survived, we have to derive understanding of the radio potential of the Samuel French edition stage version to appreciate the potential for highly dramatic sound design; particularly, when lift gates need to be rattled, characters climbing up and down the lift shaft communicate in dynamic distancing effect and rescuers call to the characters trapped below. The script references the sound of loud and hollow echoes of voices as Bert endeavours to climb back up to the lift (Jennings, 1915, p. 20).

Bert returns to inform the Liftman that as there has been 'a breakdown all along the line', they need him to go down so that they can 'take it [the lift] off the "ook" and then "lower by the pulleys"'. Somebody in authority can be heard shouting for the liftman to hurry up and he can be heard complaining about having to risk his life which is certainly worth something to him (Jennings, 1915, p. 21).

The four people left in the lift are then violently shaken and wobbled with intermittent loud bangs, troubling rattling of chains, and the frightening sensation of being pitched backwards and forwards. Jennings presents the danger and fear more as an excuse for farce with Susan scolding Leonard again for calling her dear and Leonard replying that he 'didn't dear'. As Susan says if they are to perish altogether they should do so hand in hand, Leonard takes her hand but she pulls it away. Bert says if he is to perish hand in hand with anybody it must be with Nelly because she is his choice for walking out with, and if there is to be a terrible accident he would rather face it with her. Susan preserves her haughty class superiority by clarifying that she had never proposed to walk out with Bert. Nelly, meanwhile, declares she will be with Bert, and Susan despairs at the idea she might have to die with Leonard (Jennings, 1915, pp. 23–24).

When it seems death is about to come, Susan begins to make desperate exhortations of apology and promises to be nice to everyone, that she will forgive everyone everything and would so much like to help Nelly (Jennings, 1915, pp. 24–25). She discovers that Nelly's dress was intended for her and that she was the demanding aristocrat putting her under so much pressure. She is even prepared to adopt Nelly and Bert too. They can both come and live with her because she is prepared to do anything to be able to survive her present ordeal (Jennings, 1915). But then the lights come back on. They hear a voice explaining quite reassuringly that they will all be up in a minute. Whatever the physical dislocations and ideological distortions of this crisis, the instinctive vectors of class relationship and hierarchy are maintained.

When Susan says they have been saved, she is clearly referring to the restoration of social equilibrium even though that balance is somewhat far removed from the real nature of the social equality she professed to support so enthusiastically earlier. She sets about gathering up all her bags and parasols and instructs Leonard that because she is still feeling very shaky he can accompany her home but only as far as her door. She suddenly remembers Bert and Nelly. The dress needs to be brought round to her without delay but with the concession that she will not complain this time.

Horace the liftman climbs in, and when Susan asks if the danger has passed, he says rather dismissively that they had all been in no more danger than a barrel of bloaters, which at the time was a type of whole cold-smoked herring. Horace also restores his authority by taking an extinguisher from Leonard's hands, admonishes him about breaching 'regulations' again and that he should know better, closes the gates, calls down the shaft for them to go ahead and reminds everyone there is no smoking in the lift (Jennings, 1915, p. 26).

In the 1928 version of the play published in Marriott's edited *One-Act Plays of To-day*, the liftman's line on bloaters has been changed to 'You ain't been in no more than a barrel of bananas', and with Susan's riposte being changed to 'Bananas! Oh, how nasty'! (Marriott, 1928, p. 215). It can be assumed that the later version drew more laughter from the audience. Nowadays we can certainly picture bananas in a barrel, but not necessarily have any understanding of bloaters and what they would look like in one.

Alan Beck argues:

> There is more than a dash of Bernard Shaw here. The Duchess of the 1915 stage play is obviously an intellectual Fabian, with a slight suggestion of Beatrice Webb. Could "Susan, Duchess of Wiltshire" be imagined as a guest of Lady Ottoline Morrell at Garsington?
>
> *(Beck 2000: 3.1.15)*

Beck imagines Susan following Labour in the 6th December General Election of 1923. He adds: 'Bert the bricklayer was being politicised, but in his promotion, resists being unionised. He is heading for the Tory branch of the petty bourgeoisie' (Beck, 2000).

Gertrude Jennings' one-act plays would be a mainstay of dramatic entertainment on BBC Radio in the years that followed. *Five Birds in a Cage* would be revived many times including in the early 1930s. Other plays broadcast included *Waiting for The Bus, Between the Soup and the Savoury, The Rest Cure, Me and My Diary, Poached Eggs and Pearls*, and *The New Poor*. It is intriguing that *Waiting for the Bus* first presented in the theatre in 1917 may have appealed more to the ear than to the eye given the very poor opinion of it left to posterity by George Street, the Lord Chamberlain's official censor of stage plays:

> Not so amusing as some of the author's efforts. It simply displays the obvious humours suggested by people waiting for a bus in these days of crowded business. There is a sham-sensitive woman who thinks she condescends and is annoyed by the crowd, a woman with inquisitive children, a government official dropping papers which are picked up by a comic spy, and so on. When the bus comes the sensitive lady knocks everybody out of the way and gets the one vacant place. Recommended for license.
>
> *(Street, 1917, p. 1016)*

But Mr. Street does define the realism and relationship to everyday life which listeners could identify with. Orderly queuing at bus stops in Britain did not become a public ritual until the Second World War.

Gertrude Jennings died in 1958 after a long and esteemed career as a professional playwright with one film credit *The Girl Who Forgot*, in 1940, directed by Adrian Brunel. Full-length play presentations in the West End in the 1920s were complimented by W. MacQueen-Pope: 'There was a charming comedy by Gertrude Jennings, called *The Young Person in Pink*. It did quite a little tour of the West End – such things often happened then – playing at the Haymarket, the Aldwych and the Queens' (MacQueen-Pope, 1959, p. 41). He highlighted her *Love among The Paint Pots* running to 73 performances at the Aldwych (MacQueen-Pope, 1959, p. 85) and in

1923 *Isobel, Edward and Anne* at the Haymarket for 100 performances (MacQueen-Pope, 1959, p. 106). In the fourth edition of *One-Act Plays of To-day*, the editor James William Marriott observed:

> Miss GERTRUDE JENNINGS is a prolific writer of one act plays, and is immensely popular for a multitude of reasons. No humourist is more fully aware than she that people begin to be comic when they get into an awkward predicament, and as the situation becomes more and more hopeless the fun grows more furious. Her characters are clearly defined, and usually broadly contrasted in temperament as well as in social position. The scenes are invariably plausible incidents in present day life, and Miss Jennings intensifies effects and adds a touch of farce. Her play 'Between the Soup and the Savoury' which was included in the third series of 'One Act Plays of Today', has pathos as well as laughter. 'The Young Person In Pink' is the best known of her longer plays.
>
> *(Marriott, 1928, p. 194)*

She was last produced for the BBC Home Service (now Radio 4) with the adaptation by Cynthia Pughe of her full-length play *Family Affairs* in 1950. The play described by the *Times* in 1934 as 'the perfect modern play of character' (Anon, 26 July 1934) had been a West End success with one scene actually broadcast live in February 1935 from a studio at Alexandra Palace on the inaugural BBC television service.

The Not So 'Comedy' of *Danger*

Richard Hughes' *Danger* was extensively reviewed and written about on transmission in January 1924, continued to be celebrated in the years that followed and first produced by NBC in the USA in 1927, and the first sound representation that has survived from the early part of the 20th century was a production of *Danger* by the CBS Workshop in 1935. It was the first original radio play produced for broadcast in Japan. But listening to it now is a very strange experience. The writing, culture, and production values seem so very remote and old-fashioned to the 21st century listener. This is largely true of most of the scripts and sound drama produced through the first decades of the BBC's history. But it was a landmark in audio drama development at the BBC. It is helpful to explore why this is the case.

The play has three distinctive characters: Jack, a young man; Mary, a young woman, and Mr. Bax, an elderly man with a gruff voice and rather a stilted manner of speech, plus a party of Welsh miners who say a few words and are heard singing. They are all plunged into an intense action drama in a coal mine when the lights go out; then there's an explosion and finally the mine floods with water. Will they die and experience their last moments in complete darkness or will they escape and be rescued? This is a claustrophobia disaster and horror mise en scène which is full of drama and suspense. The script of the play published by Chatto and Windus in

1928 said: 'The *Noises* required include an explosion, the rush of water, footsteps, and the sound of a pick. There must be an echo, to give the effect of the tunnel (Hughes, 1928, p. 173).

It is also clear that if it had any theatrical or stage production the audience would have to be in some kind of black box and total darkness:

> The Author was asked by the British Broadcasting Company, in January 1924, to write a play for effect by sound only, in the same way that film plays are written for effect by sight only. This was thus the first 'Listening-Play', an experiment in a new medium which has since been considerably developed. It was first produced by Nigel Playfair, and broadcast from the London Station on January 15th, 1924. For direct presentation, it should be acted in pitch-darkness, and is thus better suited for performance in a room, without a stage at all, than in even a small theatre.
>
> *(p. 171)*

We can be grateful to the *Daily Mail* for an account of 'how it was done':

> Listeners-in were advised that as the action of the play took place in the dark, they should hear it in the dark, and many adopted the advice and lowered the lights. A *Daily Mail* reporter saw the play produced at the London broadcasting station. In a brightly lit room a young woman in evening dress and two men holding sheets of paper in their hand declaimed to a microphone their horror at being imprisoned in the mine. Outside the room a young man sat cross-legged on the floor, with telephone receivers on his ears, and as he heard through the receivers the progress of the piece he signaled to two assistants on a lower landing to make noises to represent the action of the play. In a passage stood five men singing through a partly opened door leading to the broadcasting room. They were a group of 'miners' singing in another passage in the mine.
>
> *(Anon, 1924, p. 7)*

This was a play of continuous action in one setting and ideally suited for a sequence lasting just less than half an hour. Five segments of plot can be identified:

1. Jack and Mary find themselves trapped down a mine which they are visiting in Wales when the lights suddenly go out. Jack observes there must be a thousand feet between them and the surface. Mary says she has never known such extreme blackness and now she knows what it is like to be blind (Hughes, 1928, p. 176). They appear to be guided or joined there by an older man called Bax.
2. At first Mary's apparent light-hearted demeanour and language might represent the 'comedy' in the title, but her frivolity is rapidly extinguished when an explosion is heard and the rushing in of water presents the terrible threat of drowning.

She is screaming and Jack complains that she is throttling him. She is struggling to breathe and both of them are panicking as there is another explosion nearer, followed by the hiss of water. They then hear voices singing 'Ar hyd y Nos', which is the sound of the Welsh miners. Bax acknowledges their courage. The roar of the water is getting louder and drowns out the singing of the miners. Mary says she is convinced they are going to drown too (Hughes, 1928, pp. 179–181).

3. Mary and Jack express panic over the prospect of death because they feel they have so much to give the world as well as themselves. The evocative sound of Welsh miners consoling themselves with singing can be heard again in the distance. Bax says he wished he had their faith and when observing that such faith would make dying easy. Mary reacts with fear and makes it clear she does not want to die yet. Bax does his best to console her by saying that if they are to die now it would be better to do so in each other's arms. He says death would be joining them closer together. But Mary finds little comfort in his words and continues wailing that she wishes to live (Hughes, 1928).

4. There is a much more philosophical debate about ageing and death and the older man Bax challenges the contention that a long life is in any way less important or deserving of continuing than young apparently promising lives taken well before their time. He says it is harder to leave this world when 60 than it is at the age of 20. Jack undergoes some epiphanies including an appreciation of his love of Mary and the importance of his work. He is not prepared to meet death so meekly because he has so much to live for in his work and love for Mary (Hughes, 1928, p. 185).

5. As the water rises higher towards their chest and shoulders, the terror and fear provokes contrasting reactions. Bax becomes more unstable while the young couple are more stoical. Bax hoarsely despairs at the thought of dying. Jack says he is an old coward who needs to pull himself together. Mary has become calm and says she has come to terms with her fate.

As Bax repeatedly shouts for help, Jack says nobody can hear them, and it would be best to keep calm as the end is getting closer (Hughes, 1928, p. 187).

Rescuers approach and break through with their pick-axes. Bax provides the climactic surprise in character development by becoming the hero and insisting he will be the last to be hauled up by the rope. But the deadly inundation of flooding water sweeps him away before he can be saved.

The BBC's drama critic Archibald Haddon was also listening and was both complimentary and critical:

> [On] the whole the first radioplay was a triumph of the broadcaster's art. Its intention was to thrill the listener, and undoubtedly the listener was thrilled. In places, perhaps, the noises off might have been made more convincing – but I may attribute the failing to stage-craft, or transmission, or reception … the performance was a revelation of the possibilities of the radio play as a new form of drama.

Even the subtleties and niceties of literary expression 'got over,' as they say in the theatre. We seemed to be well in the dramatist's mind when he made a character say, as he stood in the valley of the shadow of death, 'Life is like a trusted friend who grows more precious as the years go by', or when he made one terrified character say to another, 'If you run you will get in a panic and go mad in the dark'. Many of us, listening hundreds of miles away, with our eyes closed, and our pulses beating, were there in spirit beside those agonised people in the stricken coal-mine … The young man who lost his nerve, played by Mr. Kenneth Kent, was particularly good when he gave way to hysterical laughter. The occasional bits of humour got over, too. I remember laughing heartily when the young man said he wrote poetry, and his elderly companion retorted 'Good God! and you call that work'!

(Haddon, 1924, pp. 160–161)

It can certainly be said that Richard Hughes demonstrates how to capture and draw in the listener's engagement in the first few seconds of a radio play after all the lights have gone out. His two central characters rapidly set the scene and urgency asking the questions: 'What's happened? Where are you'? with answers such as 'I can't find you, I can't find it' (Hughes, 1928, p. 175).

Christina L Pepler observed: 'The darkness, the danger, the sense of the characters' being trapped and helpless, literally suffering a degree of sensory deprivation, waiting to see whether they will live or die, show an instinctive grasp on Hughes's part of what the separate aesthetic qualities of drama on the air might be' (Pepler, 1988, pp. 78–79). But she also finds that Hughes has a tendency to overwrite for the listener with the melodrama and *grand guignol* in language straining suspension of disbelief and the need for realism. Hughes fails to discover or deploy the power of silence in audio dramatic pacing. The character Bax, in particular, is prolix in many of his key speeches blaming 'dithering fools' and 'incompetent idiots' for their predicament (Pepler, 1988, p. 177). He has a rather poignant speech about it not being any easier for the old to die compared to the young. He talks about life becoming more precious as time goes by. He does not want to lose what he calls his trusted friend. He is dismissive of what he condemns as imbecilic and lunatic youth. He has had 60 solid years of authentic living and not some rosy dream or trumpery shadow (Pepler, 1988, p. 182).

The excessive use of exclamation marks in the text might be a clue to the internal balance of characterisation being awry and the extent of the overwriting. Haddon though considered the speech about life becoming a trusted friend as powerful writing and had the effect of placing the listener in the dramatist's mind. Furthermore, it can be argued that Hughes does succeed in conveying considerable pathos at the end when it is Bax who sacrifices himself in order to save the young lives of Jack and Mary. Mary faints, Bax stays to put the rope around her shoulders and so she can be taken up to safety. He insists Jack goes before him as the water is rising so treacherously. After all of the deep angst about mortality and the terrors of having to confront death in such pitch black darkness, Bax says the younger man has more value in the world than he has. And he has to think of Mary. After Jack finds himself being hoisted up rather against his will, he says it ought to be Bax. By the time the rope is lowered again nothing can be heard when Bax's name is shouted over and over again, and Jack utters the final words of the play: 'Good God, he's gone!' (Hughes, 1928, p. 191).

So it is the morose older man whose chivalry engages the listener's sympathy and also a sense of dramatic irony in doing the opposite of what he led listeners to expect in the earlier parts of the play. Haddon did not like the beginning or the end: 'The ending of the play seemed too abrupt, and the beginning too sudden – a criticism which is more applicable to the other radioplays in the same programme' (Haddon, 1924, p. 162). However, Haddon did elucidate the creative capacity of the sound of the human voice in audio drama in terms of impact:

> The next thing that occurs to me in connection with these radio plays is the agreeable revelation they gave of the astonishing capacity they possess for the clear and incisive differentiation of character by the employment of vocal tones along – tones entirely unassisted by facial or gestural expression or any of the many other aids available to the performer in a theatre.
>
> *(Haddon, 1924)*

It was Richard Hughes' *Danger* which caught the attention as the significant development in the original radio play and not Gertrude Jennings' *Five Birds in a Cage*. Of course, the first was written solely for radio and the latter was an adaptation. As previously mentioned, the first Director of BBC Programmes, Arthur Burrows, in his 1924 *The Story of Broadcasting*, thought the thrilling production was the first to conjure sound drama so well with sound effects, and this opened up such a wide range of possibilities (Burrows, 1924, p. 81). Jean Chothia, in her history of British drama 1890–1940 said:

> The characters in *Danger* are sharply, if simply, delineated and the plot line very clear … Hughes created a model for subsequent radio writing as he traced emotional shifts from levity to panic, resignation and then relief. The dialogue has a realistic edge.
>
> *(Chothia 1996:249)*

Alan Beck credits *Danger* with initiating an effective demonstration of what Gordon Lea would describe as the 'self-contained method' of dispensing with the narrator and announcer within a radio play's text. He says Hughes was 'the first radio playwright to deal with description – building into the script descriptions of events and the "mise en scène." These served to compensate for the single-modality medium' (Beck, 2000: 4.2.15). Beck believes *Danger* is the first truly radiogenic play – a work of dramatic art uniquely suited from an aesthetic point of view for the radio/sound medium. At the same time he recognised that it was wordy, and operating in only one scene without any leaps of temporality and spaciality. Cecil Lewis in *Broadcasting from Within* said the play was short, 'largely narrative in form' and developed quickly, 'each voice character... [was] sharply contrasted in tone' and voice carried the story and action forward (Lewis, 1924, p. 121).

Hughes was not as experienced and successful a dramatist as Gertrude Jennings. His work had not been directed and performed in front of as many physical theatrical audiences, and it is clear that his script was rushed and always in need of rewriting. That is the craft of the playwright in any medium. There is much evidence from different sources that *Danger* was a hurried script as his biographer Richard Graves also clearly indicated in his description of Hughes meeting Nigel Playfair for coffee in January 1924:

> [M]entioned that he was engaged to put an hour's semi-theatrical entertainment on the air the next [Tuesday] evening... 'You know, Hughes', he remarked suddenly. 'I believe what is really wanted for broadcasting is something specially written for the job. A pity there's no time now to get it done; we begin rehearsing after lunch tomorrow'.
>
> *(Graves, 1994, p. 101)*

Graves explains that Hughes said he would like to have a try knowing he already had a broadcasting play in draft form that he had been working on over Christmas. Graves says it was completed overnight so that Hughes was in a position to 'read out his revised and polished work to Playfair' (Graves, 1994) over breakfast the following morning. It is, therefore, somewhat uncertain to credit Gertrude Jennings as being the main influence and inspiration for Hughes' work, though the entrapment of characters in a threatened and darkened environment is certainly a coincidence. Hughes does not reference listening to *Five Birds in a Cage*. We only know he was interested in writing for radio at around the time it was broadcast and as Val Gielgud would make very clear 22 years later, any writer who wishes to write radio drama needs to listen to it. Graves gives further information about the rapidity and improvisation which went into the play's production at Savoy Hill:

> Sir Nigel Playfair liked what he had heard. *Danger*, by Richard Hughes went into rehearsal a few hours later, and was broadcast on Tuesday 15 January 1924. It was the world's first radio play, and received excellent notices. Not only had the story been dramatic; but the special effects had worked well: hollow mine-entombed voices were produced by speaking into buckets; the Welsh miners' chorus had sung uninterrupted behind closed doors which were simply opened whenever the sound was wanted; and the press (who listened to the play in darkness from a room inside Broadcasting House [This was actually the BBC's Savoy Hill headquarters]) were particularly excited by the deafening explosion. (In rehearsal, the first 'explosion' had shattered the microphone; so in performance; while at the vital moment the press were treated to a truly terrifying bang from the room next door to the one in which they were sitting.)
>
> *(Graves, 1994, p. 103)*

The claim for *Danger* being the world's first radio play is certainly debatable given the evolution of sound drama in other countries and cultures. But Alan Beck does define it as a pioneering work which should also be recognised for the technical achievement in developing three characters who 'not only moved to and from the microphone, but that the lines demanded they embodied the action into their acting of the script, as the water rose and rose' (Beck, 2000:4.2.17). In the end, it would be more accurate to say this was a modest beginning of original radio drama writing by a young playwright learning his craft. Beck enthusiastically concluded: 'The lights went out at the beginning of the "Danger" script and lit up the whole future of writing for radio drama' (Beck, 2000: 4.2.19).

The Dweller in the Darkness

In April 1925, the *Radio Times* announced that *The Dweller in the Darkness: A Play of the Unknown,* and another half hour play by Vernon Bartlett, *Entertaining Mr. Waddington,* were being considered important developments in the art of the broadcast play:

> [I]t should be remarked that this departure represents a further state in the development of the new Radio Drama. The B.B.C desires to use fresh material in this way rather than stage plays which, however good, do not always lend themselves to wireless transmission. In pursuance of this policy, the Company has commissioned several well-known authors to write plays having particular regard both to the conditions imposed by the microphone and those experienced by listeners. It is hoped to present plays which will give a clear picture of the story and situations as the producers desire to convey them to the listener.
>
> *(Anon, 1924, p. 100)*

Berkeley's first radio play was broadcast 12 times by the BBC and during the 1920s always directed by R.E. Jeffrey who we could assume introduced him to the art of writing plays for the microphone. The story is classic radio horror. A group of people take part in a séance and the ghostly forces summoned from another world lead to murder most foul. It should also be pointed out that this was in all likelihood the first ever play written for broadcasting to be published in script form; albeit for the amateur dramatic society and touring/repertory theatre industry. No mention was made that it had begun its life as a play written specially for radio. This may account for the BBC version in 1932 presented by The Bath Citizen House Players and relayed from The Summer School of Dramatic Art, Citizen House, Bath. One scene and six characters. And an opening set out in the *Radio Times* which would eventually take the listening audience engaging with the one sense of hearing into the darkness experienced by the people in the play:

The scene is a card room at Hardenby Court, a large house rented furnished by Mr. Vyner. The room is a comfortable one, with shaded electric lights and a parquet floor. The time and the characters will be made plain in the course of the play.

(Anon, 3 Jan 1926, p. 59)

The Dweller in the Darkness stage script published in 1926 was classic *grand guignol*— a genre of theatre, Berkeley was a past master of (Crook, 2020, pp. 210–211). It can be argued that even in its short length as a one-act play having most of it played in darkness on the stage might strain the patience of a theatre audience. The booklet provides stage directions on when the lights go on and off and the direction of a revealing spot. It was produced, like with Gertrude Jennings' plays, for the amateur performance market, without any indication it had been originally commissioned as a play for performance in front of a microphone.

The clearest clue as to its radiophonic origin is in how Berkeley describes in detail the vocal contrasts between the characters. This is a vital requirement in audio drama that transcends the writing, casting, and performance. When not achieved, Alan Beck described the fatal problem of same voices in radio plays as 'clustering'.

The players are MRS. VYNER, mature, solid, with a heavy contralto voice; HENRY, lean, light-hearted and light-voiced, in the early twenties; MORTIMER, an older man, dry, sceptical, speaking in a rasping bass; and PHILLIS VYNER, eighteen, soprano …VYNER has a Scottish accent; URQUHART… thin and refined voice.

(Berkeley, 1926, pp. 6–8)

Christina L. Pepler was unimpressed with the writing: 'The thin plot, poor characterisation and cumbersome dialogue would need the advantage of radio's novelty factor. Moreover to work properly on stage the action of the play would need reworking' (Pepler, 1988, p. 106). Pepler adds, he 'used the aesthetic nature of radio more genuinely and fundamentally than perhaps he realised himself' (Pepler, 1988).

The characters are sitting down to play bridge and when the electricity meter runs out, this becomes the convenient setting to have a séance. Vyner describes how a six-foot hunchback, once lived in the house, was very fond of a knuckleduster and killed someone with it in a rage after being accused of cheating at cards. The repeated blows from the murderer 'ploughed up the man's features as though they'd been peeled off – wiped out – obliterated. It killed him' (Berkeley, 1926, p. 7).

Mortimer is cynical and makes fun of the ghost. Up until now the radio audience would have become accustomed to emotionally enjoining the characters in the play dwelling in darkness and perhaps unable to recognise or fully perceive any stranger or invading presence (Crook, 2020, p. 209). The end is somewhat predictable, but when it comes the terror created in the imagination of the listener had the potential to reach an intensity that was certainly in the *grand guignol* tradition:

MORTIMER: (*savagely*). Then get out of the way, you, whoever you are. You in front of me. (*A note of restrained terror coming into his voice.*) Get out of the way! (*Shouting.*) Get out of the way! I'll lay you out if you play the fool ... It's your own doing. Take it then!

(*The sound of a hurried rush forward; a sudden terrible gasp. A fearful blow; a dreadful crashing fall; and a horrible groan.*)

EVERY ONE: What's the matter? What's the matter?

(*A pounding noise is still audible.*)

URQUHART: ...Can't someone strike a match? (*A horrible laugh.*) Who's that laughing?

VYNER: (panting). I'll have this in a minute – Henry, there are matches in my coat.

HENRY: (*striking them*). Won't strike. (*The laugh again.*) Isn't there a light on the landing? I'll open the door. (*The door thrown open and a gleam of light from with-out.*) Now you can see a bit—(*Horrified*) What's that crouching over Mortimer?

URQUHART: Don't be hysterical, man. There's nothing there. (*The click of the switch. The light goes on.*)

VYNER: Got it.

HENRY: My God, look at Mortimer.

(MORTIMER *is lying in a crumpled heap over the sofa. They rush to him.*)

URQUHART: Turn him over quick.

VYNER: ...Horrible!... Horrible!

PHILLIS: (*screaming with terror*). He hasn't got a face – He hasn't got a face-

THE END OF THE PLAY

(*Berkeley, 1925, p. 16*)

Pepler's overall view is that the play:

> starts slowly; the dialogue is unconvincing, the explanations pedestrian, the plot overall boring, contrived ... had the charm on radio of novelty ... and even today is interesting as an attempt to grapple with the aesthetic require-ments of the new medium.

> (*Pepler, 1988, p. 107*)

Her evaluation captures the paradox of writing radio drama. A script created for the sound medium will not necessarily amount to good literature in the same way that well-written drama for the stage and in prose does not necessarily work for radio – a truth that would be confirmed by the poet and BBC producer Louis MacNeice when introducing the book publication of one of his verse scripts in 1944:

> Sound-broadcasting gets its effects through sound and sound alone, This very obvious fact has two somewhat contradictory implications: (1) A good radio play or feature presupposes a good radio script; (2) such a script is not neces-sarily a piece of 'good writing'.

> (*MacNeice, 1944, p. 8*)

Companion Website Resources

Additions and Updates for Chapter 2 The Psychology of Writing and Listening https://kulturapress.com/2022/08/12/updates-for-chapter-2-the-psychology-of-writing-and-listening/

R E Jeffrey Pioneer Science Fiction Audio Playwright https://kulturapress.com/2022/08/29/r-e-jeffrey-pioneer-science-fiction-audio-playwright/

Gertrude E Jennings – BBC's Pioneering One Act Playwright https://kulturapress.com/2022/08/10/gertrude-e-jennings-bbcs-pioneering-one-act-playwright/

Richard Hughes – Playwright and Novelist https://kulturapress.com/2022/08/10/richard-hughes-playwright-and-novelist/

The Radio Plays of Reginald Berkeley https://kulturapress.com/2022/08/17/the-radio-plays-of-reginald-berkeley/

Eric Fraser Radio Drama Artist and Illustrator https://kulturapress.com/2022/09/24/eric-fraser-radio-drama-artist-and-illustrator/

3

INSTRUMENTAL UTILITARIANISM IN RADIO PLAYWRITING

The Evolving Thoughts of Val Gielgud

Val Gielgud took over as the second director of Drama Productions at the BBC in 1929 after being part of a coup to eject R.E. Jeffrey from this position. It may well be the case he had the connivance of the BBC's Director-General John Reith. Gielgud had directed and flattered Reith in a production for the Corporation's amateur dramatic society during the year before his appointment. It can certainly be said that Gielgud had more to say about the microphone play and how to write it than he had in terms of equivalent experience and track record in writing and producing it. In 1929, he immediately set to work setting out his policy of best writing in a series of articles for *The Radio Times*. He even wrote three radio plays, directed and broadcast them, and had them published in a 1932 volume *How to Write Broadcast Plays*.

By 1946 and with the benefit of so much more experience – 15 years of script-editing, directing and indeed writing himself – he acknowledged that his earlier instructional text:

> ...is now out of print – which is just as well, considering that it is also for the most part out of date. It contained three radio plays of my own – *Exiles, Red Tabs*, and *Friday Morning* – and the late Mr. Filson Young, in a not disagreeably unflattering review of the book, remarked that it would have been more truly titled How *not* to Write Broadcast Plays. Fifteen years later it is not very difficult to agree with him.
>
> *(Gielgud, 1946, p. vii)*

Between 24th May and 28th June 1929 Gielgud had published in the Radio Times six articles 'For the Aspiring Dramatist' on what was described as 'The Microphone Play'.

DOI: 10.4324/9780203838181-3

He was setting out his own independent agenda on radio drama and how to write it. The last time anything as ambitious as this had been attempted was 1926 when the producer at the BBC's Newcastle station Gordon Lea wrote and published *Radio Drama and How to Write It* which is discussed further in Chapter 4.

It is a fact that Gielgud's entry in 1929 as productions director represented a style of 'Year Zero'. R.E. Jeffrey was history. Gielgud's agenda is dynamic and positive. He wants to bury radio drama's 'Cinderella' status. It could not be said that Gielgud did not undergo a baptism of fire in his first year. There were trenchant attacks from the Press.

Gielgud's reply to the Sunday Express Radio critic 'Mr Swaffer' in November 1929 was, to say the least, smouldering. Rather than present a rational defence of radio drama or inspire a vision on the special properties of the broadcast play, Gielgud goes for the jugular and seeks to patronise and ridicule the BBC's critic:

> It seems to me to be a little unfortunate that the critic in question should have chosen to unmask his guns upon the wrong target. He was abusing a certain 'feature programme, called "Russian Twilight," 'for being a bad play'. "Russian Twilight" was not a play; it had no pretensions to being a play; and was not called a play.
>
> *(Gielgud, 1929, p. 314)*

Gielgud scatterguns adjectives to define the newspaper attack as being 'damning', 'pillorying', abusive, 'unfair', and having responded in a highly emotional and somewhat petulant manner declares: 'But I do not propose to enter into either a debate or a slanging match with Mr Swaffer' (Gielgud, 1929). It is certainly true to say he did not enter into a debate, but it is not true to say that he avoided a slanging match. Nothing of any theoretical significance emerges from this article apart from the statement 'Radio drama is not yet set in any final recognizable mould' (Gielgud, 1929). However, he does seek to divide radio drama into three categories:

> First plays, written directly for the microphone; secondly, the story which may in its original form have been either novel or play, adapted for the microphone; and thirdly, the classic drama of the spoken word which, just because it depends upon the spoken word rather than upon anything else for its merits and reputation as a classic, can be brought to the microphone almost exactly as it was written for the stage.
>
> *(Gielgud, 1929, p. 357)*

The writing in these articles could not be described as consistent and it should be borne in mind that they were written by a busy productions executive marshalling a new role as well as managing a complex and demanding centre of creativity and live performance. Key points are extrapolated and then illustrated by what Gielgud himself describes as key or landmark productions in the year. Reference is also made to productions which are not necessarily discussed by Gielgud but certainly had a significant impact.

Article 1 was published on page 397 for the issue of 24 May 1929. It can be argued that many of the points he makes resonate as the advice and creative cultural imperatives for BBC Radio Drama up until the present day. The points made throughout the series also set out the parameters of limited 'praxis' philosophy attending radio drama as an artform. It is argued that certainly within the United Kingdom little progress has been made in understanding and communicating the potential of irony, narratology, and storytelling philosophy which might be unique to audio play.

The Wireless Play – I. For the Aspiring Dramatist

a. Dramatists should study the medium with 'special care'.
b. Stop regarding radio as a Cinderella Medium for writing. It is not in its experimental stage and does not have to justify itself.
c. There are no great financial profits for the writer, but it should be professionally remunerated.
d. As with any writing medium you need to be practical. 50 cast members and 7 acts is unrealistic. Do not waste time writing plays that 'are hopelessly incapable of performance'.
e. In 1929 the Productions Department at Savoy Hill received on average 25 plays a week. Of every 100 plays received only 2 complied with 'the special conditions for their claims to be seriously considered for production'.
f. 'Ignore Stage Technique'.
g. Scotch the idea that 'the microphone' is a poor substitute for the real theatre and 'therefore bad art'. Gielgud said: 'The time is over for this curious assertion that the broadcast play is the blind Cinderella of the drama'.
h. It is different. Radio is not a nursery slope or practice run for stage, television or film.
i. Common ground does exist: The ability to write good, witty or forceful dialogue is born, not made. Both stage and radio play need 'the ability to write'.
j. It may be easier to cover bad writing in the theatre with spectacle, good looks, pretty clothes, ingenuity of production – 'Not so with the radio play'.
k. Radio Drama has been absolutely divorced from Stage Drama. Gone are the days when 'a microphone might be put into a theatre to broadcast a play from the stage'.
l. Film broke away and made its own art-form because there was no sound. In 1929 with the advent of the Talkies, there was a need to 'break away' from the limitations inseparable from the stage.

(Gielgud, 24 May 1929, p. 397)

Coinciding with his first two articles were two highly critical letters published in the 'What the Other Listener Thinks' column that have all the hallmarks of Gielgud faking controversial points to generate debate and support aspects of his policy and agenda:

From time to time the BBC complain that writers do not appreciate the art of the radio drama, that too few suitable plays are submitted to them and so on. Setting aside the question of remuneration, let us consider what the BBC does to encourage embryo radio dramatists. Perchance the young writer will start with a one-act comedy, which will take at least five hours to write out and type, in addition to time and labour involved in planning it out. The odds are that this first born is returned with a circular, saying that it has received careful consideration, but is not quite suitable for broadcast purposes; not a word of advice or encouragement. As the play has been written especially for broadcasting, it is practically useless submitting it to any other market, and the young author's hopes are summarily shattered. Half a dozen words of encouragement might be the means of discovering a Shakespeare of the ether – Yours Disgruntled.

(31 May 1929, p 487)

A reason for arguing that Gielgud could have been the author is that it matches his concern about the low level of remuneration for writers. He was fond of referring to Dr. Samuel Johnson's dictum that only a blockhead would write for anything except money (Gielgud, 1946, p. xv).

Might I make two simple suggestions about broadcast plays? Firstly, that as the actors are not seen, the characters should be few; otherwise the effort to distinguish the voices destroys the pleasure of listening. This is quite different in the theatre, where the action is seen. Secondly, that broadcast plays should, as a rule, be short. This is not realized yet, to judge by words quoted from The Radio Times of June 7: 'The listening audience has not yet acquired the automatic habit of listening to radio plays as they have the habit of watching a play in the theatre'. Why? The answer is in the last three words. When we go to the theatre we take 'time off', and have then nothing to do but enjoy 'seeing' and 'hearing' for two or three hours. At home, on the contrary, we are liable to interruptions – a caller, letters to be written, etc., children, and the hundred and one things to be done after the ordinary work of the day. So the busy householder likes a short play – Yours V.M.C, Newbury.

(28 June 1929, p. 670)

The reason for suggesting that Gielgud may have authored this letter is that it draws attention to his article, generates a debate and reemphasises via another source the need for aspiring writers to consider the special conditions of the radio drama listener. It also, like the correspondence from 'Disgruntled', has no actual identifying feature apart from three initials and the town of Newbury in Berkshire which even in 1929 had a sizeable population.

Val Gielgud. The Wireless Play – II. Choice of Subject

a. For radio they must 'appeal to an enormous audience'.

b. Radio 'is entertainment of modern democracy'.

c. Radio has to be considered as appealing 'potentially to a far greater number of people' than cinema.

d. Consider the audience. It is easy 'for sophisticated and hyper-intelligent people to be funny at the expense of an organisation which has to make allowances for such an apparently demoded thing as family life'. 'What people are prepared to accept as entertainment under their own roofs is not the same as that which they are prepared to accept in a music hall or in a theatre'.

e. Subjects should be essentially popular.

f. Aim at the raw elements of human nature which are common to all of us.

g. There are two subjects at least on which the radio dramatist cannot go wrong: The first is a good story. The kind of story which if read in a book you could not lay down until you had finished it. Writers of tales which take their audience or their readers 'away from the ordinary incidents of life as it is lived by most of us'. A good adventure story, convincingly written about entertaining and simultaneously possible characters. The second: Attractive personalities or 'characters we can believe in'. 'Characters who, from their essential humanity, convince the audience of their existence and their friendliness; characters who produce a definitely sympathetic and charming atmosphere which makes the development of their circumstances interesting to the audience to whom they are introduced'.

h. The wireless dramatist must borrow from the novelist rather than from the playwright.

i. There is little room for caricature in radio. You need 'real people living a life that is like the life of your audience'. Radio drama gives space for 'the play of adventure and the play of human character'.

j. The Play of Musical Life. Music has great potential and the radio musical even more so. 'To concentrate on listening to pure dialogue is unquestionably a strain'. 'Mr Shaw has proved that a master of dialogue can retain our listening attention without any difficulty, but it is without fear of contradiction from Mr Shaw that I assert that there are few Shaws'.

k. Use of Music. It is used as background or as linking material to break up the monotony of human voices. However, it would be more interesting to interpolate music as a necessity of subject.

l. The time has come for authors to write microphone plays round subjects rather than to attach subjects rather painfully to microphone plays.

m. It is not a criterion of excellence to 'use as much complication in its production as possible'. The best radio plays are the simplest radio plays.

n. Poetic Drama. The microphone offers great possibilities to the play which is dependent entirely upon the beautiful speaking of beautiful words. This could be the case with work written by poets which can never be staged owing to their lack of any dramatic action. 'If a new generation of Elizabethans were to arise they would have to write for the microphone and not for the stage'. But there is no greater pitfall for the would-be dramatist than the poetic play. Gielgud warned: the poetic play to justify itself, and especially to justify itself through the medium of the microphone, must be the work of a poet and not of a 'would-be' poet.

(Gielgud, 31 May 1929, pp. 449–50)

The Wireless Play – III. Length and Method

1. Keynote – Be Practical! No play, however good, stands its best chance of acceptance for the microphone if presented in a slipshod manner. Pay attention to the requirements of length, treatment etc.
2. Preparing the script. Properly typed on quarto paper rather than 'written in longhand on the backs of brown paper bags'.
3. Sound Effects. Indicate the points at which it is necessary for sound effects to occur. Leave it to the producer 'in cooperation with the person responsible for the noise effects at Savoy Hill, to bring these indications to concrete form'.
4. Question of length? Speed of dialogue in the radio is slightly slower than that taken in the theatre. Average timing of a minute and a half to a page is a 'very fair average at which to work'.
5. In 1929, Gielgud said the 'best practical length for a radio play is an hour and a half. I do not mean that this will always be the best length or that it is the ideal length'. His predecessor R.E. Jeffrey thought the ideal length of a radio play should not be more than 40 minutes. Gielgud argued that the most important people to be considered by the radio dramatist are the audience.

   a. He explained the listeners had not yet acquired 'the automatic habit of listening to radio plays as they have the automatic habit of watching a play in the theatre'. It can be argued that at the present time in the age of podcasting and sound on mobile phones, this point may not be entirely valid.
   b. Audience interest has to be gripped and once gripped – maintained. Unusually mobile background – continually changing scenes, much incidental music and sensationally noisy sound effects contributed to gripping. Outstanding literary brilliance where dialogue by itself suffices to bind listeners to their headphones is also a key factor in maintaining audience loyalty.

6. The Simpler the Better. Gielgud wanted 'clarity of treatment'. Even then there was an active debate about the function of narrative in radio drama with two classes of thought:

   a. Retention of narrative as being essential in order to convey a clear understanding of plot development to the audience;
   b. Removing the narrative and narrator on the ground that until clarity of plot development can be achieved without these aids the true radio play has not

been produced. Gielgud's position was that there is plenty of room for both classes. He argued persuasively: 'It is not a fact that narrative is always boring or an inartistic excrescence upon the form of radio drama. Particularly is this the case when a radio play is founded upon a novel. The dramatisation of *Carnival* of his own novel by Compton Mackenzie and Joseph Conrad's *Lord Jim* by the BBC's Cecil Lewis owed very much of their success to the skilful insertion of proper passages of narrative drawn from the original books.

Or take the further example of *St. Joan*, 'where Mr. Shaw's stage directions, which were read in full, were precisely the same thing as linking narrative'.

Gielgud went on to observe that the adapter of *The Prisoner of Zenda* – his close friend and co-writer of crime thrillers Holt Marvell (Eric Maschwitz) – had made a mistake by deliberately avoiding the narrative form. It would have been greatly improved by just a little carefully chosen narrative for the sake of clarity. On the other hand Gielgud cited Tyrone Guthrie's *Squirrel's Cage* as a play justifiably without narrative: 'written straight for the microphone, and was directed immediately at the listener's ears without any thought for his other senses, not only did the play no harm, but was an essential factor in its success. *Squirrel's Cage* was written in such a manner that its meaning and its aims were alive, vivid and perfectly easy to follow, although the interludes were of a symbolic character, without any purely descriptive linking'.

Squirrel's Cage by Tyrone Guthrie was regarded as the most successful play written specifically for the microphone in 1929. It would continue to be revived and generated considerable critical coverage. Alan Bland in the *Listener* for 13th March 1929 stated that it was 'not only an excellent entertainment but also another important step in the working out of the whole problem of dramatic broadcasting'. Thematically it engaged the issues of the modernist age. However, Bland's evaluation of the first performances on March 4th and 6th included the criticism: 'Here and there were lines of the kind we have come to call "theatrical," melodramatic touches which jumped out and marred for a moment the quiet photographic realism... the voices of the chorus were not always so happy. Sometimes the rhythm seemed to flag... nor do I think that the device of the stroke on the gong followed by the screaming rush of a siren, ingenious though it was an idea, really conveyed the sensation of the rush through time and space between scene and scene (Bland, 1929, p. 333).

7. Gielgud's advice on narrative to writers:

    a. Make up your mind before you begin writing on whether to use it or not.
    b. If you do use it you must realise that narrative must be carefully chosen.
    c. Narrative passages must not be too long.
    d. Narrative passages must be balanced by other characteristics of the play. For example: if you have considerable passages of linking narrative you must balance them with considerable changes of background, plenty of music and the like.

e.   If you prefer to proceed without narrative and adopt 'the starker technique' you must take care that you do not become obscure and the essential factors in the development of the plot are not left out or slurred over.

(Gielgud, 7 June 1929, pp. 502, 513)

The Wireless Play – IV. 'How Many Studios?'

In the days of Savoy Hill and to a similar extent early Broadcasting House, the BBC used the first 'mixing panel' to combine inputs of performance and sound from different studios. In Germany, they tended to record sound in the same large studio. In the USA (at CBS for example), they followed the German model and had components of the production in the same large studio. The BBC technical mechanism was known as 'The Control Panel'. In fact Savoy Hill could mix together input from six different studios or locations. This advice needs to translate into the 21st century in terms of how many tracks or streams of sound are combined in multi-track form at any one time.

1.   '...in radio drama, as in all good art, simplicity is more effective than complication. To use six studios merely, as it were, for the fun of the thing, when the theme and characters of a play are simple and straightforward, is merely stupid'.
2.   Radio Dramatists should be aware of the artistic principle of fading and cross-fading sound which is similar to the dissolve for cinema.
3.   'Cross-fading' of parallel groups of voices is a most effective device, but it is extremely important that the voices should be sufficiently obviously different for there to be no confusion over the different sets of characters involved. While casting of actors is the prerogative of the directors, writers need to keep in mind the importance of writing 'effective differences' in characters – unless similarity is used as a specific plot device.
4.   Gielgud's postulate: To sum up: The panel (like most machinery) is a good servant but a bad master. In modern terms, this is the same as talking about the digital or analogue mixing desk.
5.   He referred to the opening of *Carnival* to explain the technique of writing to appreciate the process of sound mixing:

In one studio Mr Compton Mackenzie was reading his opening narrative. As that reached its end the producer, by turning the knob on the panel, which controlled the strength of that particular studio, gradually faded the voice of the narrator to diminishing strength. Simultaneously, by turning in the opposite direction the knob which controlled the strength of the studio in which a barrel-organ was placed, he faded up the sound of the barrel-organ, which opened the first scene in the street where Jenny is dancing. As soon as the barrel-organ had been brought up to the requisite strength, i.e. the strength sufficient to stamp the background of the scene, it was faded down sufficiently to be background and nothing else. The producer then gave the 'light cue' to the actors, again in their separate studio, by pressing a switch which turned on a green light in the distant studio, and faded in their voices against the barrel-organ background, bringing them up to a strength at which they could be heard distinctly, though the barrel-organ continued to be faintly distinguished. There you have the use of three studios in proper operation.

(Gielgud, 14 June 1929, p. 555)

To what extent has the production of BBC Radio plays changed or transmogrified since 'turning knobs' and flashing 'cue lights'? Apart from recording on location, pre-recording sequences and segueing them into live performance, the introduction of faders, multi-tracking and digital editing, it could be argued that the principles are roughly the same.

The Wireless Play – V. People of the Play

1. Wireless dramatist must do his utmost to enable listeners to visualise characters in the imagination. The means at his/her disposal were:

    a. Strong and careful characterisation in dialogue.
    b. Simplicity in the human motives which go to make up the story.

2. Gielgud talked about 'fixing' the physical identity of characters and their background. Here Gielgud was laying the ground for what I defined in *Radio Drama – Theory & Practice* in 1999 as the imaginative spectacle in audio drama (Crook, 1999, pp. 53–69). Gielgud said: 'both eye and ear are merely a means by which you make an impression on the imagination of your audience'.

3. Gielgud was dismissive of the view that radio was an abstract medium dealing with purely abstract sounds. He argued that sounds without any interpretative significance were only a *reductio ad absurdum* of a practice. He laid down his cards with this view about the more experimental plays of Lance Sieveking and Tyrone Guthrie:

    > How many of the people who heard 'Kaleidoscope The Second' could describe Sylvia's appearance or recognise her more personal characteristics? Deliberately or not, rightly or wrongly, Sylvia was a puppet. The interest of the audience was directed to the circumstances which swayed her life. They were, I think, completely unimpressed by the character of Sylvia the girl. Henry, in Squirrel's Cage, was better. At any rate, we knew that he stammered slightly. But he, too, and in the case I am quite sure it was deliberately done, ran too true to type to be real.

4. Gielgud wanted greater care and greater emphasis in 'stamping... characters and... settings to further the easier working of the imagination of... listeners'.
5. He said 'It is well known that people as a rule are not interested in other people that they do not know or have never met. Because you demand more of the imagination of your listeners than a writer for the stage, so you must provide that imagination with more material on which to work'.

6. In the course of ordinary dialogue, the little personal idiosyncrasies are slipped in, or the most important features in a scene are underlined.

7. There is no doubt that people like to follow the experiences of characters whom they can understand, whom they can recognise among their friends, and at least some of whom they can like.

8. In 1929 Gielgud argued that Britain was 'not a cosmopolitan nation. The mentality of the average foreigner is a closed book to us'. He used this point to explain why the creations of Chekhov and Ibsen were regarded as 'quite simply lunatic'. It is a sign of xenophobia that was prevalent in British culture at the time (when Britain was an Imperial/Colonial power). This is certainly not now a legitimate and widely supported social attitude of today where multicultural perspectives and viewpoints are strongly advocated and celebrated.

9. Aspiration to realism: Gielgud stated: 'Radio drama should be fixed in the minds of would-be authors for the microphone as a drama of real people for real people. Preciosity has its place, but that place is not in radio drama'.

10. Gielgud recognised critical observations about the quality and standards of contemporary radio drama. Feminist writer Vita Sackville-West had written an article before stating 'it was necessary for a woman's voice to be alternated with a man's'. This was an early sign on concern about sexism and patronymic domination of the medium by male writers, directors, and voices.

11. At the time Gielgud was emphasising the need for a special approach to microphone play writing; hence his comment: 'Except in so far that certain authors with a "sense of the theatre" are also authors of fine intellectual attainment with a gift for writing dialogue and funds of ideas, their theatrical sense is immaterial'. [That the author of a radio drama should have a sense of the theatre is the very last thing that is necessary. A 'sense of the theatre' implies knowledge of one set of tricks; a sense of the microphone implies knowledge of another set of tricks.]

(Gielgud, 21 June 1929, p. 608)

Journey's End had been a successful stage play in 1928 and 1929 and by the time of its first broadcast on Armistice day 11th November 1929 it had been performed in six different languages. It has had many BBC revivals and represents an excellent example of a theatre play which transfers effectively to the radio. The key may well be the psychology, characterisation and emotions which are highly charged and dramatised.

Gielgud provides an amusing account in *Years of the Locust* of his struggle to persuade John Reith to permit the BBC to air *Journey's End*:

> There was an occasion when I found myself in his office pleading passionately for a performance of *Journey's End* as an appropriate commemoration of Armistice Day. I could not convince him. And as I remained persistent he passed me on to the Admiral. With the latter I waxed really eloquent, almost succeeding in reducing myself to tears in a mixture of emotion and baffled

exasperation. I must have been there about quarter of an hour when Sir John looked in, and expressed surprise that I was still arguing. 'I don't understand what you want this play for', he said. 'Anyone can write an appropriate programme for Armistice Day. I could write one – if I had the time. Of course you need a lot of guns and bells and things'! And he disappeared before I could reply or comment. Again, it is only fair to add that ultimately I was allowed my own way, and was very handsomely congratulated for the success of the *Journey's End* production. I was perhaps fortunate in the fact that in Sir John's eyes the broadcasting of plays seemed rather a necessary evil, than a very serious branch of broadcasting activities.

(Gielgud, 1949, p. 70)

The Wireless Play – VI. A Practical Example

In his final article, Gielgud courageously exposes his inchoate radio dramatic career to potential attack by illustrating the main requirements of microphone drama with passages from an actual play-script which would appear to be his own script described as '"Exiles", a thrilling drama of the old Russia which may one day be heard over the microphone'.

He realised the risk he was taking:

'I am going to try to do the most difficult thing possible: To exemplify theory in practice'.

During the course of the article, he exemplified the following techniques:

1. The climax of 'Exiles' 'has two good points: It keeps a "high spot" of climax with an anticlimactic last line for its curtain – a purely theatrical but extremely effective device'.
2. The subject is 'radiogenique – (a term recently coined in France, which may be translated as "good radio" – on the analogy of "good theatre") because it deals with people in circumstances which are certainly dramatic and which are not wildly improbable'.
3. The play has a definite contest between the attitudes of two minds towards the same problem. '…this argument which runs through the play serves in the place of narrative to link up and form a background to the whole piece'.
4. The two main characters bind the scenes together and lead up to them.
5. Gielgud acknowledges the value of rhythm and pace in structure: 'The play deals with a period which can only be reproduced by short scenes and against rapidly-changing backgrounds. Further, these backgrounds are in themselves picturesque'.
6. By providing the opportunity to switch scenes from the old Imperial Court, a St. Petersburg Cafe with a tsigane (gypsy) orchestra, and a dugout on the Galician Front, Gielgud says he is creating a production framework for introducing music 'as a strictly natural background to different scenes without having to force theme – or background – music purely for its own sake'.

7. 'Exiles' is a play which is impossible to stage and therefore conforms with the demand for drama which can only be handled through the wireless medium.

8. The script ensures that although there are a good many characters involved, only two have real personal significance. 'The others are mere shadows moving in a world of memories'. The cast is therefore small.

9. Gielgud does however acknowledge that a play which requires an orchestra, a tsigane orchestra, a chorus, and various straightforward sound effects is complicated. 'Exiles' is going to be a Savoy Hill five studio production. He justifies the elaboration without admitting that he is the author of the project with these words:

10. 'A theme has deliberately been chosen which, to be properly exploited, requires these various expensive and complicated agencies, and these can be provided by the developing technique of the wireless play and could not by any other method'.

11. Gielgud claims that the author has done everything to serve 'clarity of treatment' by making his dialogue short and taut.

12. Gielgud also pays homage to influence. The scene subdivided into six sections to cover the stupendous episode of the Russian Revolution was inspired by the impressionistic methods of Tyrone Guthrie and Lance Sieveking. He says that Impressionism 'is one of the practising servants of radio dramatic technique. And the impressionist is in this case justified, because nothing else would serve to convey what is necessary for the development of the play by means of realism'.

13. Gielgud does not disclose a fundamental aspect of the play's motivation which is the special cultural and emotional knowledge and imperatives of the author. Gielgud and his family were a part of the world explored in the play. His relatives and his first wife were part of the 'White Russian' culture tossed about by the storms of Revolution and Empire.

(Gielgud, 28 June 1929, pp. 605, 668)

By 1946, Val Gielgud decided the Second World War had brought about two most important things in radio dramatic broadcasting: The technique of production was compelled to be radically simplified. And listeners turned their attention from what the machinery *could* do to *what* it could do (Gielgud, 1946, p. viii). What he meant by this was a further utilitarian imperative. The exponential increase in radio listening due to Blitz and war-time black-out conditions keeping people at home meant 'the end has taken over from the means' (Gielgud, 1946).

In answer to the question 'What is the object of writing a radio play'?, Gielgud wrote a paragraph which stands the test of time:

> The answer, in its simplest form, is the object is precisely the same as that implied in the writing of any form of fiction: the telling of a story in the terms of a particular medium—in this case, in radio-dramatic terms; the

telling of a story qualified by proper and practical consideration of both the advantages and limitations conferred upon the author by the use of the microphone, as opposed to the use of the printed page, the camera, or the stage of a theatre. It was always difficult to persuade writers for radio to keep their attention upon this elementary truth… It must therefore be stated unequivocally, at the risk of appearing both obvious and sententious, that the radio-dramatist must, before all else *write for the microphone* … it is not only desirable but necessary for the would-be radio-dramatist *to listen*.

(*Gielgud, 1946, pp. ix, xi*)

Concluding Thoughts for the Writer on the Medium with 'Unlimited Possibilities'

Extensive writing and discussion about the art of radio playwriting was taking place in the USA which during the 1930s and 1940s experienced what has been described as 'The Golden Age of Radio Drama'. It is interesting to see the parallel realisations about the best way of crafting the form and how writers and producers on both sides of the Atlantic were treading very similar paths. David R Mackey in his 1951 text *Drama on the Air* offered radio drama writers some precise explanations on possibilities and limitations in scripting sound drama in comparison with writing novels or drama for the stage and film/television.

1. **Time Element**. Because of radio's split-second timing and being continuous performance, the audience has little time for reflection.
2. **Attracting Audience Attention**. In radio, the competitive attention and audience diversion make necessary an attempt to get and hold the audience from the very start.
3. **Action**. Action in literature is *descriptive*, in theatre and television it is *illustrative* and in radio it is *imagined*.
4. **Vividness**. Radio's use of sound, coupled with the imagination of the listener, makes for great possibilities of vividness of expression.
5. **The Audience Situation**. The radio audience is an individual one, not a 'special' audience, heterogeneous, and believes its radio entertainment comes free.
6. **Approaching the Audience**. Radio always has a commercial nature and programme planners are forced to reach for the largest audience possible.
7. **Process of Communication**. In radio the listener is in control of the communication process.
8. **Thematic Freedom**. Radio is an invited guest and should act so. It does not mean radio cannot be realistic, but it should not be vulgar for vulgarity's sake.

(*Mackey, 1951, pp. 9–23*)

Companion Website Resources

Additions and Updates for Chapter 3 Instrumental Utilitarianism in Radio Playwriting – The Evolving Thoughts of Val Gielgud https://kulturapress.com/2022/08/12/chapter-3-instrumental-utilitarianism-in-radio-playwriting-the-evolving-thoughts-of-val-gielgud/

Val Gielgud – Longest Serving BBC Radio Drama Editor 1929–1963 https://kulturapress.com/2022/08/29/val-gielgud-longest-serving-bbc-radio-drama-editor-1929-1963/

Audio and Drama-Documentary Otherwise Known as the Feature in Britain https://kulturapress.com/2022/08/28/audio-and-drama-documentary-otherwise-known-as-the-feature-in-britain/

BBC Radio Drama of the 1950s https://kulturapress.com/2022/08/30/bbc-radio-drama-of-the-1950s/

BBC Radio Drama of the 1960s https://kulturapress.com/2022/08/30/bbc-radio-drama-of-the-1960s/

BBC Radio Great Play Series of 1928 & 1929 https://kulturapress.com/2022/08/30/bbc-radio-great-play-series-of-1928-1929/

4

ACHIEVING THE LONG FORM AUDIO DRAMA

Audio Drama's Key Elements

I start this chapter by going back to 1939 and then to 1940. There will be many other switches in audio/radio drama timeline continuing with travels to 1999, 2005, and then way back to 1926. Certainly, sound drama can be described as the time traveller's dramatic medium. Later we are very much in the present with analysis of an episode from an award-winning example of sound drama which is successful for legacy radio broadcasting as well as contemporary online podcasting.

In 1939, audio drama was one of the US radio industry's mainstays and most prevalent forms of programming. On 21st September 1939, the CBS affiliated radio station in Washington D.C. WJSV ran the following radio plays, series and serials:

8.45 a.m. *Bachelor's Children*. The continuing story of Dr. Bob Graham, who during the Great War, promised to care for his dying sergeant's two daughters. One daughter, Ruth Ann, eventually marries 'Doctor Bob'; the other, Janet, marries his best friend.

9.00 a.m. *Pretty Kitty Kelly*. It is murder, kidnapping, and other plots of intrigue that meet with Kitty Kelly, a young Irish lass who arrives in America with amnesia.

9.15 a.m. *The Story of Myrt & Marge*. The world of the theatre and world of life, and the story of two women who seek fame in the one and contentment in the other.

9.30 a.m. *Hilltop House*. Bess Johnson is a caseworker at the Hilltop House orphanage, struggling with the conflict between romance and her work.

9.45–10.00 a.m. *Stepmother*. Can a stepmother successfully raise another woman's children? This is the real-life story of Kay Fairchild, a stepmother who tries. Kay gave up her career in journalism to marry the widower John Fairchild, then finds it isn't easy.

DOI: 10.4324/9780203838181-4

10.15 a.m. *Brenda Curtis*. Brenda's husband fears his law office might close, Brenda considers an offer to return to the stage, Stacy Gordon returns from South America, and Gloria Bennett turns this information into a scheme of her own.

10.30 a.m. *Big Sister*. Ruth Evans is the big sister of Sue Evans, and little Neddie Evans, a cripple who has been cured by Ruth's future husband, Dr. John Wayne.

10.45–11.00 a.m. *Aunt Jenny's True Life Stories*. Aunty Jenny hosts this soap opera with a very different format. It's a new story each week, told in five daily segments.

11.15 a.m. *When a Girl Marries*. The tender, human story of young married life, dedicated to all those who are in love and those who can remember.

11.30 a.m. *The Romance of Helen Trent*. The real-life drama of Helen Trent, who, when life mocks her, breaks her hopes, dashes her against the rocks of despair, fights back bravely, successfully, to prove what so many women long to prove in their own lives; that because a woman is over 35, and more, romance in life need not be over; that the romance of youth can extend into middle life, and even beyond…

11.45 a.m. *Our Gal Sunday*. The story of an orphan girl named Sunday, from the little town of Silver Creek, Colorado, who in young womanhood marries England's richest, most handsome lord, Lord Henry Brinthorpe.

12 noon. *The Goldbergs*. Meet Molly, Jake, Sammy, and Rosalie – the Goldbergs, a warm and eccentric Jewish family living on New York's Lower East Side.

12.15 p.m. *Life Can Be Beautiful*. Carol Conrad is a young girl from the slums, taken in by Papa David Solomon, owner of the Slightly Read Bookshop. Here she becomes 'Chichi', girl of the streets, and becomes a daughter to Papa David.

12.30 p.m. *Road of Life*. Dr. Jim Brent, surgeon at City Hospital, adopts a young orphan whom he names John and draws the attention of the beautiful Carol Evans.

12.45–1 p.m. *This Day Is Ours*. The story of Eleanor MacDonald and Curtis Curtis, and as today's story begins, Curt returns home from his job search, and Eleanor is sewing and mending her meagre wardrobe in preparation for her coming marriage.

1.15 p.m. *The Life & Love of Dr. Susan*. Dr. Susan Chandler is an attractive, young woman doctor, trying to make life worthwhile for herself and her two young children.

1.30–1.45 p.m. *Your Family and Mine*. The story of Judy Wilbur, 'The Red Headed Angel' and her loves.

3.15–3.30 p.m. *The Career of Alice Blair*. The transcribed true-to-life story of a lovely girl fighting for fame and happiness, facing the problems, the heartaches and thrills on the ladder to success.

3.45–4.00 p.m. *Scattergood Baines*. Scattergood Baines is the town philosopher of Cold River, where he and his helper Hippocrates 'Hipp' Brown run a hardware store.

6.00 p.m. *Amos and Andy*. Amos Jones and Andrew H. Brown of the Fresh-Air Taxicab Company of America, Incorporated. In tonight's episode find out what happens at the Bluebird School of Singing when Andy's recital is postponed.

6.15–6.30 p.m. *The Parker Family*. Richard Parker comes home from school early and overhears an intimate conversation between his mother and a strange man.

9.00–9.30 p.m. *The Columbia Workshop*. Experimental radio theatre. Tonight – 'Now It's Summer' by humourist-playwright Arthur Kober.

In this one day of mainstream radio programming on a leading US network radio station of the time, 300 minutes or 5 hours of radio drama has been produced and broadcast. That is a total of 22 different forms of audio drama – soap series and serial and original stand-alone plays. Each nutshell description highlights the intensity of story, character, conflict, struggle, and action.

When Erik Barnouw wrote the *Handbook of Radio Writing* in the following year, it is not surprising that radio drama was one of the American radio industry's biggest employers. He described a market of 20 million words, and 17,000 different programmes every day. He advised that the 'radio script is a trio for three singers: (1) Sound effects; (2) Music; (3) Speech. At any time, any of these can carry a solo message, or they may be used in any combination' (Barnouw, 1940, p. 29). He reproduced the beginning of an *All-Sound Effect Mystery-Drama* by Richard Morenus, and *The Ghosts of Benjamin Street* by Fred Gilsdorf:

(HEAVY BELL CHIMES TWO O'CLOCK)
(POURING DRINK INTO GLASS)
(SET BOTTLE DOWN)
(DRINK—GULPING—SET BOTTLE AGAINST GLASS AND POUR
   AGAIN)
(GULPING DRINK AGAIN)
(PUSH CHAIR BACK)
(WALK ON WOODEN FLOOR AND OPEN AND CLOSE THE
   DOOR)
(WALK DOWN FLIGHT OF WOODEN STAIRS AND OPEN
   DOOR)
(TRAFFIC NOISES AT 2 A.M. AND CLOSE DOOR)

(Barnouw, 1940, p. 29)

The most well-known example of a British radio drama consisting of no words and only action sound and soundscapes is *The Revenge*, a thriller written and interpreted by Andrew Sachs and directed by Glyn Dearman, first broadcast by the BBC on 1st June 1978. The *Radio Times* said it was:

[A]n experimental play for radio; an attempt to tell a story in terms of sound alone. There is no dialogue, and no coherent speech, yet the play is a thriller with a straightforward storyline full of action and dramatic tension … recorded on location using the naturalistic recording techniques of binaural stereo.

(Anon, 1 June 1978)

In his 1940 radio drama handbook, Barnouw went on to explain how the contrasting opening of *Ghost of Benjamin Street* puts speech centre stage and then hands it over to music to provide 'a few seconds swabbing the ether with its tonal paint brush' (Barnouw, 1940).

ANNOUNCER: Fasten your windows. Bolt your doors. Turn down your lights. Draw your chairs close. For he comes once more…that amazing Spook…the Ghost of Benjamin Street…
(MUSIC: DREARY, DESOLATE, GRAVE-YARD STUFF)

(Barnouw, 1940, p. 29)

In 1999, I identified five main dimensions to the structure of communication in audio drama:

1. The word through voices: dialogue and narrative.
2. Music through instruments and choral voices.
3. Sound effects: natural atmosphere and spot effects or abstract sounds synthesised or natural sounds that have been symbolised.
4. Post-modernist use of previously recorded actuality, archive or sound history, or previously recorded narrative and dialogue.
5. The imagination of the listener: this is physically a silent dimension. In terms of consciousness it is immensely powerful. This is the existence of a significant part of the play in the imagination of the audience, i.e. the listener. It is what I have defined previously as 'the imaginative spectacle'.

(Crook, 1999, p. 160)

These dimensions are key elements in audio drama or streams of sonic narrative direction. The writing and production of audio drama involves the multi-tracking or sequencing of these dimensions, their balance, their juxtaposition, and combination or divergence.

In 2005, after studying 60 German radio plays from 1929 to 2002, Elke Huwiler in her academic journal article *Storytelling by Sound: A Theoretical Frame for Radio Drama Analysis* explained that 'music, noises and voices and also technical features like electro-acoustical manipulation or mixing, can be, and often are, used as tools to signify story elements and therefore should be analysed accordingly' (Huwiler, 2005, p. 45). She was therefore adding the 'electro-acoustical manipulation or mixing' of sound to the equation. This can be explained in terms of the positioning and movement of the characters to and from the microphone. When close, they can generate the illusion of intimacy, the idea of the interior-head, or thinking soliloquy. This is non-diegetic in the sense of being heard by the audience as listener but not the other characters in the world of the play.

When distant from the microphone, there is the potential illusion of being subject to authority, falling or leaving, an emotional sense of loss. The sound of silence has the potential to use pause for dramatic effect and provide the vacuum of emotion and imaginative participation on the part of the listener. Another sound textual element to be considered by Huwiler was the purpose of creating transitions through fading and mixing; particularly when sound design technology offered so many opportunities to multi-layer the other elements through analogue and digital multi-tracking. Huwiler's view on analysing German hörspiele and English-speaking radio plays is that there has been too much preoccupation on the dramatic and literary nature and dimension of the genre with the word being seen as the primary semiotic code of the medium and an alternative mode of expression for writers. Huwiler recognises the contribution of the Neues Hörspiel movement and other sub-cultures of production and practice where the sonic storytelling is more disruptive and unpredictable through montage, collaging, and aural deconstruction:

> They work with different musical styles like pop, opera, jingles, chorals and hip hop, and use recitals, dialogues, monologues, citations, reports and commentary as rhetorical features, while using electro-acoustical manipulation and stereophony as technical ones.
>
> *(Huwiler, 2005, p. 48)*

Huwiler decided to fashion the following template of analysis to audio/radio drama:

1. Language;
2. Voice;
3. Music;
4. Noise;
5. Silence;
6. Fading;
7. Cutting;
8. Mixing;
9. The (stereophonic) positioning of the signals;
10. Electro-acoustical manipulation;
11. Original sound (actuality).

Huwiler is engaging narratological theory in the practice of film to the practical sound texts of audio drama and quite rightly so since sound drama is becoming more of an auteur's medium – the writer is also directing and producing. Hence her appreciation:

> There is no reason why such technical features should not be as important in the analysis of radio plays, since here also the audience's understanding of what is being told is conditioned by elements like acoustical manipulation, mixing and cutting … these acoustical and technical features may be as important to the shaping of the drama as is the spoken word.
>
> *(Huwiler, 2005, p. 51)*

I think it would be wrong to assume that writers and producers of radio drama in the past have not been aware and articulated that this is an all-encompassing sonic dimension of sound storytelling instead of being dependent on and derivative of literature and physical theatre drama. In 1944, the auteur poet and radio dramatist Louis MacNeice made it very clear that:

> Sound-broadcasting gets its effects through sound and sound alone. This very obvious fact has two somewhat contradictory implications: (1) A good radio play or feature presupposes a good radio script; (2) such a script is not necessarily a piece of 'good writing.' ... Your trade is in words-as-they-are-spoken – and words-as-they-are-heard.
>
> (MacNeice, 1944, pp. 8–9)

There are other analytical factors to add to Huwiler's template which it would be good for writers to anticipate and think about. The podcast and listen-again age has changed the nature of the listening experience. It is no longer a 'here today and gone tomorrow' phenomenon. Cassettes, CDs, online listening, podcasting, and streaming means that audio drama can be written to some extent knowing the production can be paused, rewound, and listened to over and over again. It has thus retrieved a dimension of the novel, short story, and poem's audience. There is also potential writing that draws the listener into the world of the play with a much more dynamic and participating role. The listener can be the point of listening and thinking of the story's protagonist. A third additional factor to be anticipated is what is now becoming much more recognised as the phenomenological dimension of listening. What is the emotional charge and feeling engendered by the totality of the sonic texture and aural tapestry? This is what I was touching on in 1999 when I wrote:

> I believe that an essential ingredient is missing in the definitions that have been advanced to try to explain the psychological bond between sound and being, the 'sense of feeling'. So much stress has been placed on the mind's eye or the image generated by the mind, that an essential feature of human experience in drama – 'emotion' and 'feeling' – has been overlooked. ... 'the theatre of the mind is an emotional theatre, where feelings are the primary currency, mixed with mood, memories and imagination'.
>
> (Crook, 1999, p. 61)

In recent years a fuller understanding of this dimension of writing, making, and listening to audio drama has been elegantly theorised and written by Dr. Farokh Soltani Shirazi's PhD thesis developed into the monograph for Manchester University Press in 2020: *Radio/body: Phenomenology and dramaturgies of radio*.

Analysing the BBC's *Life Lines* Using Gordon Lea's 1926 Template *Radio Drama and How to Write it* – 'The World in a Buttercup and Jewels Against a Background of Black Velvet?'

Life Lines at the time of writing is an exquisite contemporary model of audio drama writing for both broadcasting and podcasting. Created and written by Al Smith and directed by Sally Avens, the action and world of the drama exists wholly in the sound world with the central character Carrie opening with the distinctive call-sign

'Ambulance Service. Is the patient breathing and conscious'? *Life Lines* is a fluid sound conduit of experience which the listener can identify with because mobile phone communications are the everyday medium and platform of social existence. This drama is the classic crisis life and death situation of the ambulance service call handler having to deal with heart-stopping situations in an almost real-time framework of the audio-drama time sequence itself. It is the ultimate in sound drama realism. Because Carrie never knows what the next call will bring, the listener is instantly apprehensive, on tenterhooks and utterly captivated and imaginatively present within seconds of each episode unfolding.

Its exposition is in the serial format. Each 15–17 minute episode has a self-contained plot line, but abiding anxieties and issues in Carrie's professional and personal life develop usually in cliff-hanger mode from episode one to episode six in each season. These episodes can be aggregated deftly and effectively in BBC R4, 45 minute structures so that one season can constitute parts one and two in the Afternoon Play slot.

Why is the writing so successful? The award-winning dramatist has carried out extensive research in an ambulance control centre so that the characterisation, dialogue, and action have authenticity. It is reminiscent of the audio-verité documentaries pioneered at the BBC in the Midlands by Brian King and Sarah Rowlands during the late 1980s and early 1990s. One series did construct dramatic sound eavesdropping narratives in an NHS hospital telephone network.

Every episode of *Life Lines* is intensely psychological, the situations emotional and acutely human. The listener is able to share the rushes in Carrie's adrenaline levels and she uses her guile, paramedic knowledge and human instinct to determine whether her calls are real cries for help from life-threatening situations or manipulative hoaxes. The sound-only telephonic mobile links to people in danger operate like umbilical cords with immediate intimacy and personal trauma vectoring into Carrie's zone of sensibility. And the genre opens up so much potential in dramatic sub-text, silences, the meaning behind what the emergency callers are not saying. This is a pure form of characterisation performing in psychological space. Every episode is often an intuitive detective story. What is really going on behind the halting, hesitant, deceiving, and concealing voices?

The dramatic entertainment also engages with contemporary politics and news events. Are there enough resources and support from management for the gruelling and relentless 12-hour shifts? The plot lines resonate with contemporary journalism: Migrants trapped in a refrigerated lorry at a motorway service station; an abandoned baby found in a refuse bin, or the victim of an acid attack. The serial plot-line beyond each episode explores whether the continual stress has led her to make the wrong decisions when a patient later dies, and how the anti-social shift patterns undermine personal and family relationships; particularly with a police officer partner with whom she has an infant child.

The quality of characterisation is excellent and simple. There are no more than two or three main characters in any episode and with action characters arriving to drive the self-contained plotlines. The production values are excellent in terms of quality of casting, direction, performance, and the realism of sound design. There is public service subtlety in teaching listeners essential and accurate First Aid skills. This is a classic BBC achievement in delivering information and education through entertainment. There is a beginning and end symmetry of impact in each episode's writing structure. There are immediate and effective questioning mysteries drawing in and hooking the listener's engagement with each episode's opening 15–30 seconds. Every episode has resonant and thought-provoking resolutions or ongoing cliffhangers which are meaningful. The listener is continually participating. The listener is inside the world of the audio drama because they know they could be there and want to be there. The participation is vicarious. Listeners are directly linked to echoes and triggers of personal experience and memory. It justifiably won the Gold Award for Best Fictional Storytelling at the 2017 Radio Academy Awards and Best Original Series at the 2020 BBC Audio Drama Awards. The intense psychological appeal of creating suspense drama in an emergency call centre has been paralleled in the film medium with Gustav Möller's *The Guilty* (*Den skyldig*) in 2018. The 85 minute Danish crime thriller about a police officer investigating an apparent murder through mobile messaging and sound actuality could succeed as impactful drama with its sound track on its own stripped of the visual narrative.

How does *Life Lines* measure up to the enduring themes of sound playwriting as an art and craft identified in Gordon Lea's 1926 book *Radio Drama and How to Write It*? This was the first book ever published on writing sound drama anywhere in the world. Around 95 years separate the book and the series. What are the parallels that can be drawn between Lea's advice at the dawn of the radio drama age and the first episode of season five of *Life Lines* when Carrie receives a call from a refugee trapped in a refrigerated lorry and makes a desperate attempt to save his life?

Lea saw dramatic storytelling sound had an obvious cultural affinity with musical expression and in appreciating the importance and value of music in dramatic construction he eloquently said: 'From out this darkness grew green music, colouring the mind and pointing the emotions to their destined end' (Lea, 1926, p. 21). Writers in sound drama are as important as composers in music: '...the one real essential is something behind the text – the idea or dramatic purpose of the author' (Lea, 1926, p. 32). The beginning of this *Life Lines* episode is certainly coming out of the darkness. Carrie and the listener do not have a camera giving filmic vision of the emergency caller. In this case, it is a foreign man with broken English, clearly in distress, and as the opening seconds unfold, he is in as much darkness as Carrie and the listener. The characterisation of Carrie as a professional paramedic unfolds rapidly as she shows how she is able to recognise the health crisis of the person calling for help, and how much of an expert she is at understanding non-vocal as well as vocal communication particularly when it is expressed with such acute distress. She asks questions that the listener wants answering and questions the listener has probably not thought of asking. It's an unfolding detective and thriller mystery. Why does he say there is no air? Where is he? There's a banging or clanking noise against thin metal surrounding a large space. What is it? Who is doing it and why? The 'green music' of emergency paints emotions and certainly the colours in the mind of anyone listening. The ideas inherent in Gordon Lea's metaphorical language are conjured so strongly in the imaginative space created by *Life Lines*.

The storytelling is not a crowd impulse but a reaching out to establish an intimate rapport with the individual listener. This is what is happening in the BBC audio drama from the get go. Lea explains:

> 'The radio drama does not make its appeal to a crowd but to an individual…
> for what will appeal to a crowd will almost certainly appeal to the individual, but it is by no means certain that what will appeal to the individual will appeal to the crowd.'

> *(Lea, 1926, p. 37)*

This is the essence of the dramatic relationship for the listening audience to *Life Lines*.

Lea and his fellow programme makers in the early 1920s had had a few years to discover how the radio drama audience is individualised in their own homes. He said 'Objectively, they see nothing, but subjectively they can see everything' (Lea, 1926, p. 38). And the writer needs to appreciate that the scripting of words conjures the voice as the agency of characterisation – the actors' shape and physical characteristics are irrelevant: 'What is written in the text will be given pure and untrammeled to the mind of the listener' (Lea, 1926, p. 39). Let us analyse how this is achieved in the first few minutes of the *Life Lines* episode.

Carrie connects immediately with the man in distress who seems to be saying he can't breathe. The Ambulance control centre supervisor, Will, is immediately engaged as Carrie explains she has a caller who cannot breathe with a call from an international SIM card and the mobile phone tower pinging the location near Soughton. By the end of the first full minute of drama, Carrie understands that there is an implication when he says 'too many for us'. Too many for what? Too many people for the air? Too many for why? He keeps saying 'SOS'. Carrie's forensic paramedical questioning accelerates the pace of the drama and the crisis which is obviously a matter of life and death. She needs to know his name, where he is, and whether she can hear traffic in the background thereby drawing in the listener's attention to the soundscape.

There are two relationships developing at this point. Carrie and Will are working together and want to find out where the emergency call is coming from. The distressed foreign man who has now revealed his name as Abbas desperately needs help. Carrie wants to provide it but requires more information in order to do so. As Will's technical mobile phone analysis contextualises the situation further, Carrie's questions continue and they have a precise homing in quality when she asks Abbas if he is calling from a service station?

Life Lines is a model example of a radio play which tells the story through dialogue and action – without any Voice of God narrator, or a character in the story communicating with the listener through interior speech, unfolding a memory and relating description, feelings and participation in past events, or even prophesising the future. The narrator in sound drama can also serve to provide the function of indirect free speech in written prose, though dramatists prefer to have the voice rooted in characterisation.

In 1926, Gordon Lea felt that there are two main styles of structure to the radio play: (1) the narrator method and (2) the self-contained method. *Life Lines* is the self-contained method. In its first season, it did interpolate action and dialogue with Carrie speaking as though she was lecturing at a training workshop or seminar. Al Smith's dialogic and intense dramatic action writing is so brilliant the narrator method is inappropriate and unnecessary. Lea explained that as an alternative using a narrator offers the chance to characterise an interesting angle and develop sympathy and tension in the way of Shakespearean drama. The narrator can create 'mind pictures' and bridge dramatic action. Narrative voice is a good and convenient method of dramatising prose/novel writing.

But all those years ago Lea preferred the 'self-contained method' and so do most contemporary writers/directors. All of the objectives and advantages set out above for the narrator method are being deployed in the self-contained form in *Life Lines*. Lea explained the narrator method is good for knitting together and making coherent long stage plays 'but as a form for original radio drama, it is not good' (Lea, 1926, p. 53). By removing the narrator the writer creates a total mental vision so that the listener can effectively overhear the drama:

> It can be made as startling and realistic as if the listener were overhearing something in the next room through a half-open door – with the advantage, that the people in the next room obligingly let the eavesdropper know all about it.
>
> *(Lea, 1926, p. 54)*

And this is what is happening in *Life Lines*.

Gordon Lea said in the self-contained method, the scenery and setting is indicated by the characters themselves and what they say:

> ...[T]his can be done quite naturally and effectively. The characters should be made to see everything objectively and to think of what they are doing objectively, so that this will appear in their speech...be made to produce an illusion of naturalness.
>
> *(Lea, 1926 p. 55)*

Lea advised writers to avoid making their characters give crude word pictures of where they are when the language is not natural to their personalities. The word picture needs to emerge gradually. Exposition needs to be subtle: '...this illusion of appearance and costume is necessary... should be done by means of the dialogue in a manner to stimulate the listener's imagination' ((Lea, 1926, p. 54), pp. 56–57).

In the modern writing workshop parlance this is 'the showing' as opposed to 'the telling' approach to writing, and *Life Lines* shows all of the following elements of the plot in Episode 1 of Season 5:

1. When Carrie and Will realise Abbas is trapped with his own child and with over 20 other families who are suffocating to death in a locked trailer of a motorway service station car park, they use sound to orchestrate rescue by police, ambulance, and fire service.

2. Abbas is asked to continue banging on the metal side of the refrigerated trailer with a piece of frozen meat and keep his mobile on so that Carrie can hear how close the siren of the police car is getting. The police officers are asked to bang on the trailer sides until Carrie can identify to them they have found the right one. Abbas passes out and we hear Carrie calling out his name and willing the rescue to get to him and his daughter in time.

3. After breaking into the trailer, police officers find the unconscious families with children. An officer called Kevin says he can only see bodies. Carrie directs him to do CPR to Abbas's child – placing her on her back and while kneeling by the side place the heel of his left hand in the middle of the chest and interlock with the right hand and pressing down to a depth of 5 cm in the following rhythm: 'one and two and three and four…and one and two and three, and four'. This rhythm of instruction and urgency is shared by Carrie and the police officers. At the same time sound drama is educating the public and the BBC's public service ethos of entertainment, information, and education are being fused with significant impact. The sound drama is also constructing all of the resonances, dimensions, and speciality of a very dramatic mise-en-scène. Gordon Lea was conscious of playing with the listener's multi-sensory perception and conjuring the colour, smell, touch, and texture of his characters' experiences. He was also enthusiastic about establishing speed and distance through movement – known as kinesics (speed) and proxemics (distance) in drama (Lea, 1926, pp. 62–64). All of this is powerfully communicated in the horror of Kevin and his colleague entering the chamber of death and fighting to preserve life and then the arrival of the first team of paramedics who define the field of tragedy and break off to say they have to get stuck in.

4. This is now a major incident with all ambulance units being directed to the lorry-park. The shock and impact of this drama are felt by Carrie when she reflects that her daughter Chloe at 5 years old is the same age as Abbas's daughter. Will enquires if she would like a break. But she decides to continue. Will Abbas and his daughter survive? Have the emergency services got there in time? All of these questions are playing in the mind of the central character and the listener of course. It is the classic cliffhanger moment in the middle of the play driving the attention of the listener to stay listening and locking the audience in emotionally.

Lea argued that exposition works better than telling. Dramatic action is better than witty dialogue:

...I started out with the theory that plays which depended mainly on witty dialogue and very little on action would be more intelligible to the listener and so be more successful. Imagine my surprise when I discovered that the contrary was the case.

(Lea, 1926, pp. 62–64)

He suggested that the radio playwright should indicate action in dialogue and combine with effects, but 'sound effects are not always as intelligible to the listener as the producer who makes them' (Lea, 1926, p. 58).

The sound design in *Life Lines* is restrained, realistic, and perfect in the way it is an agency of the plot and action and succeeds in placing the listener with this action. The ambience and tonality of the police officer change as soon as he opens the door of the trailer. There's the agonising shout 'Can anybody hear me?' and the deafening silence in return gestating the horrific implication of what has happened and been discovered. The microphone and point of listening is Abbas' mobile phone connection to Carrie in the ambulance control room.

Lea wrote that while 'the horizon of the dramatist's dreams is widened beyond all knowledge, some restraint needs to be exercised in respect of sound-effects... these should be used sparingly. An ounce of suggestion is worth a ton of irritation' (Lea, 1926). Frank H. Shaw agreed when he observed in his *Radio Times* article of the same year:

> The tinkle of a glass at precisely the right moment adds an enormous value to the spoken word [...] an enormous responsibility rests on the producer's shoulders if all synchronization of words and sounds are to be correct. I cannot remember to have been let down once.
>
> (Shaw, 1926)

The sound design in *Life Lines* never lets the listener down.

Could *Life Lines* work as well on the stage? The fact of the matter is that it has been originated and written specifically for sound and radio. In the visual medium, the camera would take over and leave the ambulance control room. Our imaginative spectacle as listeners is determined by our ear sharing Carrie's sound connection with the outside world of disasters and emergencies, and also the banal, frustrating, and infuriating.

Lea surmised that radio drama also liberates the author from the restrictions of the stage set:

> Any scene may be suggested and it will be adequate...the scene is built up in the imagination of the listener, and actual experience goes to the building. Each individual supplies his own idea of the scene, an idea based on reality, and so sees the play in its ideal setting.
>
> (Lea, 1926, p. 40)

Anything conceivable in the imagination of the writer is capable of complete expression and interpretation in radio drama: 'If he wishes to set his play in the heart of a buttercup, the imagination of his hearer will provide the setting' (Lea, 1926, p. 41). There was no evidence of any outbreak of buttercup plays on the BBC after 1926, though the concomitant imperative of modernism during this period invited and secured many imaginative expressions of symbolist plays inherent in the sound medium and exploring the disconnections and dislocations between reality, voice, sound, and meaning.

The generation of sound effects in early radio drama at the BBC (1922–1926) was limited by the technology available – single microphones with limited pick-up and much restricted frequency response compared to what we are used to now. Lea argued that sound effects and atmospheric backgrounds (so much more difficult to achieve at that time) should be mere suggestions so that the mind of the listener provided the colour, scale, hues, and shades: 'I have heard a listener say that he preferred to hear the voices of the players come out of silence; they were then to him like jewels against a background of black velvet' (Lea, 1926, p. 72). So much more is now possible in terms of multi-tracking, stereo, and surround sound. In the early 21st century, there is a fashion for sound immersion, but the nobility in simplicity and respect for what the listener can provide is still something worth thinking about. And I would argue that the voices of human character in *Life Lines* are very much like jewels against the background of black velvet modern life.

So far the analysis of the action in the plot of this episode of *Life Lines* has actually comprised of 8 minutes. The writer Al Smith, with direction and production by Sally Avens, uses a classic convention in dramatic storytelling. Tragedy is followed by comedy, the sublime by the ridiculous and the serious juxtaposed with the trivial. Here, the junction is achieved by a 'catching the breath' musical bridge derived by Portishead's iconic track *Roads* from their first album *Dummy*. The three chords are suffused with sonic sub-text. The lyrics to the instrumental which are not vocalised in the play's tapestry of sound recollect perhaps the emotions of the characters and listeners: 'Can't anybody see, We've got a war to fight, Never find our way, Regardless of what they say ... How can it feel this wrong?'

5. Carrie finds that her plaintive 'Is the patient breathing and conscious?' is met with a woman's sigh and impatient reply in the affirmative, but 'only just'. Carrie is dealing with a selfish and self-centred 25-year-old Angelica calling from the toilet/bathroom of a National Trust property where she is attending the wedding of a former boyfriend.

6. Early expressions of claims to be suffering from the advanced symptoms of hereditary bowel cancer give way via gentle interrogation by Carrie to the confession she is most likely suffering from food poisoning brought on by "salmonella ridden" cheap fish canapés financed by the tight-fisted bride. Angelica wants to be extracted by way of ambulance stretcher. Carrie's advice is to go home to bed and drink plenty of water. The sequence is comedic, particularly when Carrie's patience is tried by the revelation Angelica is wearing white at

her ex-boyfriend's wedding ceremony. The public service message conveyed with great entertainment is that 999 is a number which should only be used for emergencies.

7. The action switches to a call from a woman called Joyce with an Irish accent claiming to be walking her dog close to the lorry park and pretending to both report the abandoning of the lorry with a driver running off and her fears for migrants trapped inside. She vaguely mentions that she doesn't think those inside could get out. Now Carrie switches from being the phone detective trying to identify the nature of a medical crisis and how to maintain life and wellbeing to an Agatha Christie Miss Marple with headphones who suspects Joyce is the driver of the migrant truck and she's lying. She asks Joyce if she is near the truck as they are speaking. Can she describe the driver? Where is she now? Why did she call ambulance instead of the police? Can she go back to the scene because the police would appreciate her assistance?

8. Carrie alerts Will to bring in the police. She is clear Joyce is lying. There is no way to cross the motorway from the service station. As the location of her mobile is triangulated, Carrie keeps her talking as a police car is directed to find her with the assistance of motorway CCTV which has also identified her. She has guessed that Joyce is standing at the nearby roundabout and watching the developing ambulance and police response. Joyce is becoming taciturn and simply wants to know what has happened to the migrants so she can get away. Carrie is still stalling for time. When asking Joyce about the whereabouts of her dog, she doesn't have an answer and only wishes to know what Carrie means by the question.

9. This episode of *Life Lines* is clearly dramatising the real-life tragedies and murder/manslaughters of multiple migrant victims who have died from exposure and suffocation in the back of lorry trailers being used by people smugglers. Dramatic fiction vocalises and recreates that which we have not witnessed in a non-fictional reality.

In Chapter 5 of his book, Gordon Lea devoted a full chapter to 'The Listener's Part' and focused his analysis on the essential indigenous and significant power of the sound dramatist's medium. Critically radio and sound drama can enable a listener to participate in dramatised events and narrative if it is much more difficult to understand when engaging with journalistic and news coverage of actual events. He was encouraging writers to engage with the listener's imagination, but not by overwhelming the audience with 'mind-picture': '…in radio drama, the sense of hearing only is used. All that could be received through the other senses has to be supplied by the imagination' (Lea, 1926, p. 67). He was emphasising that listeners only need a suggestion. They can fill in the rest: 'In radio-work, this intimacy is pronounced. The listener is in direct touch with the player – there is no intervening convention – no barrier. Soul speaks to soul' (Lea, 1926, p. 69). There can be no doubt that the souls of migrant victims of people traffickers are definitely speaking to the souls of listeners in this compelling and compassionate radio drama.

It is great credit to Al Smith and the BBC production team that they have achieved everything Gordon Lea hoped for in the potential for radio drama in 1926 and the future:

> By the very fact that the listener is called upon to give so much of his own personality to the radio-play is his enjoyment and appreciation of it intensified…and he gains through the medium of the human voice a mental pageantry of colour and delight which no artist in the world can emulate.
>
> *(Lea, 1926)*

10. The last 3 minutes of the *Life Lines* episode is devoted to Carrie bringing justice to Abbas, his daughter and other victims. When Joyce pleads with her to tell her what has happened to the migrants in the trailer Carrie says she believes she can see perfectly well. This is an intense *J'accuse* and when Joyce realizes nobody is walking out of the trailer, she exclaims that she did not know there were people in the back behind her driver's cab. Carrie does not believe her. She is now police detective, prosecuting counsel and indeed sentencing judge in the court of public opinion and basic humanity. She sets out the facts rather like a judge sentencing. There were seven families and only one of them has survived. A father's daughter has died on his chest. The police are on the scene. Carrie says the little girl only came to this country to learn. She condemns Joyce for treating her as no better than the refrigerated meat her trailer is meant to carry. We hear an officer telling Joyce to hang up her phone. Joyce says plaintively that what has happened is not her fault. Carrie is not impressed. Of course it is, she says. The officer again instructs her to hang up the phone and as she does so going off mic slightly we hear that she only got involved because she needed money. This is hollow mitigation which condemns Joyce and the appalling exploitation and misery of people trafficking.

Lea was very much the stage writer and director when he began working in the radio medium. His only other publication was *Modern Stagecraft for the Amateur* in 1949, so his comparative focus is very much between sound and physical theatre and he quickly appreciated that the unstageable does not need a scene break or transition. 'Illusion once created need never be broken in the radio-play. The dramatist can be as extensive as he likes, since the whole world or any part of it can be his setting' (Lea, 1926, p. 42). Consequently, *Life Lines* is a drama where the point of listening remains largely the mobile microphone which Carrie's Ambulance control room connects with. The switch of location is as quick, fast and simple as the ear and mind connecting with any smartphone, telephone, and mobile anywhere. Lea explained that the dramatist has direct access to the listener on the emotions of the play and they are therefore immune when 'the house is made to "rock with mirth." In the quietude of your own room, you can react truly and naturally and so be sincere. All this makes for truth and reality' (Lea, 1926, p. 42). *Life Lines* is quintessential truth and reality throughout.

As already observed one traditional radio drama technique avoided in *Life Lines* is what Lea recognised the medium had resuscitated as a mainly threadbare and cliché in the stage medium; namely aside and soliloquy: 'In stage-work the "Aside" and the "Soliloquy" were incapable of sincere use' (Lea, 1926, p. 39). Lea argued that in radio-work they can be used with 'every appearance of sincerity and truth' (Lea, 1926). In radio drama aside and soliloquy are not retrogressive: 'It is simply that in radio drama we have found a medium suitable for the sincere development of this integral factor of life and action' (Lea, 1926, p. 59).

Aside and soliloquy is still an artifice in the sense that the listener is being sign-posted a direct address on talking terms or permission to eavesdrop on interior thought. But this is not needed in *Life Lines*. Such access to interiority is achieved through sub-text and an identification and participation with the central character's thinking behind the dialogue. Lea would have recognised how Al Smith as the sound dramatist had no need to write to communicate a crowd-psychology: 'In conversation with a friend you can use a direct method, an intimate method, which would not be suitable for an orator's platform. The radio-play gains just this intimacy which a stage-play can never hope to have' (Lea, 1926, p. 43).

As we have already explored in the earlier chapters, the issue of the contemporary listener's cultural memory and mind's eye association was a preoccupation in many debates about sound drama's intrinsic properties whether good or bad. Gordon Lea thought it best not to announce the actors in radio drama casts because if they knew the players 'they will visualize them as they last saw them and possibly so spoil illusion' (Lea, 1926, p. 59). Now it is conventional to identify the actors. The writer can avoid celebrity and star/name association interfering with the listener's imagination through the integrity of characterisation. The character should be identifiable by the way he or she talks and how different that is from anybody else in the play and, of course, the writer is the composer whose symphony will distinguish wind from strings, and a piano from a French horn.

When discussing the technique of radio actors, Lea recognised that voice acting required absolute control of the voice, actors needed to concentrate their thinking behind the voice enunciation and expression. Britain may well be unique in the world in having the finest audio/radio drama actors and apart from the practical consideration of avoiding paper rattle/rustle in performance, being able to adjust the volume of the voice by a determination of the position in and around the microphone, Lea emphasised that in radio acting, the performer needs to concentrate on:

> [H]is thinking and the regulation of his consciousness…his aim must be to radiate personality – the personality of his particular part – to convey atmosphere by co-operation with other radiating personalities and to do all this through the medium of the voice.
>
> *(Lea, 1926, pp. 78–9)*

In this one episode of about 17 minutes of the serial *Life Lines* we have an out-standing demonstration of the highest quality of audio dramatic direction by Sally Avens and performance by the small cast who undoubtedly merit full identification and tribute for regulating their consciousness: Carrie by Sarah Ridgeway; Will by Rick Warden; Ian (Carrie's husband and partner who is active in other episodes) by Michael Jibson; Abbas by Sharif Dorani; Joyce by Helen Norton; Angelica by Saffron Coomber; Police Officers by Justice Ritchie and Grace Cooper Milton, and the Paramedic by Shaun Mason.

While all these observations about direction and performance might seem irrel-evant to the writer, they do indicate that it is a good idea to not overwrite and to leave substantial sub-text for the actors to express and develop the creativity of their craft. It is important to give them space to bring something to the character and performance. This is what Al Smith has achieved so significantly.

Lea was discussing a new art-form in 1926 when 'radio drama is born and is in its cradle' (Lea, 1926, p. 91). He hoped that we would be able to eventually 'recognize it in its maturity' and that it would be 'full of vigour and beauty'. The last sentence of his book is 'Here is the new clay for moulding, but where are the Potters?' (Lea, 1926). This medium for dramatic expression is still welcoming new potters to mould the clay now in its second century of production after the BBC marked its centenary turning point in February 2022. And to develop the metaphor on the art of pottery, Al Smith, Sally Avens, and the BBC production team of *Life Lines* can be recognised as Ming Dynasty ceramics.

Reginald Berkeley's Bridging Achievements in Dramatising Consciousness with Modernist Technique

In 1926, Reginald Berkeley wrote a short play which provided visceral and heart-breaking emotions through the dramatisation of a child's consciousness when on the brink of life and death, having lost her mother and not knowing if her father is dead or alive. In *The Quest of Elizabeth*, Elizabeth has been run over and is in hospital Accident and Emergency talking to the nurses and doctor. This frames the symmetry of the beginning and end of the play which proceeds with her dream Alice in Wonderland fairy-tale-like journey to try to find the father she does not know has also been killed after the anaesthetic renders her unconscious from the real world:

NURSE ANDERSON: Never mind. Go on. Breathe deeply. (*she obeys.*)

ELIZABETH (*ALMOST INARTICULATELY*): Bells—ringing—in—my—head. (*A sound like sleigh bells in the far distance.*)

NURSE ANDERSON. (*GENTLY*): Don't talk. Just breathe deeply. (*The bells are nearer and louder.*) She's under. Hobday. (*The bells are nearer.*)

DOCTOR: Yes…A little more over, nurse. Yes, like that. Mind the mask…

Their voices die away. The bells grow louder…louder…nearer…They are menacing…all pervading…. Just when they are becoming unbearable they begin to die away. Strains of unearthly music blend with the ringing. The bells cease, and the strange music gradually resolves itself into a medley of nursery tunes uncommonly harmonized. Distant voices are singing a kind of marching song to the music:

(Berkeley, 1926, p. 234)

In her dream-world Elizabeth finds herself at the shore of the River Styx where the watermen Bill and Davy refuse to row her across in their boat to find her parents: '(*almost crying*). But, please, I've come all this way to look for my father. And if you say he's over there with Mummy, won't you please take me over?' (Berkeley, 1926, p. 245). As she decides to swim herself, she can hear her parents' voices far away in the distance 'Sweet-heart...Eliza-beth', 'Little heart. My baby!' as she drowns:

I'm frightened. It's too deep...Daddy!...Save me! (*Her voice is lost in a choking gurgle. There is another feeble splash; then silence*)

(Berkeley, 1926, p. 246)

Berkeley's play ignited a moral panic about radio drama traumatizing the listeners with condemnatory coverage in the *Daily Mail* which was oblivious to the fact the BBC had cut the final scene in the hospital operating theatre where amidst the faint clatter of instruments on glass surfaces, Elizabeth dies (Crook, 2020, pp. 225–231). The final lines: 'NURSE (shakily). Poor little mite. Let's hope she's found her father. THE PADRE (with grave confidence). You need be in no doubt as to that, Nurse...' (ibid, p. 247) were never heard and only read in the script later published with a public admonition to BBC Managing Director John Reith over the censorship.

Much has already been written and published about Berkeley's achievement in writing the first full-length original radio play for the BBC for Armistice Night 1925, *The White Château*, which was also the first to be published in book form anywhere in the world (Beck, 2000: 5.5; Crook, 2000, pp. 201–225). Berkeley succeeded in combining and interspersing modernist expression with intense realism by characterising how the actual building of the château witnesses the tragic events of war over time. The dialogic actions are developed through six long scenes bridged by the narration of a chronicler and a rich soundscape of originally composed music and sound effects written with the literary effect of onomatopoeia. Much has also already been written and analysed about Berkeley's 1927 modernist *Metropolis* style play *Machines* which would be wholly censored and blocked from broadcasting by the BBC because of its political content over 14 scenes (Beck, 2000:8.4; Crook, 2020, pp. 231–242; Pepler, 1988, pp. 197–229). The style of writing in my opinion is rather Shavian and does not achieve the later pace and rhythm of quick cuts between fast-moving economically written dialogue that would advance the form in the 1930s and 1940s. Beck conceded that 'Berkeley to some lesser extent still stuck to the old Galsworthy stage format' (Beck, 2000:8.4.1).

However, Berkeley does achieve a significant advance in scripting audio drama at the end of *Machines*. The play had begun with the opening traditional form of the prologue. It was preachy, polemical and is very much in telling mode: 'The Age of

Machines, in which we live, has diminished the World to an almost contemptible bulk' (Berkeley, 1927, p. 26). Pepler described the play as:

> [T]he rise and fall of a working class hero, Mansell, whose influence comes from personal charisma and what the author intends to appear as the justice of his cause, but also through the affair he has with the daughter of a powerful man on the other side, Colonel Willoughby.
>
> *(Pepler, 1988, p. 198)*

It is a play about the oppression and suffering of the working classes at that time in British social history and the inhumanity of the mechanistic machine age. All of the ensuing political drama and conflict climaxing in the murder of his lover Joyce Willoughby is closed with an ambient urban montage of the London street soundscape of the Strand. As I observed in *Audio Drama Modernism* the genius in Berkeley's writing is to present the execution of the central character 'in everyday public space rather than by melodrama in the execution block with the hangman' (Crook, 2020, p. 230).

> [*A roar of traffic in the Strand.*]
> A POLICEMAN
> …Charing Cross? Any bus going this way will take you there, madam…Pass along there, please…
> A VOICE IN THE DISTANCE
> Mansell—Execution Scene…Special!
> A MAN IN THE STREET
> Half a minute. Let's get a paper.
> HIS WIFE
> Get me a *Globe*, then—will you?
> THE MAN
> …That awful rag!
> HIS WIFE
> Yes, dear…but their face-renovation hints are the best in London.
> THE MAN
> Face-renovation!…My hat!
> THE NEWSBOY
> [*Nearer*] MANSELL—EXECUTION SCENES…SPEESHALL!…
> THE MAN
> Hi!…Got a *Globe*?
> THE BOY
> [*Pausing—husky voiced*] Yes, mister.
> THE MAN
> …I'll have the *Sun* as well [*Chink of coins.*]
> Here's your *Globe*, Elsie. [*With animation*]
> I say, Surrey all out for 72. That's a bit of a collapse, isn't it?
> THE NEWSBOY

[*His voice receding as he scurries on*] Mansell—Execution Scenes...Special!

ELSIE

[*Reading*] Listen, dear...Mansell walked to the scaffold without assistance.

Less than two minutes elapsed from the time he left his cell...Poor wretch!

THE MAN

...Who's that?...Oh, did he?...Hello! That strike's off at last. Good job.

The men have agreed to the employers' terms.

ELSIE

What does it mean...Victory of the Machines, dear? What machines?

THE MAN

Oh, I suppose something to do with the Trade Unions. They always put

that sort of rot in newspapers...Look out! There's our bus coming. Hi!

[*The sound of an omnibus drawing up.*]

THE CONDUCTOR

...No room on top. Inside...Hold tight, please...

[*Ting-ting on the starting bell. The omnibus lumbers away. A neighbouring clock strikes the half-hour. The chimes blend into the rhythmical clangour of machinery, bringing the play to an end.*]

(*Berkeley, 1927, pp. 190–192*)

It could certainly be argued that this inventive and highly radiophonic and audiogenic ending redeems many aspects of a play Pepler said was 'crude and wasteful in terms of character portrayal and not notable for convincingness of dialogue, particularly where intense emotion is involved' (Pepler, 1988, p. 204).

L du Garde Peach – *The Mary Celeste: A Mystery of the Sea* – Long Form Radio/Audio Drama

BBC Radio drama developed the long form of the microphone play through the 1920s by successful dramatisations of novels such as Joseph Conrad's *Lord Jim* in 1927 and 1928 by BBC producer Cecil Lewis, and in 1929 Compton Mackenzie's *Carnival* by the novelist himself with the variety producer and songwriter Holt Marvel/Eric Maschwitz. Mackenzie actually voiced the linking narration of his own radio adaptation. The original scripts have not survived, but reviews and articles about them have attested to the achievement of producing long stories keeping the interest and attention of the listener for one, two, or more hours in duration. In November 1929, *The Radio Times* declared:

Carnival is being 'revived' at the request of many listeners who were unable to hear it on the first occasion. The experiment of presenting the complete life-story of a character in a play of more than two hours in length, was a daring one. That it succeeded so admirably was mainly due to the special qualities of Mr. Mackenzie's story ... of London bohemian life.

(*Anon, 1929, p. 331*)

Carnival would be produced and broadcast again by the BBC in 1933, 1936, and 1960.

The BBC would describe Cecil Lewis' dramatisation of *Lord Jim* as marking 'an interesting innovation in broadcasting technique' (Anon, 1928, p. 24). Lewis divided the story into three parts, and it was described in internal memos as a first attempt at film technique with narration. The very nature of the novel's style and structure with the protagonist's direct narrative driving on the story with time reversal and the central mystery remaining unsolved lent itself to the narrator method. Prior to broadcast, Lewis said he had created: 'a photo-play technique: a large number of simple scenes, short in duration, linked together and carried forward by a storyteller' (Lewis, 1927, p. 333). He acknowledged that Conrad's novel writing provides three essentials of a good radio dramatist: '…first, the ability to tell a good plain story; secondly, the power of writing dialogue with real characters, thirdly, a fine sense of vivid descriptive prose' (Lewis, 1927).

Conrad was very skilled and successful in writing stage adaptations of his novels that ran well in the West End.

In an article in the *Radio Times* at the end of 1927 titled 'St Augustine and the Cucumber', Lewis further elaborated on the nature of Lord Jim's innovation:

> Like its vigorous and vulgar foster-sister, the cinema, radio drama ignores time and space. The author can range wide over the world. His ingenuity may be taxed in carrying his hearers with him; but there are not the physical difficulties imposed in the theatre … This may spell the death of the theatre, though through it may come the rebirth of the drama. The days of the spoken five-reel picture drama are not far off. The days of television are not far off. The combination of these with broadcasting will give a world-wide fireside drama – and its potentialities are simply terrific.
>
> …A little over a year ago, 'Lord Jim', the dramatization of a classic novel, was adapted for the microphone into twenty-three consecutive scenes linked by a narrator supplying aural sub-titles. I was responsible for this.
>
> *(Lewis, 1927, p. 711)*

Lewis had absolutely no doubt that the central purpose of radio drama was to give the listener spectacular and enduring action:

> Action! Action in a Radio play? A play without sight? A play for the blind? Certainly! Action is not only visual, it is imaginative. The eye apprehends and limits; but the ear comprehends and suggests. We see the lightning, but we fear the thunder. Reality is the prosaic stimulus. It is the inward eye which carries us up to the mountains or down to the valleys, to love or hate, to joy or sorrow. And the test of a good story-teller is whether he can carry us with him, whether he can grip our imagination.
>
> *(Lewis, 1927)*

Lewis's lively article is explaining and promoting the broadcast of his first original play for the medium *Pursuit*. This time Lewis is dispensing with the narrator method and going all out with a self-contained structure of 69 intrinsic dramatic scenes divided into three plot sections. The beginning of the play is unprecedented in British radio drama. There are six telephone pieces to the microphone. We would call them monologues now. Lewis calls them 'aural close-ups' and stipulates that there are no stage directions or mind pictures in this play. It starts with six telephone conversations, the equivalent of screen close-ups, to impress the voices of the principal characters on the mind of the listeners.

Pursuit is a detective thriller lasting one and quarter hours. Sadly it has not been published in book or performance script form, though a later production script in 1933 has been preserved in the BBC's Written Archives. Alan Beck says Lewis wrote:

> [A] popular play, really in the style of a film. The 1920s was the golden age of thriller writing. 'Pursuit' aimed to appeal to a wide popular audience as the adapted stage plays did, and as he had experimented with the adaptation of Conrad's novel, *Lord Jim*.
>
> *(Beck, 2000:8.3.27)*

Christina Pepler said the trick of the close-up telephone conversations 'works well as a means of introducing the characters, whetting audience curiosity about them and the possible connections between them' (Pepler, 1988, p. 244).

Lord Jim, *Pursuit*, and *Carnival* are just three stepping stones to BBC audio productions confidently presenting fluid self-contained and original action plays by the late 1920s and early 1930s. L du Garde Peach and Tyrone Guthrie would follow up Reginald Berkeley's enthusiasm for publishing his radio plays in book form (*The White Château* 1925 and *Machines* 1927) by bringing out two collections of their BBC plays.

L. du Garde Peach's *Radio Plays* (1931) were branded by his publisher Newnes as having 'thrilled millions'. *Ingredient X* (1929) should be avoided because of its repeated racist stereotyping of Africans and equally appalling racist language. *Mary Celeste* first broadcast in May 1931 tells a haunting and evocative mystery story over 1 hour in a fast-paced sequence of short scenes with the powerful backdrop of ocean-going soundscape.

The Radio Times and announcer cueing in the play's broadcast would say:

> This is the story of a true happening, in that *Mary Celeste* (often known as the Marie Celeste) a half brig or brigantine of 282 tons under the command of Captain Ben Briggs, did sail from New York on November 7, 1872, and was found by the brig *Dei Gratia* on December 5 of the same year, abandoned by her crew, some 380 nautical miles from Capa Roca in Portugal. Captain

Morehouse, the skipper of the *Dei Gratia*, was a friend of Captain Briggs of the *Mary Celeste*, and had indeed dined with him in New York on the night before the *Mary Celeste* sailed. That is all. When she was found, the *Mary Celeste* was under full sail and standing on her course—empty. The rest is silence.

(du Garde Peach, 1931, p. 68; Anon, 1931, p. 291)

A feature article in *The Radio Times* by John Knowles acknowledged the story, and argument was 50 years old by the time of the broadcast and writers have always been fascinated by the story: 'Joseph Conrad drew something from it. Conan Doyle wrote a history of it, and the bibliography of the *Mary Celeste*— that 'white winged wanderer' that 'phantom ship – makes in itself a small library' (Knowles, 1931, p. 263).

L. du Garde Peach wraps the hour-long play with the technique of a prologue and epilogue conversation on a liner between an Englishman and American at the very point in the Atlantic where she was found. It is a way of using dialogue to contextualise and introduce the story of a play. It is a longstanding technique deployed in the BBC Radio drama series of the 1970s dramatising Georges Simenon *Maigret* novels. Each self-contained 45 minute play of a novel would open with an imagined conversation between Georges Simenon and Chief Inspector Jules Maigret and end with a short epilogue reflecting on what the enquiry and mystery meant to Maigret himself.

In *Mary Celeste*, an Englishman and an American set the scene with a cross-fading into the past. When the Englishman asks what happened to the *Mary Celeste*, we hear the American explaining nobody knows because there was so little evidence aboard. Only a couple of long white marks or cuts at her bows and an axe stuck deep into her wooden rail. The ship's log showed the crew must have left in a hurry about ten days before she was found. The chronometer and sextant had been taken. Just as the American starts a sentence about the mystery of why they left and what had been happening aboard never being solved his voice fades against the sound atmosphere of Scene 1 which consists of waves and of wind which fades in and continues as a faint background (du Garde Peach, 1931, p. 73).

Over 20 scenes of different lengths, a gruesome and terrifying nightmare befalls the Captain, his family, and crew. It begins with the *Dei Gratia* finding her and not responding to signals. Not a soul can be seen upon her decks (du Garde Peach, 1931, p. 77). They then board the stricken vessel, thinking at first the crew are all dead or drunk. But they find absolutely no one. And the idea that drinking alcohol might be the cause is quickly dispelled when a sailor recalls Captain Briggs is a teetotaler and would not tolerate it (du Garde Peach, 1931, p. 79).

The Captain of the *Dei Gratia* decides to tow the *Mary Celeste* to port and the end of scene VI takes the focus of the drama to what happened to the people on the brigand from the time of its sailing to the disaster that befell them. Du Garde Peach writes another skilful transition for long form audio drama plot development by having Captain Moorhouse relate to his first mate Oliver Deveau, what passed between him and Captain Briggs the night before the Mary Celeste set sail. As he reports Briggs telling him a sailor needs religion to cope with the mighty queer character of the open sea, the sound of the play cross fades to the very words Briggs was telling him so scene VII can be the flashback of their last encounter and the continuing self-contained drama of what du Garde Peach will fictionalise as the course of events bringing about the crew's disappearance (du Garde Peach, 1931, p. 82).

The last 15–20 seconds of Scene XX provide a suitably *grand guignol* ending of L. du Garde Peach's mystery. We hear the frantic jumping of Captain Briggs, Mrs. Briggs, and the steward and second mate into the lifeboat. As the wave sounds grow in volume, Mrs. Briggs begins to scream and Captain Briggs cries out in terror that a giant octopus is after them and they have to row for their lives. The sound play then fades to silence (du Garde Peach, 1931, p. 110).

L. du Garde Peach's fictional answer to the mystery of the *Mary Celeste* would be produced and broadcast by BBC radio again in 1932 and then by BBC Television drama in 1956. This would have been a live production in a specially designed set. Viewers were told that the ship was:

> ...undamaged and there was no sign of confusion on board, except that the fore hatch had been opened and one barrel of the cargo of 1,700 barrels of raw alcohol had been broached. The ship's boat – she only carried one – was missing. Captain Briggs, skipper and part owner of the Mary Celeste, was a religious fanatic of the New England type, and with him on the voyage he had taken his young wife. Neither Captain Briggs, his wife, nor any member of the crew has ever been heard of since...This play is an imaginative version of what might have happened...
>
> *(Anon, 2 November 1956, p. 26)*

Tyrone Guthrie – Rhythm and Long Form

Squirrel's Cage and two other microphone plays, namely *Matrimonial News* and *Flowers Are Not for You to Pick*, were also published by Cobden-Sanderson in 1931. In his introduction, Guthrie said he feared that in future years the technique of his three plays 'will be as dead as Queen Anne, as dated as the dodo' (Guthrie, 1931, p. 8). He believed the broadcast radio play is deprived of 'all those sensual sops to Cerberus' (Guthrie, 1931) and 'the mind of the listener is the more free to create its own illusion' (Guthrie, 1931). Guthrie appreciated 'the listener's picture, created from his own associations, derived from his own experience, expresses his own particular brand of moonshine' (Guthrie, 1931, p. 9).

Squirrel's Cage was one of the most abstract verbal experimental radio plays of the late 1920s with a special Overture and Closing Music written by Owen Mase. Howard Fink explained:

The structure of the play is a cycle of man's life from birth to maturity, within the restricted squirrel-cage of middle-class social conventions. The end of the cycle is a repetition of the beginning, with the protagonist Henry and his new wife now playing the roles previously acted by his parents, and with their child now in Henry's earlier rebellious role. The play is a rather bitter social satire, full of the boredom and frustration of lives sacrificed to the system.

(Fink, 1981, p. 23)

The play certainly amplifies the potential of contrapuntally combining musical and choral verbal rhythm. Guthrie said there is no narration in the play with scene and interlude following one another without a break. After the end of each episode he plots the sound of one stroke of a bell, then the scream of a siren, suggesting a rush through time and space. Guthrie wished for the 'Scenes' to be played very intimately in rather a low key and in stark contrast to the 'Interludes' which are to be bold and reverberating, each one working up to what he hopes would be played as a thunderous climax (Guthrie, 1931, p. 14).

Experimental plays on early BBC radio provoked an uneven response from listeners and reviewers, and the analysis of *Squirrel's Cage* by Val Gielgud in Chapter 3 demonstrates this. Raymond W. Postgate in a *Listener* article discussing 'Expressionism and Radio Drama' praised the rhythmical interludes that 'all "got their effect" immediately and, what is more, got an effect which clearly could not have been got so immediately or so well by any medium other than the wireless' (Postgate, 1929, *Listener*, p. 405). He recognised that Guthrie was using a technique which was natural to radio and sound instead of being borrowed or adapted from another dramatic medium.

Postgate was not impressed with the dialogues which followed because they 'did undoubtedly drag' (Postgate, 1929). But he did recognise that:

The 'Squirrel's Cage' shows that the wireless listener will imagine for you without any demur a complete railway journey—a change in space. But he will also accept a series of more or less confused and repetitive noises as a fair representation of a whole series of railway journeys, of years and years of railway journeys—a change in time. This he does because the wireless presents no scenery or stage which will anchor him to a particular time or place: it gives his imagination freedom to visualise whatever memories are suggested by a repetition of phrases such as '*It simply means I shall have to travel by the eight-fifteen*'. A series of such phrases, repeated, varied slightly, and plastered one upon the other, is accepted by the mind as a fair record of a lifetime of railway journeys, for the reason that the mind, looking back on such a perspective of real railway journeys, recalls just such a plaster and repetition of little-varying phrases and sounds, run together by the passage of time. Now, such a process of the mind cannot possibly be evoked by the ordinary stage.

(Postgate, 1929)

Postgate was analysing the impact of 'Interlude III' which was a rhythmic puffing of a train accompanying a dialogue montage of many different voices heard when commuting by train to the City from the suburbs. The voices are all saying different things but repeating themselves (Guthrie, 1931, p. 59).

The expressionist nature of Guthrie's writing is also very well illustrated with the play's 'Interlude V' which is fragments of Interludes II and III repeated and cross-faded into one another. Guthrie seeks to create a composite image of the commuter's day so that trains can be heard fading into typewriters, and imaginatively listeners seeing in their mind's eye railway-lines merging into lines of print, the columns of bobbing bowler hats into columns of pounds, shilling and pence. He wants to create a sense of dissolving view (Guthrie, 1931, p. 7).

The Flowers are Not for You to Pick was less abstract expressionistic and when written and broadcast in 1930 succeeded in using the radio drama medium to effectively recreate the dream of a whole man's life recollected as he floats in the ocean and fights against the inevitable drowning after falling overboard. It would be reproduced and rebroadcast in 1933, 1935, 1946, 1952, and 1961.

Guthrie explained how he wanted the rhythm and spirit of his play to combine as a sound orchestration of voices and effects:

> In this play the many short scenes rise out of and sink into a rhythmic sound of splashing, moving seas. This should be complex yet symphonic ... by its rhythm and tone it may be possible to suggest not merely the waters in which Edward is engulfed, but the beating of a heart, the tumult of fear, the immutable laws and irresistible strength of Nature compared with our puny and inconstant selves.
>
> *(Guthrie, 1931, p. 140)*

The play is remarkable in opening with a traditional announcer who guides the listener into the consciousness of the central character's thoughts and past life. The announcer begins by asking listeners to recall the maxim that drowning men often see their past lives floating before their very eyes. This is what happens to a young clergyman bound for China who has had the misfortune of falling overboard. He is now struggling for his life in the ocean. The sound of the waves can be heard. His name is Edward. And as the announcer indicated Edward's past life in voice and pictures floats before his eyes with a cross-fading into the first scene (Guthrie, 1931, p. 141).

Childhood, education, family relationships, romantic entanglements, unrequited love, career struggles all unfold across 17 scenes – a life frustrated, unfulfilled, full of regrets, and disappointments, and it is towards the end that Guthrie finally gives interior voice to Edward as his life begins to fade with all the emotions and memories of his past because we are now in his present.

This is a brilliantly written stream of consciousness monologue. He echoes back to the opening words of the announcer about the past and present floating before somebody about to experience sudden death in battle. Gradually his mind and thoughts begin to focus and he realises it must now be him drowning at sea. He recalls saying to Dunwoody that he wanted him to lead the responses to the litany, but this was in the past. In the recent present, he remembers going to his cabin and then there must have been a mistake because he is now floating and bobbing on the surface. Anyone watching might see the chain of bubbles floating to the surface from his drowning person. He can see his spectacles sinking. And his last conscious articulation of thought is being thankful he will be dying still wearing his dog collar.

Guthrie in the writing then montages poignant and emotionally laden bunches of words from the people in Edward's past life – childhood, school, career, family, and relationships. They gradually become shorter and softer. They begin with Fanny telling Edward as a child to close his eyes, stand under the cedar tree, and wait until he hears them call cuckoo. The reaching out to Vanessa and life's calling, but everything beyond reach because as his mother once said to him 'the flowers are not for you to pick'.

For Edward the groping and searching for the truth is as fleeting and drifting off as the people calling 'cuckoo' from behind the trees when he was small. Vanessa has married somebody else, and he just has enough time to say 'Vanessa…I love' as the cries of 'cuckoo' get fainter and more distant and the last word heard from him is 'coming' before the waves take over and the play fades to silence (Guthrie, 1931, p. 207).

It seems extraordinary that this play was last produced and broadcast some 61 years ago. So many aspects of this script written in 1930 were in a world so different and with values and fashions so alien to the present. But the dramatic truths and artistic and creative use of the audio-dramatic medium still resonate and engage today. Guthrie brilliantly embodies the characterisation of Edward's personality and life in the only interior speech to the listener and then an evocative montage of flashbacks to one liners of incidents and memories which were life-changing and character defining.

Companion Website Resources

Additions and Updates for Chapter 4 Achieving the Long Form Audio Drama https://kulturapress.com/2022/08/12/chapter-4-achieving-the-long-form-audio-drama/

Drama On The Air USA – One Day in September 1939 https://kulturapress.com/2022/08/29/drama-on-the-air-usa-one-day-in-september-1939/

Gordon Lea – Directing and Writing About Radio Plays https://kulturapress.com/2022/08/09/gordon-lea-radio-drama-and-how-to-write-it-1926/

Life Lines – Radio Drama and Podcasting Drama by the BBC https://kulturapress.com/2022/08/30/bbc-life-lines-sound-drama-for-radio-and-podcasting/

The Radio Plays of Lawrence du Garde Peach https://kulturapress.com/2022/08/18/the-radio-plays-of-lawrence-du-garde-peach/

Tyrone Guthrie – pioneering radio playwright https://kulturapress.com/2022/08/29/tyrone-guthrie-and-radio-plays/

Audio/Radio Drama Soap Operas https://kulturapress.com/2022/08/30/audio-radio-drama-soap-operas/

5

BEGINNING THE SOUND STORY

Techniques and Devices

Analysis of widespread practice of sound drama across most cultures informs us that usually the beginning of the play needs to ask questions for which the listener wants to find and hear answers, and this process by itself engages dramatic surprises and draws the listener into the world of the play fast, furiously, curiously, and enigmatically. The generation of acute feeling, appreciation of humanity, charm, and fascination in human character always helps. Writers always need to remember that there is usually only one chance to be successful when so much of listening in social space involves competing with many distractions.

Radio/audio drama has often been described as a form of theatre and the expression 'theatre of the mind' has been in much use. The third editor of BBC Radio Drama, Martin Esslin, liked to present BBC radio drama as Britain's national theatre of the air and wrote several articles justifying the idea. All good theatre drama has, of course, the same ingredients for success. The principles are the same as those that apply to stage drama, television, or film drama and indeed written prose. The special characteristics and principles of sound drama writing discussed so far do not dominate and override the need to communicate a good story, create substantial and engaging characters, and sustain the interest of an audience. We are now more precisely aware of the differences between the theatre, film, television, and radio, but it can certainly be argued that they are not fundamental to the writing of a good script. And writing rules for any medium are there to be broken by the *avant garde*, changes in fashions and modes of listening. Consequently, the consensus that the beginnings of audio plays need to sweep the listener into an all action, enticing, enthralling, and dramatic world of crisis – a kind of material and emotional hurricane or whirlpool of suspense and apprehension should not be regarded as the general requirement and wholly prescriptive. The very concept could become a cliché.

DOI: 10.4324/9780203838181-5

Good writers acknowledge the need to respect the beginning and the risk that if this part of the play does not work during radio transmission then people will find something else to do with their smartphones or while driving switch to another channel. In recent years, listeners have been able to instruct robotic artificial intelligence such as Siri, Alexa, or Cortana to find another channel or programme. It is not good for any kind of radio or podcasting business for the contract between audio play and listener to be terminated by boredom, confusion, or the 'Ah no!' feeling. In radio, the switch off from a play that does not work will last as long as the play. And there is no guarantee that the listeners will come back to the station. They might find something more interesting on other channels. Good writers fully understand that the radio audience is not a captive one. In radio and podcasting, the audience has not been into a theatre with the doors closed behind them, the house lights turned down and effectively imprisoned for an hour and a half. When a stage play is not fully successful, there tends to be a polite social ritual of theatre-goers sticking it out stoically or heroically, though they can and do leave if there is an interval. In radio, no money has exchanged hands and the moment of departure is quick and ruthless.

The start of an audio drama should not in the style of Genesis, the first book of the Old Testament of the Bible, begin everything at the beginning of the chronological narrative. This could be a long drawn out process and take up all of the play's running time. The trick is to create a dramatic moment of arrival of the listener; almost like a parachute jump into a battle. It does not have to be a real military battle, but it would help if it was a high moment or significant moment of drama. When finding the right moment to join the story, it is advisable to avoid the slow snail's explicatory route. The background and subtext of previous histories is better explored through revelation in dramatic action. Indeed, providing the listener with a whoosh through the rapids at the beginning is good intent for the medium. Rather than 1 minute of the sound of a character snoring, a 60-second countdown to an execution, or 60 seconds after a bomb has gone off, is going to hold people's attention more.

The dramatist and script editor William Ash strongly advised writers to 'make it easy for the listener at the beginning' (Ash, 1985, p. 51). He also suggested that in structure the beginning should operate after 'working backward from the climax' (Ash, 1985, p. 52) and in the process it is very important to avoid monotony in radio drama scenes. Pamela Brooke reminds writers that the sound play needs the interplay of the five elements of characters; conflict; plot; climax, and setting (Brooke, 1995, p. 65) and these elements are standard to all genres. Clearly, the beginning cannot encompass all these factors, though it must be part of the structure deploying them and Ash reminds us of the need for the listener to be actively participating:

> The imaginative collaboration the listener enters into with the playwright, actively participative rather than passively acceptive, is the means by which subjective elements in the radio play, the passage of time, the affective

impact of words and purely sound evoked 'look' of things become objectified through the suppression, while the play holds writer and listener
together in this exclusive relationship, of all frames of reference other than
that heard and imagined realm of their joint creation. The radio play draws
the listener inside the dramatic situation by recreating the situation inside
the listener's head. In other words, radio drama provides the very intimacy of involvement which is a necessary condition for the participatory
demands it makes.

(Ash, 1985, p. 51)

Who? What? Where? When? Why, and How?

The five 'W' questions have been a time-honoured mainstay of journalistic writing
with the 'why' and 'how' referring to the source or expectant exposition of the
story on a reverse pyramid basis in terms of the most important information coming
first and trailing with paragraphs that can be liquidated by sub-editors for reasons of
space. In broadcasting, there is an argument that writing to time means that the pyramid is never turned upside down, but there is enough in the intro or lead-in bunch
of words to inform the story within itself. The seconds that follow are an important
part of the narrative and should not be cut away, for to do so could change meaning
and not succeed in explaining the news story.

The journalistic W's arise from classical rhetoric and the Latin questions: Quis,
Quid, Ubi, Quando, and Cur. The who, the what, the where and when is a good
beginning. If any are unclear, then there needs to be a dramatic purpose in the
enigma. Of course, in simple terms the why and the how are the rest of the story
in fictional drama. There is some logic in writers making some key decisions before
scripting the opening scene. For example, who are your characters and how are
they related? What is the point of view? The narrative voice, if you are using it,
might be the protagonist, or somebody else in the world of the play with the mystery of who they are and a revelation that is rooted in some future dramatic scene.
The writer is of course in control and creating here. So it might be useful to pre-
determine what happens in the story, what is it about, and is there a larger theme
being explored?. What emotions does the writer wish to engage with the listener
– laughter, sadness verging on tears or anger? Where is the story set and does it
travel across time and space to other settings? If it does, why is this the case. It is so
important to maintain the discipline that everything and anything in audio drama
needs to have dramatic purpose. The 'Why?' Question is the writer's first responsibility throughout. When does it take place – present day, past or future? When does
it take place in the lives of the characters? When is the story being told in relation
to where it takes place? Is the story narrated in present time or past time? It should
be remembered that deployment of a strong present tense mood will lend the play
immediacy. It is possible to show events from the point of view of a child character
in the past and additionally provide reaction and context from the character as an
adult in the present.

In narrative terms there is no reason why as a writer you cannot begin at the end and finish with the beginning through flashback switches. This is what Tyrone Guthrie did in *The Flowers Are Not for You to Pick*. The audio drama medium gives so much more freedom to jump from time to time and place to place. This is because a series of chronological events can be told in different ways. The writer has the freedom to select the most important points, and events in the narrative, how much to reveal them and when.

Writers need to know why their characters do and say what they do? What do they want? Why are the characters in the situation? What is their motivation? Is it a situation of their own making? Is the character's situation thrust upon them and out of their control? How are they caught in the coils of their social and economic circumstances and what are their motivating factors? All these questions will be asked by the directors and producers of a writer's play and, indeed, also by the actors cast in the roles of the characters.

In radio drama Ash says we 'have to get started with the story as soon as possible' (Ash, 1985). We have to persuade the listener to submit to imaginative involvement and participation. Once the good story is started, the listener will have an eager expectancy and want to find out what happens next. Consequently, it is a very good technique to raise questions in the listener's mind about what has gone on before, about what is actually going on and about what will happen, and the good writer deals with these in such a way that there is scene progression spurring the listener on. The sympathy is not only necessarily with the character or characters. The sympathy and perhaps even the empathy should be rooted in the opening scene itself. Ash explained 'each scene is like a playlet, having the same statement, counter-statement, rising tension, climax and resolution that is the basic pattern of all drama' (Ash, 1985, p. 52). But the first scene engages the listener with a conclusion which is a dramatic development in the story and sharply and powerfully signposts the next scene so strongly, the listener would rather stay listening to find out than do anything else.

Vissi d'arte by Paul Sirett. IRDP for LBC 1990. English Version Compared with the NRK Norwegian Version

The playwright Paul Sirett used the time frame of the soprano aria *Vissi d'arte* from act 2 of the opera *Tosca* by Giacomo Puccini to plot a remarkable and iconic opening of a radio play which gained a special mention tribute at Prix Italia and was produced in many different languages across the world. *Vissi d'arte* is sung by Floria Tosca at a time when she is reflecting on her life and her relationship with the love of her life, Mario Cavaradossi. But her fate is in the power of Baron Scarpia and she cannot understand why it seems her God is no longer protecting her. In 3 minutes Sirett establishes an immediate, clear, and present crisis which listeners can identify with, sets up the questions the listener wants answers for and creates tension through characterisation, conflict between characters, and an exciting countdown to subclimactic episodic cliffhangers. He also uses the sound medium to creatively create enigma.

There are three streams of sound multitracking in this interplay of thriller, comedy, and satire. There is the sound of *Vissi d'arte* itself being performed on the stage of a national opera house, there is the sound of the opera star Mr. Wilson doing voice exercises in preparation for his stage entrance as Spoletta, and there is the sound of the stage manager on the theatre's intercom giving Wilson his countdown cues for onstage arrival. But Mr. Wilson finds that his dressing room door is locked. He struggles to open it and then hears the voice of his aspirant impostor outside asking him if he is having any trouble, telling him the door is not stuck but locked, and when accused of preventing Mr. Wilson getting onstage explaining that he does not need to be told this because he knows the opera intimately. It turns out the impostor who has locked his rival in the dressing room had been turned down for the same part at the audition and is now taking revenge. He has dropped the key down the grate by the stage door.

Mr. Wilson is reminded of his desperate situation by the repeated calls of the stage manager who tells him there are 2 minutes to go and then the final call and demand that he be onstage immediately. He is experiencing the nightmare all actors and live performers would prefer to remain locked away as an unpleasant dream – being prevented physically by some happenstance from attending their onstage cue entrance. That along with forgetting their lines is the professional actor's worst misfortune. Now it is Mr. Wilson's reality as he plaintively calls out for help over and over again. But it is also somebody's opportunity, the hope and chance of a lifetime even though it has been stolen maliciously. Wilson had demanded to know who the hell the impostor was, but the aspiring star says that is not important now because everybody will soon know when he triumphs in the role he had been turned down for at the audition. He should be playing Spoletta. He deserves the chance. But will he get it? What happens next? Could Mr. Wilson escape when somebody walks by and breaks open the door? Is the impostor acting on his own? Won't he be recognised as an impostor when he turns up on the stage? Will he perform as well or even better than Mr. Wilson? Will the audience even notice that a different actor is playing the part?

The beginning of the Norwegian production by NRK uses the prologue technique of immediately taking the listener into a large ambient space of the Opera House with a master of ceremonies introducing the play in the location of its action. Even though listening to Paul Sirett's play in another language and culture, excellent direction and performances mean listeners can still appreciate and understand the action because sound performance is the emotional and intellectual dramatisation of thinking. Sirett's skill as a radio playwright is immediately evident in the way he has first characterised the ego, self-importance, and pomposity of Mr. Wilson through the non-verbal noises and singing of his voice warm-up routine. In the Norwegian production, the actor performing the impostor improvises a mocking by him of Mr. Wilson's voice rehearsing. As Wilson struggles and panics with the locked dressing room door, he hears his professional assassin torturing him with the very sound of the music and lyrics he will now be prevented from expressing in front of the audience that is no longer his. The 3 minute beginning of *Vissi d'Arte* by Paul Sirett has courted, hooked, and seduced the listening audience into wanting to and perhaps even emotionally needing to listen to what happens next. The character of the impostor is so intriguing. Is he mad or irrational? Is the action criminal, cultural, or political? What has happened to make him act in this way? Should we be sympathetic? Is this restorative justice in a cruel world where life is unfair and fame and riches go to the mediocre and are denied to the genuinely talented and more brilliant? The potential of the play's theme widens in reflective response to the twists and turns of the play's unfolding revelations.

Cigarettes and Chocolate by Anthony Minghella. BBC 1988

The 1980s was the age of the answer-machine – a technological innovation which revolutionised domestic and work communications. There was no longer the frustration of not being able to reach somebody because they were not there physically on the other end of the phone. And it was a device which meant you could monitor and hear who was calling and you could listen to what they were intending to say before picking up and pretending you had just got to the phone. Radio playwrights began to realise that this everyday platform for recording communications, accidentally or, indeed, deliberately recording telephone conversations had the potential to capture and resonate the drama of everyday life. It is a curious and fascinating intimate space that belongs to sound only. Sometimes these messages are the only trace of a person's life and grieving friends and relatives would cherish the sound of messages left by loved ones who had passed away or died suddenly. For some playwrights it would also be a channel of characterisation and contain all the honesties, deceptions, and ambiguities of human identity. The writer Anthony Minghella realised its potential with an iconic opening to *Cigarettes and Chocolate*, a play which received a Giles Cooper prize for best radio drama writing. His radio play for BBC 3 in 1987, *Hang Up*, would win the Prix Italia for best radio fiction in 1988.

The beginning standalone answer-machine sequence has the central character's voice asking people to leave a message after the tone, but she refers to herself in the third person when she says if you would like to leave a message for her (Minghella, 1989, p. 125). The age and accent of voice and its formal courtesy is the beginning of Gemma's characterisation. The Canadian auteur drama producer Jeff Green in 1986 used a highly produced and extrovert answer-machine message in his play *Somebody Talking to You* as a fast way of defining the personality of his main character Mercury. A short and truncated woman's voice message 'Hello?' is greeted with the *sotto voce* reply 'Ah… Mandy' containing sub-textual layers of regret over a past relationship gone wrong (Crook, 1999, pp. 178–179).

In Minghella's play, we hear from the people in her life. A similar skill in weaving messaging monologues constructs the character of Gemma who is not replying. The first message left is from Rob played by Bill Nighy in the BBC Radio 4 production. The script shows the bunches of words which is the rhythm of everyday speech with ellipses instead of properly punctuating commas and full stops. The familiarity of Gemma's boyfriend is such that he only has to say it's him followed by the imperative 'listen' (Minghella, 1989, p. 125). He thinks he has left his toothbrush at her place. Characterisation and the nature of their relationship is achieved by his instruction to not open a bottle of olive oil he had also left there because he needs something for his sister, and then the final request to come round later for sex (Minghella, 1989). Next up is the sound of one of Gemma's very good girlfriends, Lorna, played by Juliet Stevenson. They had arranged to meet up to go and see a film in the evening and Lorna wants confirmation and Gemma to remind her to bring her glasses because she can't read the subtitles without them. We are clearly introduced into a cultured and well-educated circle of friends and relationships where going out is seeing foreign films.

Next up is Rob again travelling to the office from his home and still inveigling himself to stay the night at Gemma's. His manipulative side is marked with the plaintive sign-off that she should take pity on him (Minghella, 1989). This is followed by a message from what sounds like the previous man in Gemma's life called Alistair who has to say his name perhaps to remind her (Minghella, 1989). He has written to her and now feels the need to qualify or apologise for it. It's not clear if he wanted her to read his missive, or not. When he says she should not think of it as a problem or even as a not very good poem (Minghella, 1989), we have a clue as to why the relationship is a past one. It is also possible this is a platonic friendship becoming difficult for Gemma because Alistair is seeking romantic intimacy and a step too far for her. The quality of the writing opens up imaginative speculation and enigma in the minds of different listeners.

It seems dramatists cannot resist bringing mothers into answer-messaging dramas because that is who calls Gemma after Alistair. Mother seems to know much more about Gemma's character and tendency to listen and not pick up the phone. She uses the word 'suppose' when referring to Gemma being out and makes it very clear she would appreciate her daughter picking up the phone when she gets in or decides that she is in (Minghella, 1989, p. 126). Rob's next interactions get shorter and pacier with the rising exasperation of his inability to hear from her. First name, time check and where he is, next name check and then just a sigh before putting the phone down (Minghella, 1989, pp. 126–127). The last interaction is another classic representation of communication and characterisation with non-verbal human sounds.

Between the accelerating sequence of messages from Rob, we have a long meandering monologue from another girlfriend, Gail, who had to ring in again after using all her message time and is eventually cut off the second time as she reveals her anxiety over a hospital scan, possibly for cancer. She wants and needs company and wants Gemma to be there with her, but then is cut off by the answer-machine for exceeding the message time (Minghella, 1989, p. 126). Her last word is 'hate' and presumably refers to her frustration and dislike of answer-machines which guillotine callers. Lorna rings again from a callbox opposite the cinema and does not conceal her impatience and irritation with a queue building, the film starting and a pretty cross message to hurry up (Minghella, 1989).

Now we know something is wrong and we want to know why. Up to this point, we have not heard a word of Gemma's voice in real time. The production switches to the BBC's announcer revealing and confirming to the listeners they are hearing a presentation of a play by Anthony Minghella. All of the foregoing is more than enough to have hooked, engaged, and achieved imaginative and emotional commitment from the listening audience. Gemma speaks next in direct narration, interior speech, or voice-over mode with a morning ambience and the sound of Bach's 'St Matthew Passion' as if playing through open French windows. Quickly and clearly she narrates about the day she stopped talking being a perfect one to have in England (Minghella, 1989, p. 127). It seems she had been on holiday in Italy with all the people in her life. She speaks of Italy being like a glass of dark wine swilled in the mouth. Minghella is giving his character a dramatic line which is poetic and imaginatively conjures the sensation of Italian Barolo wine, rich in taste and deep red in colour.

Gemma refers to speaking to them all, loving them all, and then enigmatically refers to suicide, stopping talking, and killing oneself (Minghella, 1989). Another subclimactic crisis raises urgent questions and opens up a mystery about the character Gemma and her friends and mother all of whom we now care about in terms of human interest and understanding as listeners.

Sorry, Wrong Number by Lucille Fletcher. CBS 1943.

It can be argued that Lucille Fletcher is an author who scripted two of the most famous radio plays in US broadcasting history: *The Hitch-hiker* (1941) and *Sorry, Wrong Number* (1943). Both plays won awards and would be repeatedly reproduced by the CBS network from the time of their première in the early 1940s to the end of that decade and throughout the 1950s. *Sorry, Wrong Number*'s success in the sound medium led to development as an equally successful feature film in 1948.

The idea for a thriller about a woman who loses control when confronted by something she seemingly has no control of was inspired by Lucille's altercation with an elderly woman who had complained that Lucille had pushed in at a queue in a drug store on Manhattan's East Side. She had gone to buy medicine for her sick husband, the celebrated radio and film music composer Bernard Herrmann. Herrmann said the play was Lucille's revenge on the woman who had patronisingly demanded to 'know who this interloper is!' Lucille had only been innocently conversing with the pharmacist, a long-time friend. A 1959 version produced for the CBS radio series *Suspense* received the 1960 Edgar Allan Poe Award from the Mystery Writers of America for Best Radio Drama.

What is so striking about the presentation of the play in the CBS *Suspense* programming strand is how well American radio sold their plays to the audience. The following is an example of the time-honoured advice on how to communicate to an audience which has been attributed to so many different sources: 'In the first part I tell 'em what I am going to tell 'em; in the second part—well, I tell 'em; in the third part I tell'em what I've told'em'.

MUSIC: SPOOKY THEME MUSIC UP THEN BED UNDER ANNOUNCEMENTS AND HOLD TILL END

ANNOUNCER: Suspense.

MAN IN BLACK: This is the Man in Black… Here again to introduce Columbia's programme Suspense. Our star tonight is one of the most compelling actresses in America today. Here in a new study in terror by Lucille Fletcher called Sorry, Wrong Number.

This story of a woman who accidentally overheard a conversation with death and who strove frantically to prevent murder from claiming an innocent victim is tonight's tale of suspense. If you have been with us on these Tuesday nights, you will know that Suspense is compounded of mystery and suspicion and dangerous adventure. In this series of tales calculated to intrigue you, stir your nerves, to offer you a precarious situation and then withhold the solution and so it is with Sorry, Wrong Number and the performance of Agnes Moorehead, we again hope to keep you in…

MUSIC: Stab

Suspense!

MUSIC FADE

(Fletcher/CBS, 1943)

For all intents and purposes, this is a classic narrative where the listener is being told are you sitting down and listening because I am going to tell you a story; I have told you the story; and I have told you that I have told you and now listen to the rest of the story with those parts, obviously the key parts, I have not told you about. This wrap-around presentation is usually not in the gift of the sound playwright, but it remains very instructive of how in narrative mode, Erik Barnouw's 'Trio for Three Singers' of music, sound effects, and speech, can be so simply and directly orchestrated to defeat all of the distractions of listening to radio or podcasting in the cacophony of the 21st century everyday soundscape.

The presentational hard-sell at the beginning of so many 'Golden Age' US radio drama is rather reminiscent of the old Music Hall or touring repertory theatre tradition of a 'Master of Ceremonies', director or lead characters themselves going out into the town/city square, village cross, or green to 'hear ye, oh hear ye' call the audience into the pageant or carnival of performance. It is also a bit like starting the show with a film-like trailer. Barnouw says the introductory material is often the 'where, when, and who of the story to follow. Sometimes only one or two of these elements happen to be important, and may be given exclusive attention' (Barnouw, 1940, p. 72). In some ways, this is what the BBC and Minghella did with the opening answer-machine sequence of Cigarettes and Chocolate. Over 3 minutes and 45 seconds we are introduced to the characters one after the other in the messages they leave, rounded off with Rob's sigh and the final electronic tone before the heavily branded BBC Radio 4 continuity voice of the time intones: 'We present Cigarettes and Chocolate by Anthony Minghella' and then straight back into realistic ambience of the central character Gemma opening up the French windows to the garden of her London home.

In 1940, Barnouw offered an example of what he called 'semi-dramatized intro-
ductions' from a *Great Plays* series with the narration split as a very effective device.
But the reference and illustration relates to radio dramatisation and representation
of literature and storytelling in US culture more than 80 years ago which would
be justifiably reframed and interrogated by African-American dramatisation in the
present time when phrases and tropes such as 'COLOURED VOICE' and 'FAST
NEGRO MELODY' are neither appropriate nor acceptable, perceived as offensive,
and where issues of identity and voice need to undergo a transference in point of
view and power:

BURNS MANTLE: …And now for the characters in our play. First there is Mrs.
   Pyton of Plantation Terrebonne in Louisiana.
(MUSIC: Background through:)
MRS. PEYTON: …O sir, I don't value the place for its price but for the many
   happy days I've spent here. My nephew is not acquainted with our customs in
   Louisiana but he will soon understand.
MANTLE: Her nephew is George.
GEORGE: I have never met in Europe any lady more beautiful in person or more
   polished in manners than this girl Zoe.
MANTLE: The inventive Yankee overseer is Salem Scudder.
SCUDDER: I reckon this picture taking machine o'mine will be a big thing some
   day.
ANTLE: And Zoe of course is the Octoroon.
ZOE: My father gave me freedom. May heaven bless him for the happiness he
   spread around my life.
MANTLE: But Jacob M'Closky has more definite ideas.
M'CLOSKY: Curse their old families. I'll sweep these Peytons from Louisiana and fair
   or foul I'll have the Octoroon!
(MUSIC: Swells to quick finish.)
MANTLE: And now—Dion Boucicault's great melodrama of 1859. The Octoroon
   or—
COLOURED VOICE: Life in Louisiana!
(MUSIC: Fast negro melody, fades under dialogue.)
                    (pp. 73–74 notated to The Octoroon, *from the* Great Plays *series.*
                    Adaptation by Joseph Bell. NBC sustaining)

The African-American playwright, Branden Jacobs-Jenkins, explained in an interview for the British National Theatre in 2022 that an 'octoroon' is a very antiquated
word used to describe a person considered to be 'one-eighth black' – so crude-
ly-speaking the equivalent of having one black great-grandparent. At the time of
the play's composition, to be even 'one-sixteenth black' in many states was to still
be 'black enough' for the legal system to discriminate against you (Branden Jacobs-
Jenkins, 2022). When the Irish playwright Dion Boucicault wrote *The Octoroon*
in 1859 he was a white man using theatre to dramatise the debate about slavery

and mixed-raced relationships rather like the popular novel of the time *Uncle Tom's Cabin* by Harriet Beecher Stowe.

Boucicault was ventriloquising non-white characters and the racial and political lens of representation led to contrasting endings when the play was performed in England and the USA. In England, it would be given a happy ending with the mixed-race couple Zoe and George united and apparently living happily ever after. The tragic ending with 'Octoroon' Zoe taking poison *Romeo and Juliet* style because she believes they could never be together was deployed for American audiences to underscore and perpetuate the ideological message that mixed race relationships had to be avoided.

In 2014, Branden Jacobs-Jenkins rewrote and dramatised Boucicault's play using the original characters and plot, but vocalising much of Boucicault's dialogue himself as 'BJJ' – a black playwright and criticising the original play's portrayal of race using Brechtian devices. The work is retitled from the use of the definite article *The Octoroon* to the indefinite article *An Octoroon*. The male characters perform using blackface, whiteface, and redface, and the female characters are portrayed by performers cast to match the characters' actual racial identity. *An Octoroon* was ranked in a 2018 poll of *New York Times* critics as the second-greatest American play of the past 25 years.

In his 1940 *Handbook of Radio Writing*, Erik Barnouw offered a shorter and now less controversial method of vivid radio play beginning from a series of the time titled *Criminal Case Histories* which can be seen perhaps as a resonating echo for the current popularity of true crime podcasts in the documentary and dramatised genres:

NELSON CASE: Tonight, Warden Lawes tells the story of case history No. 581–753.
VOICE: I'm in the death house. But I didn't do it. I swear I didn't. I don't care if it was my gun. I'm innocent. I never shot that tax collector. I'm innocent— I swear I didn't do it. (FADING)
NELSON CASE: I suppose all condemned men say that. Warden Lawes.
WARDEN LAWES: Some do—and some don't! Sometimes of course we know they're lying—and sometimes we're not sure.
(Barnouw, 1940, p. 74 from Tom McNight and Associates)

This opening generates multiple questions of suspense and interest for the listener: the need to know more about the voice of the central character: how did his gun end up being used by the real murderer? Can he ever prove his innocence? Is he really lying because Warden Lawes (what an excellent name for the chief of a federal penitentiary) says all condemned men say that? Or is this a case where there is a real miscarriage of justice? And if it is, will the truth be found in time to save him from the death house? Another driving imperative for listener curiosity is an abiding fear in everyone that they too can be accused of something they never did.

Most of the exemplars of effective sound plays parachute the listener into a crisis and dramatic moment of the central character's story. And this device is a very good tip on how to find inspiration for creating and beginning a play. In drama workshops, I used to hand out an archive photograph from the autumn of 1914 taken just across the road from Charing Cross railway station in London as the First World War was developing with intensive fighting in Belgium and France. This would later bog down into trench warfare on the Western Front. The flow of casualties from hospital ships landing at Dover and Folkestone became a flood as the regular army of 'Old Contemptibles' would need to be replenished by volunteers and eventually conscripts.

The photograph shows the forlorn, anxious, and ruminating faces of the crowd outside what used to be the Accident and Emergency entrance to the old Charing Cross Hospital about 30 yards across the Strand. This is now part of Charing Cross police station. Only months earlier these crowds had been cheering their heroes off to a war expected to be won by Christmas but would eventually generate another 4 years of carnage, misery, and destruction. There are so many grievously wounded soldiers arriving at the Channel ports, after disembarkation from the Charing Cross railway station platform, there is a convoy of ambulances queuing up to take them in. I would then follow the distribution of the photograph with a copy of the imagist poem by Ford Madox Ford titled *From Antwerp*.

This is a powerful poetic representation of the photograph. It seems Ford had been a witness to these scenes, and emotionally he enters the mind of a grieving mother who is there to see the return of the wounded who will not include her beloved son:

> This is Charing Cross;
> It is midnight;
> There is a great crowd
> And no light.
> A great crowd, all black that hardly whispers aloud.
> Surely, that is a dead woman – a dead mother!
> She has a dead face;
> She is dressed all in black'
> She wanders to the bookstall and back,
> At the back of the crowd;
> And back again and again back,
> She sways and wanders.
>
> *(Jones, 1976, pp. 81–82)*

I would suggest that it is possible to imagine Ford Madox Ford's lost women of Flanders are among the people depicted in the photograph. They who 'await the lost that shall never leave the dock' (Jones, 1976) at a Charing Cross eventually 'past one of the clock' with very little light and 'so much pain' (Jones, 1976). Either the photograph or the poem can be the source of a writer's inspiration and arising dramatisation. Such sources of writing are very wide-ranging and writers have great licence in how they can develop creatively from any source of this kind. Original writing can be achieved by basing a script on a personal experience, an idea, real life, documentary research, and as in this case even a still photograph and a few lines of poetry, prose or philosophy, or even a headline from the news. Tom Stoppard was able to create a full length and memorable stage play from the fleeting and brief lines of Hamlet's childhood friends Rosencrantz and Guildenstern. Shakespeare's *Hamlet* becomes the almost irrelevant backdrop to *Rosencrantz and Guildenstern Are Dead* with the eponymous characters now centre-stage in an absurdist and existential tragicomedy.

The setting of the photograph of the entrance to Charing Cross Hospital in 1914 and Ford Madox Ford's poem present so many individuals and their living true and poignant personal crises: The soldiers fighting for their lives, the doctors, and nurses striving to save lives and put back together broken ones; the friends, wives, mothers, sisters, and brothers of the men at the front not coming back, still fighting or coming back with the reality of war now so greatly impressed upon them.

This can be seen as a way of summoning the ghosts from the past and giving them full bodied humanitarian and poetic characterisation. The audio drama medium has the potential to memorialise and the effects can be profoundly moving. None more so than in Stephen Wyatt's Tinniswood award-winning play *Memorials to the Missing* first broadcast by BBC Radio 4 in 2007–2008. This dramatises the story of Fabian Ware's campaign during the First World War to establish an Imperial War Graves Commission to properly record the graves of those killed in action. This would eventually become the Commonwealth War Graves Commission.

Wyatt is an outstandingly accomplished radio playwright and teacher. His play begins with the voices of the ghosts of soldiers 1, 2 and 3, each of whom exclaim 'I'm one of the missing' with the background of a voice reading from the roll call of names on the memorial at Thiepval in France. Their characters develop through the play as haunting and interloping spirits when stirred by the struggle to identify what remains of their traces on the battlefield. They are on their own journey of remembrance. Ware in voice over narration describes how his team become battlefield detectives trying to make sense of bodies destroyed beyond recognition, identity discs rotted to nothing and 'tiny battered relics scooped from the mud' (Wyatt, 2008, p. 20). Ware is joined by a Nurse searching for her cousin who has been reported missing in action and Ware shows her some of the objects he is examining.

When looking at a compass which survived the shells we hear the ghost of Soldier 1 identifying it as belonging to him. Ware is trying to make out the initials nearly getting them right. The listener hears Soldier 1 correcting him and then in the world of the play the nurse makes them out correctly and Soldier 1 informs us they are his father's initials (Wyatt, 2008, p. 22).

This is a beautiful and moving play which is unique to the radio dramatic form. The traces of the dead are so sacred. Wyatt writes with the sensitivity of a priest giving the last rites to the dying and comforting their grieving relatives. At the end of his 45 minute play Wyatt parallels and synchronises the poetic imperative and resonances of the beginning. Soldier 1 describes how his presence on the memorial makes him a witness to his parents' visit to Thiepval and their weeping when they see his name. Soldier 2 sees his wife Agnes visiting with the son he never knew and reciting the lines from his favourite Shelley poem *Adonais* which finishes with 'And grief itself be mortal' (Wyatt, 2008, p. 50). Soldier 3 explains that nobody visits him, but he takes comfort and consolation from a sergeant in today's army bringing his squaddies along to contemplate with some discomfort how they may well end up. One of them even reads his name.

In *Sorry, Wrong Number* Lucille Fletcher characterises Mrs. Leona Stevenson with huge sympathy. The breakdown in personal equilibrium, and the panic, fear, and loneliness caused by the catastrophic failure of modern technology and communications is something listeners can identify with.

The play begins with phone dialing and Mrs. Stevenson's sighs and frustration in not being able to reach her husband for around 45 minutes. The robotic voice of the operator says she will try to put her through, a man's voice answers but is talking to somebody called George and neither can hear her. Whatever she says the two men continue what turns out to be a dark and menacing discussion about the commission of a contract killing. The man is the broker between a client and George who is to do the killing. The coast is clear for tonight. George has the address. At 11 o'clock a private patrolman goes to a bar for a beer. He needs to keep the lights out downstairs and wait until 11.15 when a train crosses the bridge. Even if the window is open and the woman victim screams nobody will hear her. The client also wants it to be quick, with a minimum of suffering and as little blood as possible. George recommends using a knife. And he is reminded to remove rings, bracelets, and jewellery from the bureau drawer to make it look like a simple robbery.

A shaken and traumatised Mrs. Stevenson is immediately back in contact with the operator to say she has heard a murder being planned and demanding the call to be traced. But all the operator can do is repeatedly ask her the number she was calling (Fletcher/CBS, 1943).

The seemingly accidental connection through a crossed line with something so horrible as a plot to murder raises so many questions. The indifference of the technical controllers, the inability to get help quickly, and the apprehension of what will happen at 11.15 when the train crosses the line, all summon the listening audience into the heart of a compelling and unforgettable thriller.

The flaws in Mrs. Stevenson's character raise the question to what extent her impatient character and rudeness to the phone operators contribute to her making herself her own worst enemy. These are only the first few minutes of the play. The plot clearly invites a direction of storytelling where the suspense is intensified by a growing realisation on the part of Mrs. Stevenson herself that she might well be the intended victim of the murder contracted by the unidentified client. How can Mrs. Stevenson persuade the police to take seriously her claim to have heard a murder plot when the phone company is unable to locate and rewind any recording of what she heard, or indeed trace the connection to the numbers of the two men making the arrangements to kill for money.

They are so nonchalant in their demeanour and matter of fact small talk that we could be fooled into thinking we are listening to engineers on the phone booking a home visit in order to repair a boiler. Will she ever be able to reach her husband and if not, why has he made himself so unavailable? The beginning of *Sorry, Wrong Number* has the active participation of the listener because the questions being asked generate multiple imaginative possibilities true to each individual listener.

The War of the Worlds by Howard Koch for Mercury Theatre on the Air CBS 1938

Much has been written about the Halloween night 1938 hoax radio drama event and with extensive analysis of why the nature of the writing and production created the socio-psychological impact that it had (Crook, 1999, pp. 105–114). Richard Hand and Mary Traynor also extensively analyse why the adaptation by Howard Koch under the direction of producers Orson Welles and John Houseman became such a successful transference of novella storytelling by H. G. Wells to radio drama by Mercury Theatre on the Air (Hand & Traynor, 2013, pp. 22–32). However, the script discloses many of the routine techniques and devices that according to Erik Barnouw identified in 1940 as contributing to excellent audio dramatic engagement with the listener. The very fact that it had convinced so many US listeners that they were hearing genuine news reports about an invasion of their country by creatures from the planet Mars is a tribute to the verisimilitudinous quality of the radio drama script and the production's aspiration to realism.

The War of the Worlds 1938 radio version begins rather like the original prose upon which it is based with Barnouw's routine technique of 'The First Narration'. Orson Welles begins with 'We know now that in the early years of the twentieth century this world was being watched closely by intelligences greater than man's, and yet as mortal as his own…' (Koch, 1971, p. 33) and ends with a signpost on how Mercury Theatre On The Air are going to use the familiar texture of contemporary radio broadcasting as their storytelling frame. He explains its 1939, business is better, fears of war are diminishing, unemployment is down, and the economy is picking up in an America where on Halloween night 32 million people are listening to the radio (Koch, 1971, p. 36).

This is Barnouw's 'Scene-Setting Moment' (Barnouw, 1940, p. 75) where like in a film the listener's mind-world horizon is panned or dissolved sonically to eavesdrop on the sound of a radio station. Radio Drama has enveloped the drama of radio broadcasting with its weather and news bulletins, and live music from the Meridian Room in the Park Plaza Hotel in New York City. The texture of the writing and production uses the simulation of a radio station's broadcasting to operate with Barnouw's technique of 'overlapping of narration and scene' (Barnouw, 1940, p. 79). The announcer's news bulletins operate as narration while switching to actuality and outside broadcast scenes including the Princeton Observatory where Carl Phillips interviews Professor Richard Pierson, the famous astronomer, and Carl Phillips again, out at the Wilmuth Farm, Grovers Mill, New Jersey with Professor Pierson.

They managed to get there apparently in 10 minutes though the magic of radio dramatic time-shifting achieved the transference in considerably less time. Barnouw would have approved how in the 'Scene Shifting' between radio station, Ramón Raquello's orchestra, and the outside broadcast interviewing and commentary on the Wilmuth Farm, these scenes begin with 'Atmosphere dialogue' (Barnouw, 1940, p. 76) where the first 5 or 10 seconds are often devoted to the job of bringing the scene alive. For example, Carl Phillips in the ambience of an echoing room with the sound of a ticking clock explains that he is standing in a large semi-circular room looking out through an opening at a sprinkling of stars. There is a ticking sound coming from the vibration of the clockwork in the observatory (Koch, 1971, p. 38–9).

At Grovers Mill we hear the sound of crowd noises and police sirens first and Phillips rapidly engages his reporting role with the words: 'Well, I... hardly know where to begin, to paint for you a word picture of the strange scene before my eyes, like something out of a modern "Arabian Nights"' (Koch, 1971, p. 43). As the escalation in crisis, threat, and fear of the unknown accelerates with the Martians preparing to and then emerging from their spaceship, the script and production creates two of the most effective examples of what Barnouw describes as 'Pause transitions' (Barnouw, 1940, p. 82). The first generates anxiety in the minds of listeners that their live outside broadcast connection with Phillips is perhaps not as secure and certain as it should be. They lose him as he moves to obtain a better position to be able to tell them what is going on. He talks about a most extraordinary experience, but then he can't find the words. He has to pull his microphone to find a better vantage point and asks the listeners to hold on while he does so. Back to the piano faded in by the radio station, but this is a very short interlude as Carl Phillips is back on air more breathless and having to reassure himself he's returned to live broadcasting from the Wilmuth Farm at Grover's Mill. He is on the back of a stone wall getting a sweep of the whole scene (Koch, 1971, p. 50).

The next pause transition is as devastating as it is possible to imagine. And Orson Welles directing the production live in the studio where he is performing with his cast uses a hand holding gesture to maintain the dramatic silence for three whole seconds. Screams and unearthly shrieks are heard. Phillips sees something wriggling out of the shadow like a grey snake, followed by others, all looking like tentacles. The creature as big as a bear is glistening like wet leather. Although it is indescribable, Phillips continues to describe the alien life – eyes black and gleaming like a serpent, saliva dripping from rimless lips, quivering, and pulsating. Then there are the beams of light against a mirror, a jet of flame, striking men head on, turning into flame, the whole field on fire, explosions spreading all over and engulfing woods, barns, and vehicle petrol tanks. Then it is coming his way about 20 yards to his right. There is the sound of a man shrieking in agony. But the transmission is cut. There is an abrupt dead silence lasting nearly 3 seconds of dead air.

The radio announcer says they are unable to continue the live outside broadcast because of what he describes as circumstances beyond their control (Koch, 1971, pp. 51–2). These 16 minutes and 39 seconds of audio drama are, of course, iconic, memorable, and a significant moment in broadcasting history, but they also demonstrate so magnificently how to build dramatic tension in subclimactic peaks, vary pace, and rhythm with sound effects, music, and speech, intensify anticipation through scene switching between the pleasant dream of light music, the urgent information of interrupting news flashes and the nightmare of death and destruction as the invasion of aliens becomes a reality in the orchestration of radiophonic motifs and textures of live news broadcasting realism.

All the while characterisation unfolds with Carl Phillips performing the role of the listener's inquisitorial journalist broadcaster, and Professor Pierson, the initially confident and authoritative expert on astronomy and extra-galactic phenomena surprising himself and shocking the listeners with the growing realisation that with all his knowledge of science 'I cannot account for it' and 'I don't know what to think' (Koch, 1971, pp. 40, 48). Even Mr. Wilmuth, owner of the farm has been created with the authenticity of his 'willing to please disposition' in dialogue that would have been familiar to the conducting of *vox populi* interviews on the radio at that time. When asked if he was frightened, he is hesitant saying he was not quite sure, but 'kinda riled'. Phillips wants to move on to do more interviews, but Wilmuth asks him if he wants him to tell him some more and Phillips replies first with a 'no', then a 'that's quite all right' and presumably as Mr. Wilmuth's enthusiasm presses upon him further, a final 'that's plenty' (Koch, 1971, pp. 46–7).

Richard Durham's Origination of Characterisation in Radio Play Openings

Richard Durham researched and scripted 91 of the *Destination Freedom* programmes. Why is the creative and cultural success of this project so important? Nothing like it has ever been produced in US broadcasting history, or indeed in the history of UK broadcasting. It is not enough to say that Richard Durham is considered the most significant African-American dramatist in broadcasting history. It would be right to say he is one of the most significant radio dramatists in English-speaking radio history throughout the world. He combined history, art, journalism, culture, politics, human rights, and drama to make a contribution in storytelling that had impact and represents a milestone in the literature of human struggle and progress. Durham created 91 unique chapters of drama charting US black history which resonate across the panoply of understanding human history.

Professor J. Fred MacDonald's 1989 volume published by Praeger includes 15 scripts for: *Dark Explorers*; *Citizen Toussaint*; *Denmark Vesey*; *Railway to Freedom*; *The Liberators I: William Lloyd Garrison*; *The Story of 1875*; *The Heart of George Cotton*; *The Long Road*; *Peace Mediator*; *The Death of Aesop*; *Tales of Stackalee*; *The Trumpet Talks*; *The Rime of the Ancient Dodger*, and *Premonition of the Panther*. The *Destination Freedom* series premiered on NBC/WMAQ 27 January 1948, and ran for 2 years. His programmes are mainstream icons of significance in radio history because of their innovation in style, subject and genre, and the quality of writing, production and performance. He was particularly brilliant at opening his plays with innovative ideas for characterisation. I have selected four examples where he gives voice to a human heart, the Chicago slums, to Louis Armstrong's trumpet and the spirit of a pioneering baseball player through the music and lyrics of a folkloric balladeer performed by Oscar Brown Jr.

The Heart of George Cotton was about the accomplishments of pioneering heart surgeons, Dr. Daniel Hale Williams (1856–1931) and Dr. Ulysses Grant Dailey (1885–1961) and was first broadcast 8th August 1948. They were responsible for the first successful suturing of the human heart. MacDonald praised the narrative role assumed by a human heart for offering a compelling perspective on the medical technique developed by the two medics, and the repetitive sound of heartbeats heard during much of the script for adding a relentless urgency to the unfolding story line (Durham and MacDonald, 1989, p. 117).

The Heart is the character who speaks first in this play followed by his beat slightly faster than normal. Drums are brought into the mix to emphasise and deepen the beat. As the heart beat works into a rhythm, Heart says he is the spirit's rhythm. He describes his form, the size of a fist and living in a cavity between two lungs. Durham gives Heart the voice and function of human civilisation for he is the timekeeper of life. He is as old as the Neanderthals and equal to the Roman, Tartar or Turk. Durham's writing is sensationally poetic and elegiac. The heart talks about being the lion, lamb, and the hate in men. He wishes to tell the story of how scientific and medical inquiry has fought to heal him whenever he has been split and left outstretched on an operating table in the breast of a dying man. Here the sound design slows down the heart beat which then become ponderous and bedded underneath the sound of a patient with laboured breathing and in such a crisis that his own heart's beating is like a drum in his ears. (Durham and MacDonald, 1989, p. 118).

In *The Trumpet Talks*, Durham's dramatisation of the life of Louis Armstrong, the cohesive narrative voice is provided by the trumpet which Armstrong will play into legend as one of the world's most influential jazz artists. It was first broadcast 31st July 1949 and the drama begins with the Trumpet playing the prologue of Armstrong's 'West End Blues' and when speaking – it is the embodiment of words and music.

Durham writes that the Trumpet should sound sanguine and like a man who has been in high and low places, is modest but knows his power and is worldly and mellow. The Trumpet proudly states that he is the trumpet that is being blown in the music and describes his curved brass cylinder and cup-shaped mouth with three valves and a thousand notes. Again as in *The Heart of George Cotton* Durham gives his unique characterisations of organs, objects and forces a spiritual and historical place in the world. This is not just a musical instrument but something able to call home the quick and dead when the angel Gabriel touched his lips to his mouth. He has been blown by the Roman when their empire ruled the earth and he has been blown for Caesars, Napoleons and in the highest and lowest of places. Durham then holds the rhythm of the Trumpet's speech as though holding a note in a symphony or pausing a jazz improvisation so that he can talk about the time the 'kid' aka Louis Armstrong blew him. Until that time he was not aware of the scale he could climb or the tones he could command. Louis Armstrong gave Trumpet a voice free and strong so his own voice could be (Durham and MacDonald, 1989, p. 215). What a magnificent and brilliant way to begin a radio play dramatising the early life of Louis Armstrong.

The beginning and unfolding drama in *Anatomy of an Ordinance*, first broadcast 5th June 1949, is further proof of the stature and quality of Richard Durham as a radio playwright. In this dramatisation of the Black Alderman Archibald Carey, Durham characterises with voice and political and philosophical ontology the force of the Chicago slums. He makes them metaphysical, giving them a single person-ality and consciousness which is menacing, cunning and the force of indifference, cynicism, injustice, and indeed evil. Slums is the Shakespearean Richard the Third of urban squalor and deprivation. He begins by saying a good morning and how do you do and boasting about how happy and healthy he is particularly in having so much fun at work. That's jamming six families into a run-down flat with dark stairways, the roof coming down, the streets dirty outside, the rents sky high, and sickness all around.

By the way he also hopes the area is segregated along racial lines. He then goes on to mock his nemesis – the very Reverend Archibald Carey who has been calling him, the one and only 'Mr Slums' the cemeteries of the living. How dare he? Slums says this 'windy city Alderman' has to go. And that is what the play is going to be all about – the battle to stop Slums being run out of town (Durham, 1949b).

Durham's ability to invest dramatic identity, characterisation into inanimate or indeed biophysical and chemical forms shows how his understanding of the radio dramatic medium was supreme and originally creative. Durham could write for sonic imaginative reception and understood the phenomenology of the listener. His writing art in the sound medium was utterly exceptional. This is further demonstrated in the beginning and continuing script of *The Ballad of Satchel Paige*, first broadcast 15th May 1949. Leroy Robert 'Satchel' Paige (1906–1982) was an African-American league baseball and Major League Baseball (MLB) pitcher who is notable for his longevity in the game, and for attracting record crowds wherever he pitched. The drama of his life is unique for the creative use of ballad singing as the narrative imperative throughout the play (Durham, 1949a).

The production opens with folk guitar music being played and faded up and Durham succeeds in combining so many compelling cultural forms to begin telling the story. The music hails from African-American Spiritual, Blues, Jazz, and American folkloric traditions. This was the age of Woodie Guthrie and Pete Seeger, highly influential folk singers and social activists of this time whose songs would have been played on US radio. And then Durham the lyri-cist combined with the spine-tingling and warmth of Oscar Brown Jr's singing begins telling the story of Satchel Paige. The seven lines of the first verse are classic Durham drawing on history, poetic description and turning stories into legends.

He begins by explaining that nobody can remember when Satchel ever played on the baseball field. Perhaps it happened when he was putting out Caesar at the same time Judas was trying to do his stealing, and that he learned his throwing curves watching Cleopatra when she was being courted by Anthony. There is no truth that his catcher was ever Methuselah. And most importantly of all, his playing may have stretched back a long way, but nobody cared to ask about his age. This is because he was the best pitcher in baseball God had ever blessed the world with (Durham, 1949a). All of these ideas are orchestrated into music and song and lyrics rhyming and half-rhyming mellifluously. Durham also purposes the folk balladeer as a narrator in radio drama in a way very few future radio and sound producers could ever do. Certainly Norman Corwin's direction of words by Millard Lampell and music by Earl Robinson in the CBS broadcast of *The Lonesome Train* in 1944 could have been influential (Crook, 2014). In Britain the format would be developed as drama-documentary radio ballads from 1958 by Charles Parker, Ewan MacColl, and Peggy Seeger.

Opening the Long Form – Caryl Phillips *The Wasted Years* (1984) and Nigel D. Moffatt's *Lifetime*

The Wasted Years by Caryl Phillips is long-form radio drama which when broadcast on BBC Radio 4 on 12th March 1984 ran for 87 minutes and 50 seconds. As is explored in more detail in Chapter 10, it had the space and length to interweave multiple and related plots. But its beginning features the central character, Solly, in conflict with his teacher Mr. Teale in what will be one of Solly's last lessons at school. The play opens with classroom noise as the bell has just gone for the end of the day. Mr. Teale, for we never get to know his first name, is trying to maintain control of class 5C. As the kids can be heard jeering he is reminding them that school is not a Saturday afternoon down at the match. Solly can be heard saying a boy called Deakin who has been told to put a chair back in order shouldn't have to do it as the school day is over.

Teale picks up Solly's disruption and does not take kindly to him saying nothing in reply to his question. Tagley, who is Solly's best friend, has been told, to shut his 'stupid mouth' and the confrontation ratchets up when Teale makes Solly Daniels the centre of the trouble. The crisis point for him and the interest for the listener is what happens next after Teale tells him he is still waiting for an answer (Phillips, 1984, p. 87).

In *Lifetime* (1987) the Jamaican born playwright Nigel D. Moffatt manages to achieve one of the most difficult forms in audio drama – a full-length monologue which played on BBC Radio 4 for 29 minutes and 3 seconds. What is so skilful and beautiful about his writing is the way the richness of Archie's account of his 'lifetime' becomes a tender, complex and deeply moving biography and characterisation of the love of his life – Marcy. The language is Jamaican patois – the rhythms, feelings, and subtext utterly Shakespearean. Marcy is a woman who gives him a lifetime of being watched. In lyrical writing, Moffatt has Archie talking about feeling her eye 'burnin' out me backbone. In the first minute there is much warmth and mischief in Archie's account of always being asked 'Where you goin'? 'Where you goin'? and the opening reaches a quick peak of humour when Archie compares himself to the men who can go to a toilet and stay up there for an hour, but 'Me don't even get time to wipe me arse' (Moffatt, 1987, p. 73).

It has sometimes been argued that the monologue form is not sound drama. I would most heartily disagree with that. The appreciation, analysis and attention I gave to Lee Hall's brilliant and award-winning *Spoonface Steinberg* (1997) as 'an enormously successful manifestation of aesthetic expression in the field of radio drama' (Crook, 1999, pp. 136–148) I would argue is ample evidence of my position. Nigel D. Moffatt's *Lifetime* was its equal 10 years before and never ceases to move me whenever I re-read it or have an opportunity of listening to Rudolph Walker's performance as Archie. Archie may only be sitting on a park bench but his is the voice and character which dramatises his life, his wife Marcy, and their world in Jamaica and Britain. Monologue as narrative is the drama of showing through the point of listening and performance of one character. It is not the voice of God telling the listener something in narration.

Verse Plays by Norman Corwin and Benjamin Zephaniah – Some Model Beginnings

Benjamin Zephaniah's *Hurricane Dub* was selected as one of the winning scripts for the BBC 1988 Young Playwrights' Festival. It is a verse play with dialogue written to be spoken to the reggae beat. It is a brilliant synthesis of dramatic poetry, sound design, and original musical composition by Dennis Bovell and remains an audio drama classic. The action takes place on the night of what would be described as the Great Storm of 1987 when hurricane force winds swept over southern England overnight on 15th October of that year. Samuel and Maxine are kept awake in their London flat.

Zephaniah begins by writing in words the opening of what could be described as the equivalent of a radiophonic symphony. First there is the wind, slowly but then quickened faster and loud into a definite rhythm. This then segues into music with the wind holding the basic rhythm. Next the music fades leaving only the wind throughout the play. The soundscape is punctuated with occasional tin cans blowing, dustbins crashing, cats crying, and bottles falling. For we now hear the verse of Maxine and Samuel tucked up in bed. Zephaniah directs that Maxine's voice is heard in time to the wind.

This is the experience of a couple with the heritage of Caribbean hurricanes and the arrival of a British one in London is an acute crisis on so many levels for Maxine says:

'Me can't get to sleep and me count so much sheep,
And me want to sleep, doctor say me must sleep,'

And Samuel says:
'It sound wild. Could give a weak heart a fright,' and Maxine confirms:

'Well it keep on boddering me'.

(Zephaniah, 1988, p. 13)

The brilliance of the writing is self-evident. Of course listeners want to know what happens next. Characterisation has a hurricane force impact, and the rhythm, rhyme and beat of the dramatic poetry has fundamentally connected with how the listeners are feeling from a musical as well as imaginative point of view.

In 1945, the auteur radio drama producer Norman Corwin crafted a verse play in the trial format to interrogate the concept of nuclear power that would detonate in only a matter of weeks after its broadcast with the nuclear bombs dropped on Hiroshima and Nagasaki. *The Undecided Molecule* puts the atom 'X' on trial because Corwin says he'd 'had doubts about the stability of matter ever since I almost blew up a house at 36 Perkins Street, Winthrop, Massachusetts, when I was a high-school student' (Corwin, 1947, p. 35). An instructive aspect to evaluating the beginning of the play is that the published script has a sequence in the opening from pages 3 to 6 involving the Vice-President in Charge of Physio-Chemistry speaking on the telephone. In the live production for July 1945, all of this is jettisoned. Corwin and his cast have realised the original script was overwritten and the entrée to the drama of trial X needs to get underway pronto. Corwin even manages to versify the opening announcement in the style of the ensuing play. The listeners are told how lucky they are to dial into a programme in time to watch a trial and Corwin then develops the verse by rhyming knack with back, stations with congratulations, and half-rhymes fool with molecule (Corwin, 1947 , p. 3).

Corwin's friend and colleague R. LeRoy Bannerman said Corwin's writing itself was musical:

> It soared. Moreover, he possessed an unusual ability to mix lofty, Olympian prose with everyday vernacular to provide an intimate, personal touch, yet affect an abstract, artistic approach that exceeded the commonplace convention of radio literature. He gave radio a language and a style which elevated the medium to new heights of artistic endeavour.
>
> *(Bannerman, 1986, p. 9)*

After the playing of musical fanfares the Clerk of the court convenes the hearing, demanding that everybody stands and bows to face 'the justice who will adjust this case'. The Judge invites the Clerk to present the charge to the undecided molecule and the rhyming indictment is an excellent and typical example of the burlesque, entertaining and witty verse writing throughout. It is accessible and of course delightfully sayable:

> CLERK. Unwilling to be named.
> Rebelling when defined.
> Declining to be blamed,
> Objecting when assigned,

Protesting when selected,
Resisting an attack,
Refusing to be directed,
And talking back.
    (Corwin, 1947, pp. 3–7)

The play may be in an expressionist genre of fantasy and verse, but in these first 2–3 minutes of courtroom session, the listener is hooked with the fascination of putting science on trial, wondering how X will be presented and indeed plead. Two of the characters, Clerk and Judge, have practically sung their roles in verse, and even when courtroom ritual fills time with the declaration of the indictment, the Judge, played by Groucho Marx, can be heard in the recording of the live production responding with non-verbal sounds of surprise, intrigue and even disapproval. This is an excellent example of avoiding what Erik Barnouw described as the danger of 'the vanishing character' (Barnouw, 1940, pp. 56–57). He explained a character not talking is like the door not in operation. It soon 'slips from the listener's mind into a cloud of non-existence' (Barnouw, 1940).

Conclusions

Keith Richards advised on the importance of the opening to audio drama: 'Whatever you do it must catch the ear, whether it be by music, by sound effects, by arresting words, or indeed by all three, it must have an impact (Richards, 1991, p. 22). He said the listener needs to be caught up in the action, and so it is often a good idea to begin where the action is (Richards, 1991, p. 24). It is vital to hold the listener's attention and not a good idea 'to begin in an ambiguous way, or to switch styles. A confused listener is not going to stay around if there are unexplained stylistic changes or if the piece starts in one genre and moves without reason into another" (Richards, 1991, p. 31).

Donald McWhinnie emphasised that radio playwrights cannot afford to waste words, sound, music, and time because there can be none of the concessions experienced in theatre-land when the audience settles in their seats, unwraps chocolates and the slow intrigue is expected to unfold:

> His sense of drama or poetry or music must operate immediately. It is easy enough to conceive a 'shock' opening in the work of suspense or terror, but every radio script must begin by creating some kind of anticipation, by posing some sort of question. The writer must at least imply some inner tension, which is ultimately to be resolved, if he wishes to involve the listener. It may be through situation, character, atmosphere, or shock tactics, although 'stunt' openings for the sake of it are liable to fall flat; whatever the method, the initial tension must come from the heart of the programme, and the first sounds

we hear should seem pre-ordained and inevitable – an impression which should subsequently be confirmed and consolidated.

(McWhinnie, 1959, pp. 113–114)

Claire Grove and Stephen Wyatt re-emphasised the consensus on audio-drama openings:

[I]t's very easy for a listener to lose interest or switch off if their attention isn't caught in the first few minutes. So, within those two or three minutes, a writer has not only to capture the listener's attention but also let them know something about the nature and tone of the piece.

(Grove & Wyatt, 2013, p. 31)

Richard Hand and Mary Traynor advised writers to conjure openings that 'will engage and intrigue a listener. Does it make sense? Does it puzzle us enough to want to hear more? Does it shock or scare us? Does it make us laugh?' (Hand & Traynor, 2011, p. 119). Annie Caulfield, in her discussion of openings, described the advantage of a character operating as a proxy detective for the listener in striking up important questions that need to be answered so that eventually 'the listener should then start asking their own questions' (Caulfield, 2009, p. 28).

Vincent McInerney reinforces the writer's duty to begin with an immediate and intriguing plot 'because if your play looks as if it is going nowhere then neither are you' (McInerney, 2001, p. 106). The writer is there to tell a story 'as simply and as economically as possible. Part of this economy should be directed to exposing the substance of the plot as quickly as possible' (McInerney, 2001). Shaun MacLoughlin adds 'In radio you do not have a *captive* audience, who have paid for a seat, who might be embarrassed to leave and who will therefore give the play a chance to develop' (MacLoughlin, 1998, p. 22). He quoted the legendary pioneer of British television drama in the 1950s and 1960s, Sydney Newman who said rather vividly 'Catch them by the goolies as they get up to switch the set off and you've got them for half an hour' (McInerney, 2001). The beginning is vital – an important conclusion:

The switch off button is never far away. As a writer you probably have about a minute, two at the outside, to engage your listener. However wonderful the rest of the play, if your beginning does not captivate the listeners, they will never stay to be enchanted.

(McInerney, 2001)

In 1943 Morton Wishengrad was commissioned by Milton Krents of the American Jewish Committee to write a radio play on the rebellion that year by young Jewish fighters in the Warsaw Ghetto taking a stand against the liquidation and the deportation of men, women and children to concentration camps where they were being annihilated. It was an event largely ignored by the world. Wishengrad said 'The more I read, the more inadequate to the task I felt. Several times, I asked Krents to get another writer. He refused' (Barnouw/Wishengrad, 1945,

p. 32). It was an experience where he was unable to sleep as he wrote, rewrote and discarded drafts that littered the floor. He recalled: '...my wife made me sit down, and I talked for nearly three hours about the Warsaw Ghetto. The script opened up after that. I wrote the opening and closing narrations first' (Barnouw/ Wishengrad, 1945, p. 33).

This is a descriptive analysis of beginning of *The Battle of the Warsaw Ghetto* by Morton Wishengrad. The style and writing is direct, urgent, haunting and dares to tell a story about the fate of people the listeners have already been told are now dead. The narrator is a dramatic character who transitions us into the actuality of what happened. And the opening Voice, as we will find out in Chapter 10, operates as symmetrical lamentation. Wishengrad said he was motivated to:

> [P]resent the tragedy of the people who gave the world its monotheism, its morality, and its concept of the sacredness of human life. I wanted to present Jews as they are, without self-pity, without anger, and with the terrible conviction that, to paraphrase Theodor Herzl, if you cannot march, you must at least remain standing.
>
> *(Barnouw/Wishengrad, 1945, p. 33)*

The production begins with the Jewish Cantor singing 'El Mole Rachamim' unaccompanied for 20–30 seconds and this fades under the Voice who sets the dramatic events the listener is about to hear in the context of Jewish and Second War history. The Voice speaks closely and softly to the microphone and identifies what is being heard as a prayer for the dead. The Voice advises listeners to hear him with reverence because this is a prayer that is not in the least ordinary and neither are the people for whom the prayer is being offered. These are the dead of the Warsaw Ghetto, the people who have been starved and beaten to death, and deported to their deaths in gas chambers.

The Voice says these are the scapegoats of centuries of history stretching back thousands of years to when the priest robed himself in linen and stood on Mount Sinai at the convocation of ancient Israel. The people brought to him a live goat chosen by Lot and he laid his hands on the goat's head and confessed over it all the iniquities of the people. The goat was called Azazel meaning scapegoat and after it was released by the priest, it fled into the wilderness.

But the Voice declares there was no release for the thirty five thousand Jews who stood their ground and fought the army of the Third Reich. Twenty five thousand gave their lives in that battle and now sleep in common graves. They have vindicated their birthright. The Voice says let the Cantor sing and hear him with reverence for they have made an offering by fire and an atonement unto the Lord and they have earned their sleep. The Cantor's voice is faded up to the finish of the prayer. A music theme is established to prepare for the action of the story (Barnouw/Wishengrad, 1945, pp. 34–5).

At this point Wishengrad has the narrator simply introducing himself as Isaac Davidson who has been living in the Polish city of Lublin with his wife, Dvora, and their son Samuel. After Poland was invaded they have been herded into a cattle car and transported to the Warsaw Ghetto. Davidson says it is a place of purgatory around which the occupiers have built concentric walls of brick, barbed wire and soldiers armed with bayonets.

The music fades as the listener is provided with a scene from inside the Ghetto where Nazi soldiers are harshly ordering new arrivals to quickly pick up their blue cards. The Davidson family, Isaac, Dvora, and Samuel are receiving one each. Isaac explains they are stamped with the letter J. These are the bread cards which are as precious as life itself. Each entitles the holder to just one pound of bread a week. This is the opening of the play as the family of three shuffle to the tenement in the Twarda District, which Isaac says is the place where they are to live.

(Barnouw/Wishengrad, 1945, p. 35)

Companion Website Resources

Additions and Updates for Chapter 5 Beginning the Sound Story https://kulturapress.com/2022/08/12/updates-for-chapter-5-beginning-the-sound-story/

Norman Corwin and Radio Drama https://kulturapress.com/2022/08/29/norman-corwin-and-radio-drama/

Anthony Minghella and Radio Drama https://kulturapress.com/2022/08/27/anthony-minghella-and-radio-drama/

The Radio Plays of Lucille Fletcher https://kulturapress.com/2022/08/18/the-radio-plays-of-lucille-fletcher/

Richard Durham and Radio Drama https://kulturapress.com/2022/08/29/richard-durham-and-radio-drama/

The Radio Plays of Caryl Phillips https://kulturapress.com/2022/08/13/the-radio-plays-of-caryl-phillips/

The Radio Plays of Susan Hill https://kulturapress.com/2022/08/18/the-radio-plays-of-susan-hill/

The Radio Plays by Angela Carter https://kulturapress.com/2022/08/18/radio-plays-by-angela-carter/

Radio Drama and Representation of the Holocaust and Final Solution https://kulturapress.com/2022/08/29/radio-drama-and-representation-of-the-holocaust-and-final-solution/

6

CHARACTERISING THE SOUND STORY

Techniques and Devices

Characters Unique to the Audio Drama Medium

From the plays referenced across much more than a century of sound drama writing and production, we should now be familiar with the medium's potential to characterise beyond the human form. Reginald Berkeley's characterisation of the *White Château* building itself (1925) was a chronicling vocalised witness to all the follies of war between 1914 and 1918, Richard Durham gave human spirit, personality, and voice to a trumpet, to the Chicago Slums (albeit rather malignant), and to the human heart. Rosemary Horstmann highlighted all of the potential of corporeal audio drama characterisation with her quotation from J.C.W Brook's play *Giving Up* (1978). This is the story of a man getting up, going to work, and deciding to give up smoking. Ostensibly a simple scenario until the central character divides into a comedy of body parts such as the ears, nose, mouth, arms, legs, fingers, private parts, and, of course, the brain. The point of view and listening becomes the various organs in his body – the inside story as it were:

The listener first hears sleeping noises from all over the body. It could be a platoon of soldiers in a barn. Right Ear and Left Ear then begin to compete for Brain's attention. Right Ear says to Left Ear to keep out of it because Right Ear heard it first. Left Ear insists Left Ear has a job to do and will report anything heard. There are grunts and groans and other bestirring noises from all over the body and Omnes tells the ears to shut up, go back to sleep, and stuff some cotton wool in their orifices. The Brain is waking and making incoherent noises getting the brain into focus and operation. Ears are almost shouting that there is an alarm clock on the go, it's time to get up and the flow of ringing alarm noise comes echoing through them. What is a Brain to do first thing in the morning but to say 'Oh dear…' and Right Arm like an over eager dog which wants to run after its bone says it is ready to do the usual. Brain says please but what is the usual? We hear the Right Arm

DOI: 10.4324/9780203838181-6

stretching, perhaps to hit the button to turn off the alarm, but it could easily be to grab a cigarette (Horstmann, 1991, p. 27).

Horstmann praises the developing conflict in the play between the characters Brain, Will, and Conscience, and she argues this is 'extremely ingenious, highly effective radio, and would be hard to realise in any other medium' (Horstmann, 1991 p. 28). This was a 45 minute script for BBC Radio 4's Afternoon Play strand, and it appears it was only broadcast once. Horstmann says radio drama characters should have an aurally recognisable personality and talk consistently all the way through. There are two tricks often used by script editors and directors. Conceal the names of characters and randomly drop their lines into a pool of mixed up dialogue. Is it possible to identify which line is likely to belong to each character? Read all the lines belonging to one character aloud and listen carefully for anything that jars and simply does not belong to that particular character.

There can be no doubt whose words these lines belong to in an extract selected by Shaun MacLoughlin from *Lobby Talk* by Juliet Ace. This is from a radio play about Coco the parrot who occupied a cage in the bar of a hotel in Beirut frequented by journalists and became hugely popular because he would swear in 22 different languages.

The play begins with Coco talking to the listener while covered with a cloth that has been thrown over him by the barman Walid.

Coco begins inevitably with a few squawks and explains that although his name is Coco he would have been happier if he had been called Dwight, Charles, or Winston. His real owner had been a journalist whose name he finds rather difficult to recall. The hotel manager, Fouad, thought that because of the civil war in Lebanon and ongoing conflict involving the Palestinians, Syrians, and Israelis, most of his clientele were reporters from abroad and needed some friendly company. Coco fits the bill because he speaks to them in their own languages. In the anthropomorphising Juliet Ace cleverly gives Coco a claim to empathy. He knows those dark moments human beings have far and away from home and family; particularly in a hotel lobby at 3 o'clock in the morning. He is the parrot always around with sympathy and squawks and able to parrot in more languages than any other parrot he has heard of. He is high-ranking and internationally famous even though he does not have the powers of those parrots who feature in magic realism novels.

He wants the listener to understand that he hears all languages as if they are one and so his speaking and hearing vocabulary now extends to millions of words, has no accent, and is more complex than Esperanto.

At this point, Walid tears the cloth off Coco's cage to wake him up. The sound design lets in the better-established ambience of the hotel. Their fractious relationship is obvious when Coco calls Walid a boring little man, after Walid tells him to behave himself. Coco demands a large scotch, calls him a fool, and whistles the first two bars of the Marseillaise and always hits the wrong final note. While shouting 'shut up'! over and over again, Walid also curses Coco with the threats he might be shutting him up for good, and there will be a day when the beak squawks once too often (MacLoughlin, 1998, pp. 14–16).

When Israel invaded Lebanon in 1982 and was bombarding the city, the jealous barman Walid eventually shot the real Coco the parrot. But is this what happens in the radio play? Hopefully, the BBC will rebroadcast it on BBC Radio 4 Extra at some stage so you can find out.

The characterisation of a disruptive parrot called Loreto is central to Tiziano Scarpa's Prix Italia award-winning RAI play of 1997 *Popcorn* which opens with Loreto locking himself inside Luciana bathroom, preventing her getting ready to go out for the night. Loreto is outraged at being denied his proper lunch for three days and instead been assailed with the absolutely dreadful boiled chicken, hard boiled eggs, and then today roast chicken. He's convinced she is doing it on purpose. A parrot needs his proper lunch of popcorn. Scarpa's writing is clever because in these dramatic opening lines he plants loaded words as clues behind the row between them.

Luciana is banging on the door furiously. She tells him that she has been putting food on the table and if he is not happy with the house menus he is more than welcome to flutter down to the park bench outside and wait for old ladies to be charmed by his usual stories and crumble up a cracker biscuit for him. Loreto cries out that he doesn't tell stories. The listener wants to know those stories Luciana is so angry about. Why is a parrot telling stories and to whom? (Scarpa, 1997)

Pamela Brooke advises that characters should be people listeners are attracted to, a bit larger than life, recognisable, familiar, 'slightly exaggerated for dramatic effect' (Brooke, 1995, p. 65) and 'interesting enough to generate strong emotional reactions' (Brooke, 1995). She talks about audio dramatic characters being so imaginatively real to listeners that they will 'worry about them and cheer for them as they would a close personal friend' (Brooke, 1995). Brooke titled her 1995 book *Communicating through Story Characters* because she is committed to authentic characters to develop stories and 'probe deeply for the genuine and generally hidden conflicts that cause real people to do things even when they know and believe that the consequences can be dire' (Brooke, 1995). She sets out the following guidelines for effective characterisation in radio drama:

Limit the number of main characters with names and personalities to avoid confusion;

Give incidental characters generic names to avoid slowing down the action with unimportant information;

Avoid clustering same age, sex, temperaments, and speech styles with your main characters – it is always better to contrast in age and gender;

Generally leading characters will be opposing each other in dimensions of conflict and struggle;

Make sure you clearly identify the character with the point of view (POV in film) or point of listening (POL) in audio drama;

Make sure the listener's allegiance and sympathy with the main character is not at
the total expense of the others because listeners need 'to understand and care
about the characters they disagree with' (Brooke, 1995, p. 67);

Ensure your characters have clear, realistic, believable, and not over-complicated
motives. These should have causation and the consequences should have the
potential of revealing strengths and weaknesses in those characters.

Creating the Character and Effective Use of Characterisation

Pamela Brooke identified a consensus among audio drama writing authors about the
need for a main protagonist character in any sequence of drama who represents a point
of view which the listeners can believe in and identify with. Unity of action requires
characters that always have function and dramatic purpose. The main character and
other characters must be active. There needs to be a dynamic relationship between the
activity of the character and the urgency of the plot (Crook, 1999, p. 183).

I have often debated and discussed which should come first. Should we be creating a plot first from which the characters hang, or should we create our characters
first from which the plot hangs? Previously, I relied on John Galsworthy who said
that the writer who does the former rather than the latter is committing a cardinal
sin. I still hold to the view that he was right, though I also accept many a good
writer can adopt other strategies to achieve the same result. The creative impetus of
character generation benefits from coming first. It is better to begin with the idea,
follow with the characters, and then tell the story (Crook, 1999, p. 184). There
remains merit in my previous argument that the plays which have survived their
periods tend to be those dominated by the power of their central characters such as
Shakespeare's *Hamlet, Macbeth, Romeo and Juliet,* and *Richard III.*

I would offer the following guidelines on the creation and profiling of audio
dramatic characters:

1. Attempt the profiling before a word of the play is written;
2. Make sure you have writer's control in determining the background, anteced-
    ents, and history of your main characters and that you know their strengths and
    weaknesses, ambitions, aspirations, and insecurities;
3. Depending on the kind of play and genre do consider whether you need to
    have a full understanding of each character's anxieties, fantasies, what it is that
    they hate and love about themselves, and perhaps even how they are capa-
    ble of deceiving themselves. In *Radio Drama: Theory and Practice*, I set out a
    series of questions that you could ask and answer as the creating writer of your
    character:

    What was the worst thing that ever happened in your character's life and how
    did the character come to terms with that experience? What is the best thing
    that ever happened in your character's life and how has that experience res-
    onated intellectually and emotionally? What was the character's relationship

with the mother and father and any siblings? What is the experience that your character has had with grief and profound emotional suffering? What experience has your character had with death and serious injury? Has your character stared death in the face? Does your character fear death? How would your character want to die and what would be the worst way of dying for your character? What are your character's religious and philosophical beliefs? What has happened in the past to change them? What is your character's sexual orientation and history? What was your character's first sexual experience and how did he or she lose their virginity? Has your character been in love? How many times? How would your character exhibit attraction to another person? Has your character suffered from a broken heart? What would it take to break your character's heart? What does he or she want out of human relationships? What drives the force of envy and jealousy within your character? What does your character think about his or her body? How would you pitch the quality of your character's self-confidence? How does your character day-dream? How does your character respond to fear and danger? How does your character exhibit extreme anger and what would provoke your character to this point? What would reduce your main character to gales of laughter and how does your character have fun? What was the most foolish thing your character ever did? What is your character most ashamed of?

(Crook, 1999, p. 185)

4. Be aware that audio dramatic characters have an internal and exterior existence and consciousness, and the exterior is not necessarily determined by the interior although they often have direct cognisance of each other;
5. Do not forget how interior and exterior consciousness are sometimes in conflict, and this complex juxtaposition can set up interesting paradoxical manifestations of dramatic expression (Crook, 1999).

Characterisation in sound drama will be mainly achieved by dramatic narration and dialogue. The resulting script is somewhat similar to a musical composition. The creative notation in words for the character allows and anticipates the performance and interpretation of subtext. This is why teachers of creative writing often advise authors and dramatists to write less in order to mean more. Donald McWhinnie demonstrates the principles at play here by taking the opening 11 lines of Giles Cooper's radio play *Without the Grail* (1958) and incorporating directorial notes based on the actual performance. He set this out in his book, *The Art of Radio*, published in 1959 to show how good scripts are usually always underwritten (McWhinnie, 1959, pp. 124–125). He repeated the analysis in the introduction to the BBC's publication of six of Giles Cooper's seminal radio plays in 1966. The original script, equivalent to a composer's score handed over to the conductor of an orchestra is seemingly stripped to everyday small talk between a couple long familiar in each other's company.

The central character Innes is packing to go away, and his wife Hazel is trying to help him while at the same time questioning the purpose of the journey and actively discouraging him. Innes concentrates his vocabulary by using nouns and facts such as toothbrush, razor, tooth-paste, soap, and towel, the place in Assam where the man he is going to see lives, socks, handkerchiefs and avoiding giving the answer she wants by using the words, 'confidential' and 'secrets'. Hazel's questions are a series of 'whys': What sort of job, why all the way to see one man, and why all the mystery if he is just seeing a tea merchant (Cooper, 1966, p. 127).

McWhinnie set out his directorial interpretation of how to draw out and identify the playwright's subtext. This is also very much a case of identifying the director's subjectivity as well as a likely reflection of any discussion between the director and living author. There is so much more potential for this kind of consultation during the production of modern drama for radio and podcasting. In this analysis and script scoring, he shows so well how the harmonics of well-written drama are waiting for the acting instruments and direction they are going to be matched with.

McWhinnie identifies ways of performing each individual line as well as determining the attitude and thinking of the individual character, and, as all professional actors know so well, acting is thinking before speaking and movement. Consequently, Innes' mood and feeling varies in terms of being 'disinterested under his breath', 'long-suffering' because it is the third time he has answered the same question, snappy and then reasonable. Hazel journeys through sadness, exasperation, putting on 'half-hearted humour' and then 'wide-eyed innocence':

INNES: (*Evading it*) Confidential. (*Matter-of-fact*) Let's have those socks.
HAZEL: (*Not critical, not sorry for herself*) Honest, love, anyone would think you worked for the Secret Service, not a tea merchant.
INNES: (*Almost gaily*) We have our secrets. (*And quickly, before advantage can be taken*) Handkerchiefs. (*Pause; rather more politely*) Thanks.

(Cooper, 1966, p. 13; McWhinnie, 1959, p. 125)

Notice how the director's notes and actors' interpretations are longer than Cooper's original script. As McWhinnie says so pertinently 'in radio you only have the words, and mere words are so much sound unless there is a nuance of character or emotion in and between every line. A good writer puts it there to be dug out' (McWhinnie, 1959). There is no doubt that Giles Cooper was the wizard of radio dramatic subtext. I have argued that your understanding of your characters is potentially as intense an intimacy as you will ever experience in your own personal relationships. And Giles Cooper proved that successful characterisation does not depend on mythological extroverted heroes.

McWhinnie said he could not recall any hero in a play by Giles Cooper because he seems to deal with inadequate people who in trying to solve their problems only succeed in creating more problems for themselves. In focusing on the apparently understated and non-celebrocratic individuals in human society, Cooper invested nobility and profound sympathy in characters who are usually invisible. A charming and I would argue rather intensely sympathetic example of this style of characterisation is Bundy in *The Disagreeable Oyster*. The listener cannot fail to engage a sense of compassion with Bundy. As McWhinnie explains:

> [H]is characters are undistinguished and, on the face of it, uninteresting; the individual never wins, however much he asserts himself, and though he may think that he is a free agent his chances of fulfilling himself become increasingly remote—even when he asserts his authority, he usually finds a higher authority frustrating his ambition.
>
> *(McWhinnie, 1959, p. 11)*

Cooper gives nobility and dignity to the losers in life. He divided Mervyn Bundy into two parts – Bundy Major and Bundy Minor. Bundy Major is the exterior character who would never say what Bundy Minor wants to say and can only be heard within himself. Cooper and his Director McWhinnie cleverly inveigle Bundy into the continuity announcement of the play. It is as if the leading actor of a theatre show runs through the aisle of the audience stalls in costume and blurts out some comment on the play they are about to see before jumping onto the stage centre and disappearing behind the curtain. In this case it would be two actors, Bundy Major and Bundy Minor – perhaps taking the stage left and right:

ANNOUNCER: This is the BBC Third Programme. We present a play by Giles Cooper entitled, 'The Disagreeable Oyster'.
BUNDY: You can say that again.
ANNOUNCER: 'The Disagreeable Oyster'.
BUNDY: They do disagree with me, but how was I to know when I stood on the steps of the Rosedene Family and Commercial Hotel, thinking that the world was my oyster that ...
BUNDY MINOR: Begin at the beginning.

(Cooper, 1966, p. 85)

Bundy Major explains that the beginning of what will inevitably become a complicated and bizarre story is something altogether ordinary, mundane, and yes, perhaps on the face of it a little boring. It is 12 o'clock on a Saturday morning in his office at Craddock's Calculators Ltd. It could be said unlucky people had to work on Saturdays in those days. Bundy says the office he works in is not particularly nice. Even the typists can see a very narrow bit of St Paul's, but alas he is poor old Bundy. The listener than hears Bundy Minor reminding him that he does have a first name. It's Mervyn.

Bundy Major is still preoccupied with the humiliation of his office view – the upper part of a mercantile bank. Bundy Minor interjects with a 'Well?' and Bundy Major continues with the narrative. It's a fine May morning. What should Bundy do? Is it worth beginning anything before the weekend? A door opens loudly. Mr. Gunn appears. How good it is that Bundy is still around. There is a crisis and Bundy should sharpen his ears and pay attention. Bundy Minor can only see the ginger hair growing out of his ear (Cooper, 1966).

Some listeners may have picked up in this opening that for some reason Mervyn Bundy, usually addressed as Bundy even though we are going to get used to two versions of himself, has started at Craddock's Calculators Ltd. and ended up at the Rosedene Family and Commercial Hotel. What happens in between? We need to be told. Will we find out why there is a Bundy Major and Bundy Minor? Will they become the one and only Bundy? Will one leave the other? And how will the events change them? And how does Mr. Gunn's crisis become a disagreeable oyster?

Shaun MacLoughlin says characters in radio drama are successful in terms of being recognised by the auditory imagination if they are described, identified by speaking, or being spoken to. Too many characters confuse the listener; writers should be as economical with the language of their characters as possible. Interest in characterisation grows and intensifies when the plot and story develops and deepens their emotional resonance. Characters need to evolve and evoke. He also pointed out that the fewer the characters in a play, the greater the scope for actors to bring their creativity to the subtextual dimensions of the characterisation (MacLoughlin, 1998, pp. 77–78).

William Ash recommends writers categorise characters as thematic and illustrative. The main ones will be thematic, giving the play its shape, and striking up the conflict and showing the story conceived by the writer. They will be developed and changed by what happens (Ash, 1985, p. 26). Illustrative characters are derived from the storyline instead of determining it. Thematic characters usually reveal subjectivity and what is going on internally in their minds and hearts. He said this 'brings about dramatic changes in a pattern of human relationships, or perhaps it is a dramatic change within a single character that provides the climax of our play' (Ash, 1985, p. 27). Ash argued that a significant outcome of creative characterisation in radio drama is achieved when 'internal developments in characters will make all the more impact if some inner change becomes objectified in overt action which becomes an external force for the other characters' (Ash, 1985, p. 28).

Vincent McInerney offered a precise definition of the aim of character creation and their development when he said they can be said to be set in motion and explored by the expedient of either putting an ordinary person in extraordinary circumstances or putting an extraordinary person in ordinary circumstances (McInerney, 2001, p. 121). He repeated the much emphasised point that the main character(s) 'must, at the play's close, have developed from the manner in which they were portrayed at the outset' (McInerney, 2001). Characterisation needs to be a journey in which a crisis is resolved or precipitated. He agrees that mentally the listener has a limited capacity in holding attention and engagement with characters in radio play worlds. Too many will mean the necessary identification and appreciation of a substantial main character will be undermined. In a half hour drama, four main characters would be the limit. McInerney recommends writing to achieve immediate identification with the acronym SCRAM standing for sex/class/regional/age mix (McInerney, 2001, p. 122). He also warns against stereotypes which can always be avoided by giving every character 'the individuality that befits all individuals' (McInerney, 2001, p. 125).

Keith Richards recommends that radio dramatists keep in mind the relationships between the main characters of their plays:

> They must have need of each other, for the only reason that they are brought together in the artificial environment of a fiction is that they have something to work out, and one of the other characters, or perhaps more than one, can help them work out just what that is. Their needs can be quite disparate but they all must have them. Any character without needs is a passenger and should be excluded.
>
> *(Richards, 1991, p. 57)*

Richards emphasises the needs for emotional as well as intellectual tension between the main characters which is worked through and resolved in some way: 'We need to know where the characters have come from and what they have brought with them, providing that this can be done in the writing without an overload of exposition' (Richards, 1991). The characterisation needs to be achieved through causality and not coincidence, through dialogue and not description.

Effective and successful characterisation is impressively present in many online podcast series and serials which at the time of writing are accessible online and funded by sponsorship and/or advertising. It is a tremendous skill and achievement to develop and sustain characterisation across many episodes of series or a serial run.

The scripted audio drama *Bronzeville*, which ran on multiple digital audio platforms between 2017 and 2018, is a ten part weekly series written by Academy Award and BAFTA nominee Josh Olson with a cast of actors, including Tracee Ellis Ross, Wood Harris, Omari Hardwick, Lance Reddick, Cory Hardrict, Lahmard Tate, and Brittany Snow. The characterisation in the setting of 1940s Chicago is centred on the Copeland family and begins with newcomer Jimmy Tillman fleeing Arkansas after killing a white strike breaker in self-defence. When arriving in Chicago, he makes friends with Casper Dixon 'a smooth talking numbers runner' for a racket controlled by the Copeland family in the predominantly African-American neighbourhood of Bronzeville. The drama is achieved through consistent successful character development and changes through dialogue and self-contained drama with captivating subplots and cliff-hangers driving the listener's interest from episode to episode. The mark of its success has been the commission of a second season of ten further episodes released in 2021.

Moving from the crime to the romantic comedy genre, another outstanding exemplar of long-form audio dramatic characterisation is brilliantly achieved in the series written and directed by Faith McQuinn, *Margaritas and Donuts*. The six part series was released online in 2019 and centres around the story of Josephine, a paediatrician, who is largely unlucky in love. With some coaxing from her best friend Katrina, Josephine starts a relationship with Malik, an ophthalmologist who works in the office across the hall from hers. Malik appears to be exactly the person

Josephine needs in her life, but perhaps she does not quite realise it yet. McQuinn's writing is subtle, sublime, and has a unity that is captivating and engaging for the sound medium. The three main characters of Josephine, Katrina, and Malik are developed in a comforting style with warmth and affection. The relationships between them are exquisitely and elegantly developed in finely crafted dialogue throughout. It is sound drama that romances the auditory imagination rather than shocking it.

Conclusions

Audio drama thrives with main thematic characters who have public and private dimensions, external dialogic relationships, and interiority. When dramatists script the expression of private moments for their main characters, this allows listeners to feel and access their hearts and minds. Writers are sharing the privilege of knowing and understanding them through the powerful opportunity of dramatic revelation. Character change and development enriches the intensity and quality of listening as well as enhancing the appreciation of the story.

Immediate engagement and rapid identification of characters through dialogue and action is essential. If listeners can fully imagine an audio drama's main characters from the beginning, the natural course of the characters' impulses will help to write the rest of the play. Placing a central character in a specific social, physical, and emotional environment where there is conflict and tension will generate a nexus of dramatic storytelling. In tragedy, the impetus of dramatic characterisation is determined by a striving for a goal that the hero can never attain. The tragedy is accentuated by the unrelenting failure to overcome the obstacles thrown in the hero's path. Tragedy tips over into melodrama when the dynamics of the social and physical environment of the play dominate the focus of characterisation. In comedy, the drama depends on the dramatic portrayal of the central character's response and reactions to the social and physical environment. In farce, the dramatic entertainment tends to be derived from the dynamic force of the actions on character rather than character on actions. Comedy and tragedy are the drama of characterisation. Melodrama and farce are the drama of situation (Crook, 1999, p. 186).

Giles Cooper's plays provide paradoxical truths on the concept of hero and heroine in character construction. Listeners generally appreciate main characters who are transcendent people in transcendent moments and succeed in overcoming adversity. One of the most enjoyable plot developments in characterisation is the transference of the hero from the obvious to the humble and that is certainly the case with Bundy in *The Disagreeable Oyster*. I am happy to fully subscribe to my observation that by investing greatness in apparent inferiority as a writer, you can engage 'the well of human generosity which thrives on a recognition of the potential for human dignity' (Crook, 1999).

Characters who resonate conviction and intensity and have charisma will obviously serve dramatic exposition well. Listeners will be drawn to imperfect people because they can identify with them. Drama requires conflict which can only be generated when characters are different externally and internally and have been invested with believable motives which underpin the conflict between them. Consider maintaining a polarity between the main characters and ensure they undergo internal and external changes as a result of the twists and turns of the plot. Secondary and illustrative characters should be more singular in their characteristics. One way of appreciating this is that at the moment of the listener's arrival into the story, secondary characters should already be committed while the central character is still weighing up the options.

Listeners must like and care what happens to the main character. They should dislike and have the potential to feel real animosity towards any character operating with the role of antagonist. It is also a good idea to modulate charm with alarm and alternate tension with humour in the realm of any central character's thoughts, emotions, and utterances. The advantage of powerfully contrasting sympathy for the protagonist character and antipathy towards the antagonist character is that the conflict becomes competitive and the opportunity to surprise with ambiguity by revealing the bad in the good and the good in the bad so much greater. And in the overall context, I would continue to advise writers to

> Strike the colours of the world of your play with detail so there is a rich imaginative atmosphere setting mood and emotional, cultural or political ambience ... Keep surprising the listener all the way through the plot and tantalise the listener with a cascade of fascinating and demanding questions followed by intriguing dramatic answers.
>
> *(Crook, 1999, p. 187)*

Characterisation in Morton Wishengrad's *The Battle of the Warsaw Ghetto* (1943)

The play is short in running with a duration of 25 minutes and 38 seconds. Wishengrad respects the rule of having less than four main characters in any time sequence of less than half an hour. A religious and spiritual 'Voice' opens and closes the drama with the background of the Jewish prayer for the dead *El Mole Rachamim*. This is a narrative characterisation of lament for the hundreds of thousands murdered in the Ghetto and killed by the Germans putting down the revolt. The key central and thematic characters are Isaac Davidson, his wife Dvora, and son Samuel. The action impacts and changes each of them catastrophically. All the other characters are illustrative and contribute to the telling of the story from the urgency and threat to life of their arrival from Lublin to the revolt of the fighters and violent battle and suppression of the Nazi occupiers and persecutors. They include Nazi 1, Nazi 2, Nazi 3, Ghetto Woman, Teacher 1, Teacher 2, Girl, Instructor, Plumber, Doctor, Conductor, and Pole. It could be argued that Teacher 1 as a fighter giving his life in the struggle to show that the Jews can stand and fight is a hybrid of illustrative and thematic characterisation. He changes his fate and that of others and he is changed. He enters the play subjugated and resorting to his role as continuing educator and trying to continue some semblance of normality when instructing Samuel: 'And now, we'll see if you have learned your lesson …There are seven marks of an uncultured man and seven marks of a wise man. Do you know what they are, Samuel'? (Barnouw/Wishengrad, 1945, p. 36). The dialogue is evocatively ironic. He leaves the play at the end of his life after being mutilated fatally in battle, but defiantly exclaiming: 'It is not for thee to complete the work, but neither art thou free to desist from it. Yes, tell them to mark that on our graves' (Barnouw/ Wishengrad, 1945, p. 44).

Characterisation, writing, and dialogue are pared to the bone, a model in economy of expression and compression of meaning with the intensity of emotion. Isaac Davidson is the main central character dramatically performing in narration and dialogic scene. He is a poignant witness, chronicler, and victim. He talks of their degradation in having to divide dead men's bread in the Ghetto of Warsaw. He asks the listeners if they have ever tasted dead men's bread. Because if they had, they would find out that the taste is bitter and because the saliva does not flow in such conditions, the mouth is dry. This is what we are, says Isaac Davidson and this is how we lived (Barnouw/Wishengrad, 1945, p. 40).

Companion Website Resources

Additions and Updates for Chapter 6 Characterising the Sound Story https://kulturapress.com/2022/08/12/updates-for-chapter-6-characterising-the-sound-story/

Margaritas & Donuts by Observer Pictures (Written and Directed by Faith McQuinn) https://podcasts.apple.com/gb/podcast/margaritas-donuts/id1482406262

Bronzeville https://podcasts.apple.com/us/podcast/bronzeville/id1199964972

Giles Cooper and Radio Plays https://kulturapress.com/2022/08/30/giles-cooper-and-radio-plays/

Harold Pinter and Radio plays https://kulturapress.com/2022/08/30/harold-pinter-and-radio-plays/

Independent Radio Drama Productions IRDP https://kulturapress.com/2022/08/29/independent-radio-drama-productions-irdp/

Kwame Kwei-Armah and Radio Drama https://kulturapress.com/2022/08/29/kwame-kwei-armah-and-radio-drama/

Lance Sieveking and Radio Drama https://kulturapress.com/2022/08/29/lance-sieveking-and-radio-drama/

Lee Hall and Radio Drama https://kulturapress.com/2022/08/29/lee-hall-and-radio-drama/

Louis MacNeice and Radio Plays https://kulturapress.com/2022/08/29/louis-macneice-and-radio-plays/

7

DIALOGUE AND THE SOUND STORY

Techniques and Devices

Writing Dialogue – Key Principles

Good audio dramatists script dialogue to have the rhythm, cadence, and spoken word idiomatic nature of speech, and at the same time they avoid writing naturalistic language without dramatic purpose. Dialogic drama is not just the conversation of real life. Spoken language has to be a response to a plotted situation or action and serve the purpose of developing characterisation and advancing the storytelling of conflict, tension, struggle, and the journey imperative of any play. Any exchange between characters will be dramatic if there is purposeful response between them. William Ash says dialogue is the *sine qua non* of a radio play:

> In no other dramatic medium does the word in its full range of denotation and connotation, the word with all its associated ideas in train, the word unqualified by any gesture or facial expression, the word freed from any visible context whatsoever come more richly and significantly into its own – creating opportunities for the writer by means of dialogue alone to scale the dramatic heights and show us our world stretched out below, or, by dialogue misused, to tumble into some bathetic pitfall.
>
> *(Ash, 1985, p. 34)*

Dialogue can frequently provide comic relief during intense and emotionally overladen sequences, but writers vacillating charm and alarm to variegate emotions and peaks of intensity of feeling should always bear in mind that dramatic comedy is rooted in character and how the response to a situation reveals and impacts on character. It is not merely old-fashioned Music Hall routine or stand-up comedy.

Timothy West created a parody of the very worst in radio dramatic writing with the play *This Gun That I Have in My Right Hand Is Loaded*. It has never actually been

DOI: 10.4324/9780203838181-7

broadcast by the BBC since it was written as a training exercise in 1959. Rosemary Horstmann included it in its entirety as the third appendix for *Writing for Radio* published in 1991. It is certainly instructive on how not to write dialogue. It is used widely in creative writing courses throughout the world and even a sound production is available to listen to online.

It is a spoof play and opens with 1950s style cliché sound effects of music, traffic noises, wind with ship's sirens, barking dog, a hansom cab, echoing footsteps, key chain, and door opening and shutting. Laura wants to know who is coming into the house, only to be told who do you think, with her name check, identifying himself as her husband and then for full measure announcing himself as Clive as if she didn't know. Their son Richard says hello to his Daddy, just in case his father needed reminding, and Daddy says hello to his son and just in case anybody listening wanted to know his son's name, calls him Richard. Clive observes he is getting to be a big boy so listeners have some idea what he looks like, but what is his age? Might as well ask his son. Richard reveals he is 6 years old. The information is clearly rather overwhelming because Laura, Clive's wife, and Richard's mother, decides that Daddy is tired and Richard needs to go upstairs and wait to be called when it is supper time.

Just in case there is no doubt about what happens next, Richard agrees to do what Mummy says and can be heard running heavily up the wooden stairs. Laura wants to know what Clive has under his arm. As if she can't see, Clive says it is the evening paper with another name check for Laura and a rattle of paper noise for good measure. Clive says he has been reading about the Oppenheimer smuggling case. There is a big effort noise before he exclaims 'Good gracious' and describes how nice it is to sit down after the long commuting train journey home from work, which he feels obliged to describe as the insurance office in the City of London.

Laura says she will get him a drink and gives him a name-check adding 'darling' after. We hear lengthy pouring of a drink and then a clink so it is clear the drink was poured into a glass. Clive says thank you with name-check Laura and adding 'my dear'. This presumably is to demonstrate how much they are in love, or perhaps they are husband and wife just in case this might be in doubt. But what is he drinking? We must be told. So after clinking, sipping, and gulping Clive says it is Amontillado which he describes as good stuff. But what will Laura be having to drink? Laura says she will have a whisky, 'if it's all the same to you'; not that she had to say that or that it has any subtextual meaning whatsoever. Or does it?

Having whisky sounds are established with clinking, pouring, and syphoning. So much is happening in this scene, or rather is not happening, but we do not know what Laura looks like do we? And Clive, for some reason, thinks and says whisky is a strange drink for an 'attractive auburn-haired girl of twenty nine'. Perhaps it is time for Clive to ask is there, with a bit of a pause after 'there', anything wrong? Laura, says to Clive – we know because she name-checks him when saying – no, it is nothing, but she does have something to say. Clive says 'yes' interrogatively. Laura is still shy of saying what she is thinking and feeling:

LAURA: No, really, I –

CLIVE: You're my wife, Laura. Whatever it is, you can tell me. I'm your husband. Why, we've been married – let me see – eight years, isn't it?

(Horstmann, 1991, p. 103–104)

This has been another opportunity to inform the listener that Clive is Laura's husband and Laura is Clive's wife and furthermore they have been married for 8 years. And it is because of all these reasons Laura can tell him whatever it is that is wrong.

The comedy here rests in the overwriting, the excessive, and clichéed use of sound effects and usurping the whole function of imaginative engagement on the part of the listener by the deluge of ludicrous detail. The parody is more farce than actual comedy because the language deracinates characterisation. It is deliberately superficial. There are two contrasting scenes from the canon of *Dad's Army* series episodes written by Jimmy Perry and David Croft for BBC Television between 1968 and 1977 which amplify the difference of dialogue with comedy arising out of the words only and dialogue rooted in dramatic character responding to plot development, and also intrinsic to the action of the scene.

It is not widely appreciated that many of the television scripts were dramatised for BBC Radio by Harold Snoad and Michael Knowles between 1973 and 1976. This included the production of episode 14 'The Loneliness of the Long Distance Walker' based on the script of a television episode that was not archived and no longer exists. One of the memorable scenes from the radio drama episode is a meeting between Captain Mainwaring and Sergeant Wilson of the Walmington-on-Sea Home Guard platoon (part-time unpaid WW2 soldiers) and a Brigadier at the War Office in London. They want to persuade him not to call up Private Walker into the regular army for active service because he is the platoon's spiv and black market dealer who provides them with whiskey, cigarettes, and other luxuries subject to shortages and rationing. Of course, they cannot tell that to the top brass of the military. At the same time, the opportunity for comedic misunderstanding is accelerated by the fact the Brigadier is struggling to recruit long-distance walkers for his brother-in-law's army physical training unit. The Brigadier thinks he can find suitable men for his 'mad keen heel and toe merchant' brother-in-law. There might be some champion walkers among the ranks of Home Guard soldiers waiting to go into the regular army.

The Brigadier tells Mainwaring and Wilson they have 5 minutes as they are ushered in. Magnificent fast dialogue repartee flows after the Brigadier enquires as to the walker's name, only to be told it is Walker. Do they really have a walker called Walker? Yes, indeed they do. Such coincidences are not so unusual. The Brigadier's Captain called Cutts says in the radio version he knew of a tailor called Tailor and in the television version a butcher called Butcher.

Naturally, if the Home Guard platoon has a walker called Walker he must have a record and the Brigadier wants to know what it is. But Mainwaring thinks he is asking about Walker's criminal record. The Brigadier wants to be reassured he has got a record surely. Mainwaring always turns to his Sergeant, Wilson, when in difficulties or not knowing the answer to a problem or question. Has Walker got a record, Mainwaring asks of Wilson. Wilson in his usual laconic style ventures to suggest that he doesn't think his criminal racketeering has ever been found out, so no record for Walker.

The Brigadier begins to get nonplussed when told his prospective long distance walker has no record. But is Walker any good as a walker without a record, the Brigadier asks? Perhaps he is one of the 'London to Brighton walkers' like his brother-in-law? But Mainwaring says he is one of the Walmington-on-Sea Walkers. Croft and Perry continue to draw out the comedy based on a classic routine of two sides to a confusion getting worse with the audience knowing what neither of the two sides actually know. Sea Walkers? asks the Brigadier, J. Walker says Mainwaring, but why is Walker Jay-walker demands the Brigadier. All Mainwaring can say is that J for Joe Walker is his full name.

The Brigadier already knows what his name is but needs to be reassured that he is a walker. Mainwaring explains they know because Walker told them so. Wilson tries to help by saying that he distinctly heard Walker saying 'I'm Walker'. But surely says the Brigadier, Walker had said 'I'm a Walker?' By the time Mainwaring says 'No, no sir. No. Not A Walker. – he said 'I'm J. Walker', the Brigadier has had enough. He cannot wait for Captain Cutts to see them out. There is an air raid and Mainwaring and Wilson are directed to the shelter in the basement. Should the Brigadier follow them, asks Captain Cutts? The Brigadier tears up the Walker file, says Mainwaring and Wilson are up the pole and he would rather take his chances under the Luftwaffe's bombs in his office than spend any more time with the lunatics who have just wasted 5 minutes of his time and life. (Perry & Croft, 1998, pp. 65–68) [Adjusted to match the radio adaptation].

Perry and Croft feared this scene and its dialogue sounded like Music Hall routine when they first wrote it, but they were surprised how 'remarkably well' the live audiences responded to it in television and radio (Perry & Croft, 1998 p. 66). This is largely because the delightful dialogue is wholly based on the developing joke about the army wanting a walker when the Home Guard platoon want Joe Walker to be discharged from his call-up. The comedy is not directly related to their character, unlike a scene between Captain Mainwaring and Sergeant Wilson in another episode 'Keep Young and Beautiful'. The middle-aged soldiers take drastic measures to appear younger so as to avoid being dismissed from the Home Guard for being too old. Mainwaring has mocked Wilson for wearing corsets, but then feels remorseful.

He apologises for pouring scorn on his Sergeant. He accepts he has no right to do that because he too has taken steps to look more virile. Wilson hopes the Captain has not resorted to monkey glands which in the early 1930s was a rejuvenation technique for men and involved surgical transplantation in a rather sensitive area of a man's anatomy. Wilson is reassured by Mainwaring that he has done nothing as drastic as that. All is revealed when he takes his hat off. For Captain Mainwaring has invested in a toupée. Wilson responds with a long sequence of repressed laughter, trying to be polite and saying how it is both terribly and awfully good and eventually breaking down into uncontrollable laughter. Captain Mainwaring replies with one of the sitcom's iconic comedic ripostes which was added to the everyday catch-phrases associated with the series 'Well be careful. You'll snap your girdle' (Croft & Perry, 2002, p. 50) [Adjusted to match the radio adaptation].

It can be argued that in this scene, Perry and Croft have written dialogue that arises from the abiding competitive and class tensions between Captain Mainwaring, the grammar school educated Bank Manager with a chip on his shoulder, and Sergeant Wilson, the privately educated and Honourable Arthur Wilson who because of his social connections has no trouble getting into the local golf club and is on first name terms with the local aristocracy. The writers give the actor playing Wilson, John Le Mesurier, so much scope for subtext and feeling when laughing at the sight of his commanding officer and superior line manager in the bank where they both work during the day appearing so ridiculous in ill-fitting black toupée.

Dialogue should also be written and constructed so that scenes are connected. Such lines and exchanges can serve as effective conscious and subconscious transepts.

The quality of dialogue is determined by the presence of active, direct, and emotional language as opposed to reflexive, passive, and neutral communication. Believability is increased by specificity. Quality is also improved when dialogue is more specifically constructed in relation to a character's background and emotional state. If dialogue is reacting to action or situation then it must be dramatic and poised on polarities. The goals of the characters in each scene should be different and the language should explicitly or implicitly dramatise this. A sublime example of these objectives is fully represented in a further scene from Anthony Minghella's *Cigarettes and Chocolate*, and was selected by Keith Richards for his book *Writing Radio Drama* in 1991. We rejoin three of the people important in the life of the central character Gemma who has decided to give up speaking for Lent. At the beginning of the play we were introduced to them leaving messages on her answer-machine. Now they meet each other and we find out so much more about them when they gossip and talk about their mutual friend. Their conversation conveys familiarity, intimacy and a certain casual brutality in disrespecting Gemma's feelings and welfare. The listener is being invited to interpret the language literally or to regard it as the trendy middle-class banter then associated with the growingly affluent and fashionable Islington area of London.

Gail thinks Rob and Lorna have met for a romantic assignation. Gail jokes about the possibility of a threesome. Rob invites her to jump in. Gail asks after Gemma. Rob clearly lies when he says she is great. Gail calls her an old bag for not ringing back and responding to messages on her 'bloody machine'. This is because she is flat-hunting and needs her company. And it is also how she discovered the café. Rob is thinking about something else when asked if he thinks the café is nice, and replies emptily 'Yeah'.

Gail is meandering on and one part of her brain wants to ask Lorna a question and the other compliments them both on the tan they got when they were in Italy together. Was it wonderful, she asks? Rob replies that somebody called Tom was wonderful and the grown-ups did fine, but Stephen cheated at scrabble. Lorna reminds him that he cheated too. Rob says there is a difference between cheating openly which is something he does and pretending not to cheat like Stephen. Consistent cheating is not cheating at all in his view. Listeners are no doubt wondering if he is referring to relationships as well as Scrabble. Gail continues with her two-stream thinking and talking. While asking if Gemma had a good time, she also calls them both pigs because she loves Italy and would have liked to have gone as well.

On the subject of Gemma, Lorna says she was fine, but political. Rob disagrees. Lorna explains Gemma wanted to adopt a baby from Vietnam outside the Uffizi in Florence. Gail asks why. Lorna asks Rob why. Rob questions the implied criticism and ascribing politics to Gail's motivation. It was all about context. They were having such a good time. Gail is getting witty and cynical. She says that as she is having a nice time at the moment, she thinks she will adopt the Vietnamese boy. Perhaps he is for sale. Rob does not see the funny side. He thinks the boy had Dutch parents because they wore funny and ugly shoes you can get in Covent Garden. Gail wonders if he is talking about clogs.

Rob continues with two-stream thinking and talking. The shoes were not clogs. They looked like a pair of Nature Treks run over by traffic. And the Vietnamese boy was 'extraordinarily beautiful'. She asks Lorna if she agrees with him, but the waitress arrives with the coffees. Rob has another thought, perhaps wanting to change the subject. Does Gail want anything else? 15 pounds perhaps, which they could get her, implying they are used to her asking to borrow money. The taciturn Lorna makes to leave by saying she is going to metaphorically get her skates on shortly. Rob seems surprised and disappointed. Should he cancel the hotel room then? Lorna replies in the affirmative while saying 'Sorry' (Minghella, 1989, pp. 129–130).

Minghella's scriptwriting offers the essence of everyday speech with ums and ahs, repetition and unfinished sentences, but at the same time captures character through what Richards described as the 'impression of reality while in fact, being largely artificial' (Richards, 1991, p. 91). Minghella also brilliantly demonstrates the dramatic skill of scripting a character to use words that carry more than one meaning. Hence providing the direction of 'Yes' subtextually for Lorna's reply in 'Sorry'.

McInerney confirms how dialogue serves to 'isolate, delineate and develop character' and additionally 'informs the audience of the plot, and indicates through "signposting" (hints) in which direction the plot will be going' (McInerney, 2001, p. 130). As has already been demonstrated, dialogue describes the people in the play, the mise-en-scène and surroundings that contain their dramatic life. He agrees with Richards and others on how the writing is highly contrived and artificial though appears completely natural (McInerney, 2001). In short, plays are not life; they simply represent life and the primary purpose of dialogue 'is to edit the slice of life under consideration in an effort to make it palatable and of an acceptable strength to the listener' (McInerney, 2001).

It can also be advantageous to write dialogue which advances continuity by characters using their lines to tag across scenes by repeating a last word or phrase and usually with different meanings. The dialogue of each character must relate to his or her dramatic function, so it is perfectly acceptable to mix direct and indirect dialogue between two characters when they have different goals.

In audio drama, dialogue is the arterial motorway providing the essential highway of the story's exposition. Keith Richards set out an impressive list of expository devices that can be deployed by writers usually in the dialogic form. They are not exhaustive, but enormously helpful:

1. Direct questions. Characters who ask questions elicit information that can advance a plot;
2. Interrogation. The pressure of authority investigating through formal or informal questioning can accelerate back-history and understanding;
3. Indirect questions. A more subtle and by-the-way method of providing information along the lines of 'I don't suppose you might know or remember?;
4. Leading statement. Declarations which invite debate, challenge, and discussion;
5. Storytelling. A time-honoured technique as old as human time and can effectively open up and develop important advances in the plot with a character saying something along the lines of 'I think you should be told.' or 'I've got something important to tell you';
6. Explanation. Often achieved through characters who are expert or have been consulted for advice, guidance and diagnosis;
7. Clarification. Excellent for unravelling misunderstandings;
8. Correction. Such a device works well when characters are in conflict or doubt each other;
9. Argument. A device which can electrify an entire scene and channel considerable amounts of significant information in support of plot and characterization. A mainstay of the trial format;
10. Recollection. In danger of being over-used. Better deployed in relation to one character afflicted or burdened with the baggage of problematic memory;
11. Confession. A direction of communication which often involves the unburdening of guilt and other powerful emotions;
12. Gossip. Characters who indulge in this have the capacity to cause much mischief;
13. Trivia. The everyday exchange of information expressed through humour, joshing and joking;
14. Advice. Those who give it can exercise much passive aggression and it may not be wanted. Offers great potential for dramatic impact, conflict and tension;
15. The Media. Using broadcasting, print and now online media has a longstanding legacy in radio drama. The recreation of live radio broadcasts in the CBS *War of the Worlds* broadcast of 1938 was regarded as a hoax too far at the time, though it is still celebrated for its socio-psychological impact. Richards feels it is a not so subtle device often over-used by inexperienced writers;
16. Telephone/mobile and smartphones. In audio drama this expository platform can contain the entire mind-world for the listener as created in the BBC series *Life Lines*. Richards cautions against one-sided electronic communications as these can be 'confusing, laborious and frustrating';

17. Recordings. The digital information age offers so many creative ideas for leaving messages from the past, present and future which catalyse action, precipitate mysteries, enquiry, and investigation;

18. Letter. The epistolary form can work well in audio drama as a way of expressing a character's inner feelings and thoughts. This can be an intimate and direct connection with interiority. Characters may wish to say things in letters that they cannot say face to face in dialogic scenes. It can be an excuse and opportunity for avoiding confrontation.

(Richards, 1991, pp. 81–83)

Dialogue can be divided into two major styles. It is possible to mix them, but more often playwrights tend to commit to one style in single plays. Ken Dancyger described heightened language as the language of the theatre and having a 'high octane' quality communication. He explained that when crafted for scriptwriting this heightened method of speaking often has poetic and philosophical undercurrents usually fundamentally charged with authorial intention and expression. Consequently, the writing is utilitarian and functions in serving the interests of plot and character development, but also provides the view of the writer. It is the vehicle dramatically communicating the very idea at the core of the play.

As the word is the main weapon of choice for sound dramatists, apart from the options of music, sound effects, and silence, it could be argued that sound drama is the natural medium for heightened dialogue. It has a greater capacity for description, and expressing a writer's conviction. Longer words and more complex use of metaphor, simile, and vocabulary are further signs of a heightened style of writing. Norman Corwin's verse play *The Undecided Molecule* (1945) is a classic example of heightened dramatic writing.

William Ash cautions against writers who find the imaginative potency of the spoken word to be tempted into 'verbal indulgence, into an intoxication with the sound of words, and the effects the technical staff can create to go with those words which ceases to have any narrative line at all' (Ash, 1985, p. 40). He adds there is no reason 'why we should not have an interesting thematic sound collage – as long as it does not pretend to be a play' (Ash, 1985). However, Corwin's representation of the female advocate to represent the Animal Kingdom in the trial of the atomic particle X is arguably free of any excessive lexicographical flourish. This is flowing dialogic drama, heightened in style, but charming in meaning and purpose. He also has much fun scripting the playful attraction between Anima's lawyer and the Judge who asks her to go on because he is getting so 'goose-pimply and blistery':

ANIMA: I could tell of a bird named the smew
      and another yclept urubu—
      Of the dziggetai, dzo,
      And of zingel roe—
JUDGE: And a fish that is called inconnu.
ANIMA: Quite true.

JUDGE: And a monkey that's called wanderoo.
ANIMA: Quite true.
JUDGE: Oh, I just love to listen to you.

(Corwin, 1947, pp. 46–47)

This inventive dramatic verse is modern, satirical in places, entertaining, accessible and free of any obscurantist and modernist effect. Corwin is using the poetic rhythm of the English language to celebrate the animal world as well as giving an opportunity for his characters Judge and Anima to flirt outrageously in court.

Bannerman said the rhymed fantasy *The Undecided Molecule* was one of Corwin's all-time favourites and he found it 'a particular delight' (Bannerman, 1986, p. 170). Corwin also pioneered the use of non-verbal electronic sounds to articulate the dialogue of the molecule 'X'. This was achieved using a development of the oscillator called the theremin. Corwin explained it:

[C]an be made to flutter, whine, or imitate the inflections of speech ... I myself (every director is a ham at heart and wants to perform in some way or other) operated the spark key and tuning dial that gave expression to the molecule's inner struggle.

(Corwin, 1947, p. 42)

Some radio producers like to go out on location and explore realism. In these situations there is a tendency to accentuate the use of naturalistic dialogue with more simple language. There is less use of vocabulary in the exchange between characters, shorter words and a relationship to action and characterisation. Lines between characters are often crossed-over and crashing into each other. This tendency is normally a sign of a struggle by both characters to say something first. This extract has two parents communicating to their son in a short story radio drama written in 1988 to stimulate debate in a phone-in discussion programme about the impact of divorce on children. The language is in short halting bursts. There is none of the sentence structure found in prose literature. And the fact that we don't hear words from the other side of the conversation invites listeners to imagine the thoughts and feelings of their son whose audiogenic presence is only represented by the sound of his cycling:

FATHER: I know you think I'm a bastard ...I probably am ...I didn't give you the bike as some sort of ...you know sop ...the sweet before the left hook ...Huh! ...We ...we ...both of us ...went together to buy it for you ...because we still love you ...whatever happens we still love you ...Do you understand that? ... It's not going to make any difference ...We're still a family ...Even when we're apart ...You can still see me ...anytime ...Well you'll have to phone during the week ...not during the day of course ...I'll be working ...but later ...On second thoughts why don't you write ...it'll be cheaper ...People don't write enough nowadays ...Well I don't think so ...You write ...and I'll ring ...that's a promise?

[SOUND OF DOMESTIC DESTRUCTION. FASTER BICYCLE ON GRAVEL.]

MOTHER: Subtle wasn't he? ...A 12 speed racer and a Piss off ...I hate your mother ...I'm shacking up with some slut ...I'll introduce you later sort of thing ... Don't look at me like that ...It's not my fault ...I'm not the one who's been screwing around ...I'm not running out on you ...I'll still be here ...Washing, and cleaning, and cooking and working now ...I'll be working now ...To keep you in the style to which you're accustomed ...Yeah! ...I'm bitter ...I'm sorry ...but how can you know what I'm talking about? ...at your age ...What do you know about bitterness ...12 years ...That's how old you are isn't it? ...12 years ...You ...Yes ...You ...One of life's accidents really ...

[SOUND OF DOMESTIC DESTRUCTION. F/X BICYCLE. CONTINUOUS RUN ON ROAD. TRAFFIC PASSING.]

(Crook, 1999, p. 194)

Keith Richards emphasises dramatic dialogue is not recorded speech and writers must avoid superfluous domestic conventions of greetings and pleasantries because listeners do not want to be concerned or confused about the exiting and entering of characters unless these actions have dramatic purpose and meaning. Dialogue should be compact and not dense and impenetrable. He explained:

> Dialogue is heightened language, but it is not necessarily poetic or rhetorical language. It is usually not particularly grammatical. Passion can play havoc with syntax, and people whose normal speech may be basic and colloquial can still be made to speak in a powerfully dramatic and, at the same time, perfectly credible way.
>
> *(Richards, 1991, p. 94)*

Donald McWhinnie says realism can 'be a wasteful method, just as real conversation is wasteful of words and only tolerable because we ourselves are indulging in it' (McWhinnie, 1959, p. 60). McWhinnie also says description through dialogue requires the utmost discipline from writers by combining the economical with the imaginative. Levels and depths of perception need to be expressed through refined and heightened dramatic speech in the space of a few seconds. He selected a scene from Giles Cooper's *Without the Grail* as a brilliant example of what he described as 'highly selective, indirect description' (McWhinnie, 1959). Shaun MacLoughlin quoted the same scene when explaining what the word has to accomplish in establishing scenery, people, and depth of feeling in the continuum of a radio play (MacLoughlin, 1998, pp. 56–57), and it has also been included in a 2021 volume of papers *Audionarratology: Lessons from Radio Drama* where McWhinnie's views on sound drama writing are contextualised in the history of developing the audio dramatist's critical vocabulary in Great Britain (Bernaerts & Midlorf, 2021, pp. 32–33).

The scene begins with the fade in of a running car which slows to a stop. Innes asks his Indian driver what the problem is and is told they need to cool the engine. Innes accepts the situation. He accepts it is the driver who makes these decisions and, of course, they are in the hot jungle. Innes says it is very dusty all around them, but the driver explains it is the road which is making it look like this because inside the jungle is green. Innes sees a railway line and asks where it goes:

DRIVER: No place into the jungle, stop.
INNES: Eh? ...Why?
DRIVER: Military reasons. Now abandoned.
INNES: Wartime?
DRIVER: Yes, wartime. In Assam there were armies all the time. Now in the jungle here live all things.
INNES: Er—animals, you mean?
DRIVER: No, *things*. Wheels and chains gone rusting. Old guns and tanks not moving. In one place were fifty thousand teeth-brush, abandoned. All Abandoned.
(*pause.*)
(*Car starts and moves off. Fade out.*)

(McWhinnie, 1959, pp. 52)

In less than a minute, Cooper has conjured the atmosphere of heat and exhaustion, vividly painted in the imagination of the listener the locale where most of the play's action will take place, provided new insight and revelation about the central character, and carried the plot forward. McWhinnie said it was 'rich in overtones' (ibid) and who can fail to be fascinated and inspired by the idea of 50,000 toothbrushes abandoned among rusting old guns and tanks in the middle of the jungle. All that is missing is the image of 50,000 dentures.

In *The Battle of the Warsaw Ghetto* Morton Wishengrad had to find a way of using dramatic dialogue to tell the story of how disease as much as deportation to concentration and extermination camps destroyed human life. This he would do by making the tragedy agonisingly personal to his central character Isaac Davidson who describes his family and everyone around them having to deal with hunger then followed by plague. Of the 17,800 people who died from spotted typhus in Warsaw, 15,758 were Jews. Isaac says he is speaking without irony when observing that imprisoning plague behind a brick wall became a great achievement in medical science. Wishengrad scripts Isaac repeating the figure of Jewish deaths at 15,758, and then after a pause, says Dvora Davidson his wife made the figure 15,759. Statistics in scale, sometimes so difficult to imagine, become human, emotional, and deeply personal when a name, human character, and life can be added by a single factor of one.

Isaac now moves from the narrating voice into the dramatised agony of consoling his grieving son in the shared room that is their home in the ghetto. He gently urges Samuel to leave her as he cannot help her any more. All the while his boy is crying out for his mother and sobbing. In perhaps the most poignant and tender dialogue ever written for a radio play Isaac asks his son to come to him because she cannot hear him anymore. He asks him not to cry as he washes his face as his mother would surely not want to see him like this. He asks Samuel to do something for him and the boy says he will try if he can.

He asks him to go into his corner and try to sleep, but Samuel says he is not able to do that at this time. So Isaac asks him to turn his face away, right to the wall so that he is unable to see what his father has to do next. Samuel asks his father not to hurt her. But Isaac says no one can hurt her now. He has to take off her clothes which he describes with such pathos and heart-breaking detail: her apron; her dress; and the shoes given to her by Uncle Avrum. He quotes from *The Book of Job* in the Bible's Old Testament: 'Naked came I out of my mother's womb and naked shall I return thither' (Job 1:21). Samuel is struggling to suppress his sobbing when he says he realises his father will be carrying her body outside into the street.

This is something Isaac has to do. He will do this after dark because he has to. She must be left there cold, naked, and nameless. Father and son know what has to happen. They must not know who she is because of the bread cards. They will take away her bread card which Isaac and Samuel both need to stay alive, if she can be identified in any way (Barnouw/Wishengrad, 1945, p. 39).

Wishengrad uses dialogic dramatic exposition to tell a story which Allied governments and their mainstream news media struggled to comprehend and report in 1943. He said 'The scene in which Isaac disrobes Dvora was written in a few minutes. I reread it and threw it away. My wife found it on the floor and made me reinstate it' (Barnouw/Wishengrad, 1945, p. 33). This was the first telling of the operation of the Nazis' Final Solution for European Jewry through radio drama. Wishengrad was determined it would also be the first to dramatise their defiance and resistance.

Companion Website Resources

Additions and Updates for Chapter 7 Dialogue and the Sound Story https://kulturapress.com/2022/08/12/updates-for-chapter-7-dialogue-and-the-sound-story/

US Radio Drama History https://kulturapress.com/2022/08/29/us-radio-drama-history/

Winsome Pinnock and Radio Drama https://kulturapress.com/2022/08/29/winsome-pinnock-and-radio-drama/

Radio Drama and Dramatising Classical and Modern Literature https://kulturapress.com/2022/08/29/radio-drama-and-dramatising-classical-and-modern-literature/

Short Story Radio Drama – Broken Porcelain by Tim Crook https://kulturapress.com/2022/08/23/short-story-radio-drama-broken-porcelain-by-tim-crook/

Independent Radio Drama Productions IRDP https://kulturapress.com/2022/08/29/independent-radio-drama-productions-irdp/

Arch Oboler and Radio Drama https://kulturapress.com/2022/08/28/arch-oboler-and-radio-drama/

Archibald MacLeish and Radio Drama https://kulturapress.com/2022/08/28/archibald-macleish-and-radio-drama/

8

SUSTAINING THE SOUND STORY

Techniques and Devices

Ironic Transposition of Character in Audio Drama Play Development

There is an argument that in any 5 minutes of audio drama the listener requires an intensity of dramatic experience and expression, which is in a sense mini-climactic. The main character or a subsidiary character needs some epiphany, developmental learning, or character changing event that is intensely entertaining and for the purpose of achieving continued attention from the audience asks further fundamental questions of the character and plot. If it can be constructed with a dimension of ironic transposition and understanding between the central character and audience, it can be argued that you would be achieving a higher plane of playwriting. This can often be achieved when juxtaposing and sharing diegetic and non-diegetic knowledge between the characters and listening audience. This is certainly a vehicle for improving the political, cultural, and literary resonances in sound drama writing.

A major inspiration for this technique can be derived from the end of Joseph Conrad's novella *Heart of Darkness* where the messenger or journeyman narrator, Marlow, who is of course the central character and a kind of Jason of the Argonauts or Achilles, has witnessed the complete degradation and breakdown of the charismatic adventurer, journalist, and traveller Kurtz. Instead of bringing civilisation and enlightenment to Africa, he has brought all the evils of colonial exploitation and Conrad implied he had introduced the exigencies of genocide. The narrative unfolds an appalling depiction of what would now be condemned as crimes against humanity. Marlow is fundamentally disillusioned and is present when Kurtz leaves his legacy and final words: 'the horror, the horror'. Kurtz has entrusted to Marlow his papers which on reading appear to be incoherent ramblings and passages of a memoir written by somebody whose personality has descended into madness.

DOI: 10.4324/9780203838181-8

Such an experience is fundamentally character changing for Marlow; not only in his reflection on the European colonial experience in Africa but also in how he, the woman to whom Kurtz is betrothed, and the Belgian European community are supposed to survive and renew themselves after his death. He has to visit Kurtz's fiancée in Brussels who has been seduced by Kurtz's fake ideology and is grieving terribly. While Marlow, and we the audience, have understood the meaning of the 'horror, the horror', what would be the point of the fiancée knowing? Would she be able to understand? When Marlow is confronted with her demand to know Kurtz's last words, Marlow knows he has to lie for the purposes of compassion, to protect himself from having to deal with confronting her with the truth and we are left with intense moral ambivalence. This is how the final scene in Conrad's novella was dramatised in 1989 for UK independent radio and NPR USA. The adaptation dramatised the narrative voices of Kurtz, Marlow, and Conrad himself into a chorus of witnesses, chroniclers, and viewpoints:

INTENDED WOMAN: Ah, but I believed in him more than anyone on earth. more than his own mother, more than... himself. He needed me! Me! I would have treasured every sign, every word, every sign, every glance.

MARLOW: Don't please ...

INTENDED WOMAN: Forgive me... I – I have mourned so long in silence – I... silence...You were with him – to the last? I think of his loneliness. Nobody near to understand him as I would have understood. Perhaps no one to hear...

MARLOW: To the very end...I heard his very last words...

INTENDED WOMAN: Repeat them... I want... I want... something... something to... to live with...

VOICE OF KURTZ: (Heavily echoed) The horror, the horror, the horror, the horror!

INTENDED WOMAN: His last word... to live with... Don't you understand, I love him – I loved him... I loved him!

MARLOW: The last word he pronounced was...your name.

INTENDED WOMAN: I knew it. I was sure! (She begins to weep with grief)

VOICE OF KURTZ: I wanted justice...only justice...

VOICE OF MARLOW: I couldn't, I could not tell her.

VOICE OF KURTZ: The horror, the horror!

VOICE OF MARLOW: It would have been too dark, too dark altogether.

Thames river actuality.

VOICE OF CONRAD: Marlow ceases talking, sitting apart, indistinct and silent, in the pose of a meditating Buddha. The offing is barred by a black bank of clouds, tranquil waters of the Thames flow sombre... flowing under overcast skies to the uttermost ends of the earth.

VOICES OF CONRAD, MARLOW AND KURTZ: ...leading to the heart of an immense darkness.

[THE END]

(Crook, 1999, p. 193)

Has Marlow done the right thing? He has limited options. He does not want to tell her the truth. He could say Kurtz was not able to say anything. But what he does say reveals something about his own kindness and complicity in the crimes he has witnessed in the Congo and the cover-up he has become a part of. He is furthering deception. He says to her that the last words Kurtz ever uttered were her name. Why can the audience be deeply affected by this? As a result, the love the Intended woman has for Kurtz becomes a fantasy and a lie, and the reality of what Kurtz has done to himself and his society and culture is covered up through false consciousness. This compounds the colonial brutality of the Belgian imperialist project in the Congo. The ironic transposition is that we have also become part of the limited circle of people in the mind world of the novel who know the truth of Kurtz's own indictment and judgement of himself. All that he has contributed and left to the world is horror and more horror. Those who know include Marlow and anyone in the boat with Kurtz when he died. Everybody else in the world of the story, the other diegetic participants of the narrative are left in ignorance.

However, the irony here is not fully appreciated by the Nigerian writer and academic, Professor Chinua Achebe, who argues the novel has been written by a racist. He had been attracted to Conrad's book as a child and found him seductive, but as he grew up and became educated about the power relationships between Europeans and Africans, he became appalled at the portrayal of his fellow Africans as unattractive beings and the use of inappropriate language. Achebe argues Conrad creates a setting and backdrop which:

> [E]liminates the African as human factor. Africa as a metaphysical battlefield devoid of all recognizable humanity, into which the wandering European enters at his peril. Can nobody see the preposterous and perverse arrogance in thus reducing Africa to the role of props for the break-up of one petty European mind? But that is not even the point. The real question is the dehumanization of Africa and Africans which this age-long attitude has fostered and continues to foster in the world.
>
> *(Achebe, 1988, pp. 251–261)*

Ironic Transposition – from Conrad to Bleasdale

There are three powerful examples of ironic dramatic transposition in Alan Bleasdale's controversial television drama series from 1986 *The Monocled Mutineer* which I would like to highlight. For many years, the series was largely forgotten and only available for viewing on DVD. However, it was resurrected in 2017 and rebroadcast by the BBC. Bleasdale takes the Conradian 'horror, horror' concept into the middle development of his central character Percy Toplis. As a mouthy and truculent Royal Army Medical Corps (RAMC) corporal he is detailed to do execution duty for a court martialed officer called Cruikshank who is to be shot for cowardice. In taking up the anti-war counter-cultural ideology of the 1960s, primarily driven by the radical rebellion of youth culture against the Vietnam war and the canonisation of First World War 'pity of war' poets, Bleasdale dramatises a 'horror, horror' firing squad scene where Cruikshank does the very opposite of dying like an officer and gentleman. Ratings in the firing squad cannot shoot straight and after the condemned prisoner is given the coup de grâce, some of them are shown to throw up. Cruikshank is pathetic throughout. Crying and sobbing, he has to be forcefully tied to the chair for the firing squad. After being grievously wounded and before being shot through the head, he convulses in the mud and gravel howling 'mother, mother' and with the potential ironic distortion of his cries sounding like the German word for mother – die Mutter, which when spoken into the ground through tears and dirt could also sound like murder.

This shockingly realistic execution scene explains why Toplis decides to reinvent himself as an officer through impersonation. The logic in his thinking is also ironic. If the military can arbitrarily strip an officer of his commission so he can be executed as a private as they did with Cruikshank, why shouldn't Toplis choose to take on a commission of his own volition to have a better life and avoid being ordered to participate in needless slaughter and become cannon fodder?

Having now taken on the identity of an officer, Toplis decides to visit Cruikshank's beloved mother who has been deceived about her son's death through an army cover-up. Toplis tells her only part of the truth in the sense that he conveys the accuracy of Cruikshank's last words that he was crying out for his mother, but not in the context of a humiliating and disgraceful execution for cowardice. He pretends this happened while in action and the ironic transposition is most intriguing. What we know and Toplis knows and the grieving mother does not know is that he died in a most disgusting and unjust manner, but we also know that ideologically it was also a form of 'action' in the sense of being war's hopelessness, and in a meaningless wasteland of humanitarian reality. We share with Cruikshank's mother the sense that her son made as much of a contribution to the Great War as anyone else. So the cover-up of his being reported killed in action and included on war memorials is emotionally, philosophically, and ideologically ironic. The dramatic intensity and suspense in the scene is driven by what we wonder Toplis will say to her and our curiosity about his motives which are perhaps both selfish to himself and also compassionate to the memory of Lieutenant Cruikshank and the feelings of his mother. At the end of his apparent mercy mission, he asks to borrow money so he can afford to stay in a hotel in York.

The impersonation, in itself a moral deception and actual crime, becomes the opportunity for the central character to express and determine truth through irony. As with Conrad's Heart of Darkness, again a grieving relative wants comfort and the messenger has to balance compassion and kindness with truth and brutal reality.

But the significant difference in this play of irony in The Monocled Mutineer is that Toplis does two things: He tells the truth as well as ensuring that he was using words that could give her solace. This turns the brutality and injustice of what happened to Cruikshank and all the other soldiers executed for alleged cowardice into something noble and poetic.

Dramatic Ironic Transposition Through Interiority

Later on in the series, Bleasdale presents another scene with ironic dynamics that inform and change the central character. Toplis is depicted with his own mother – an alcoholic who had more or less had to abandon Toplis when he was a child. She has never forgotten him, has gone blind, and lives on her own in abject poverty. He visits her as an adult pretending to be a doctor. As she cannot recognise him physically and he does not wish to reveal that he has been prepared to see her, out of love, they are in a position to express things about each other that they would not be able to do if they had confronted each other with the knowledge of their real identities. In the process both characters are able to learn things about how much they mean to each other when they find themselves compelled to reference each other in a plane of misunderstanding and subterfuge.

Bleasdale has intensified the ironic understanding through rendering blind aspects of each character's existence: Mrs. Toplis has a physical blindness and the moral blindness of not realising what she has done to her son; Percy Toplis has the moral blindness of cowardice in not being able to retrieve his mother's love as an adult, to forgive her for her past mistakes, but at the same time he discovers that the subterfuge of his existence as a fake and conman enables him to reach out to his mother in a way that he could not if he visited her openly as her son.

Deceit in the performance of everyday life by Toplis operates as an external shield and body armour when the emotional agony of what he is confronting is too overwhelming and unbearable to face in his true self and identity. There is something inherently tragic that Toplis cannot achieve the necessary emotional and human connections with those he loves and respects without pretending to be somebody else.

The ironic resonance of Conradian and Bleasdale dramatic construction of irony when messengers convey condolences, memory, and legacy to their loved ones after witnessing catastrophic events in human history further inspired a key moment in the stage play *Devils On Horseback* (2018). This dramatised the secret trials of conscientious objectors at Deptford Town Hall London during the First World War. One of the characters, Haskett, is a working class builder whose short-tempered personality undermines his application for exemption before the tribunal. His service on the Western Front breaks down into outbursts of anger and insubordination directed at officers. He is court martialled and pays the ultimate price for angry and repeated breaching of the code of military discipline.

As he is made an example before the firing squad, conscientious objectors being punished for refusing to wear the King's uniform are forced to attend his court martial where he is condemned as a warning of what they may face. When Haskett is told he is going to be shot at dawn he repeats his character's catchphrase – the first word being an Anglo-Saxon four letter expletive beginning with the letter 'f'. Henry Albrow is one of those conscientious objectors who survives the Great War and by the time of the Second World War has become a lawyer working for the Ministry of Labour. He is trying to mediate a different approach to pacifists in wartime:

A YOUNG SPITFIRE PILOT IN UNIFORM AND WEARING DEC-
ORATION OF DISTINGUISHED FLYING CROSS POPS HIS HEAD
AROUND THE DOOR.

PETER HASKETT (HARRY HASKETT'S SON): Mr Albrow?

ALBROW: Yes, that is I. Sorry for all the commotion.

PETER HASKETT: You sent me a letter. About my father.

ALBROW: Ah, you would be Flight Captain Peter Haskett?

PETER HASKETT: Yes, sir.

ALBROW: I'm so pleased you could come.

PETER HASKETT: I haven't much time. I'm flying out to Canada to take on a
training command.

ALBROW: I'd heard.

PETER HASKETT: All a bit of a funk. Far rather be on operations.

ALBROW: Your experience in the Battle of Britain will be vital to pass on to
the new pilots perhaps?

PETER HASKETT: I suppose so.

ALBROW: I've been tying some loose ends from my past. Bit of a coincidence.
Here I am doing legal work for the war, and it just so happened I was…

PETER HASKETT: So you knew him, my father?

ALBROW: Yes, I did.

PETER HASKETT: He died over there in France. I'd hadn't even been born.

ALBROW: Yes, I know.

PETER HASKETT: My mother won't talk about it.

ALBROW: A lot of people would rather not.

PETER HASKETT: Were you there? What was he like?

ALBROW: Fire in the belly. He was a…a warrior. Yes…he hated the injustice
of it all.

PETER HASKETT: Were you there when he?

ALBROW: No. No… but just before. Such courage. Such passion. We all
admired him for it.

PETER HASKETT: Thank you. Thank you. I've been trying to find out something. Nobody seems to know anything.

ALBROW: Well, there were so many who didn't come back.

PETER HASKETT: Can you remember?

ALBROW: Remember what?

PETER HASKETT: The last thing you heard him say?

ALBROW: Ffuah! (STOPPING HIMSELF) Forward! He said: 'Forward to
Victory'. And then laughed. ('FORWARD TO VICTORY' IS THE
SLOGAN ON DEVILS ON HORSEBACK RECRUITMENT
POSTER – SOME OF THEM COULD BE ON THE WALLS OF
THE COUNCIL CHAMBER)

PETER HASKETT: Forward to victory?

ALBROW: A joke you see. He had a great sense of humour. We all loved him
    for it. Made us all feel better. Particularly when he was riled you know.
PETER HASKETT: Thank you. I really appreciate that.
ALBROW: My pleasure. The least I can do.
PETER HASKETT: Well I'd better be…
ALBROW: Of course. Thank you for coming.

(Crook, 2018)

Ironic Transposition Through Tagged Words, Phrases and Sounds Between Scenes

Word and phrase tags combined with sound effects which bridge scene changes, cross-fading sound effects as sound symbols in the switch between time-frames, and interior and exterior characterisation offer further opportunities for ironic transposition. The film director Alfred Hitchcock was expert at transposing time with flashbacks in his films and using sound only for this purpose. This would not be the first time I have expressed appreciation of how he achieves this in the 1935 film *The 39 Steps* (Crook, 2011, p. 15) when the main character Richard Hannay is recalling what the woman secret agent told him before her murder. The cleaner enters Hannay's flat and discovers the knifed woman's body, she turns round and screams, but instead of the scream of the actor we hear the screech of the Flying Scotsman's steam engine whistle. Tagging can also be the use of one kind of sound and then cross-fading or jump editing that with another in the following scene. In *The English Patient* (1996), the film's sound designer, Walter Murch, tags/cross-fades the tapping of a character's pen with the rhythmic drumming of Bedouin in the North African desert to bridge a flashback.

I have detailed the sound symbolism or tags transitioning interior narration with past recollection of realistic exterior existence in my direction of the radio play *Coffee and Tea 90p* by Tony Duarte from 1991 (Crook, 1999, pp. 165, 176, 179–180). The beginning of the play builds tension as the apparent trauma on the part of the central character involves rerunning his memory to an event that had a catastrophic impact on his relationship. The swooshing cafeteria till bell sound used as the junction is an antique cash-desk bell sound being reversed and vary-sped.

Tom Stoppard scripts imaginative word and sound tag bridges between the scenes of his classic radio play *Artist Descending a Staircase*, first produced and broadcast by BBC Radio 3 in 1972. Three very old artists, who have been friends since early manhood, share an attic. Now one of them is dead. The circumstances are mysterious. Evidence concerning the manner of his death exists on a tape-recording. But what is Truth? The detail of the inventive and imaginative plot design is discussed in Chapter 9, but Stoppard constructs scene changing backwards and then forwards.

In the junction between the first and second scene, Beauchamp says he thought he was paying Donner the compliment of allowing him to hear how his master-tape recording work was progressing. In the flashback, Stoppard directs the fade up of the sound of Beauchamp's 'master-tape' as a bubbling cauldron sound mix of squeaks, gurgles, crackles, and 'other unharmonious noises'. Beauchamp lets this play for longer than anyone would really listen to. When Beauchamp asks Donner what he thinks of it with the proviso that he takes his time and chooses his words carefully, Donner says he thinks it is rubbish (Stoppard, 1994, p. 119). The description of the role of a tape-recording in the first scene segues into the sound of the tape in playback in the flashback scene.

The same bridging tag of words and then sound is used between scenes 2 and 3. Donner is recalling a past event when he was convinced Martello was telling him the truth. He had damaged a figure he was working on when he brought him a cup of tea. In the flashback junction, Stoppard writes that Martello is scraping and chipping, clicking his tongue, scraping again, and then sighs. Donner is heard saying 'That's it—help yourself to sugar' (Stoppard, 1994, p. 125). In this reverse time bridging, the sound is intriguing; particularly in the context of having tea and being offered sugar while doing artwork.

Ironic resonances and transpositions give audio plays an enticing and driving imperative for following the story and plot. They also sometimes resonate as one of the most memorable dramatic moments of a play. I would put forward an excellent example in a BBC radio drama production of the Georges Simenon novel *Maigret Sets a Trap*. Denholm Elliot is playing Chief Inspector Jules Maigret with an adaptation script by Aubrey Woods. The powerful moment marks the climax of an important scene, but it is not the end of the play.

This is the story of a serial killer dominated by his mother and wife. They compete for his affections and control over him. While he is already in custody for five murders of women on the streets of Paris, Maigret suspects either his mother or his wife has tried to imitate his modus operandi by killing another young woman victim to bring about his release.

Maigret confronts both of them with the killer Marcel Moncin also present. When the mother confesses, she begins to flounder when asked to describe the colour of the victim's dress. One short line 'The dress was blue' is uttered by his wife who up until now has said nothing in the scene. Maigret, in the style of Sherlock Holmes, sets out his theory of why he knows the latest victim is either Moncin's mother or wife. He acknowledges the killing was ostensibly like all the other ones because of the presence of stabbing and clothes slashing. But there is one key and significant difference. The young woman killed at the corner of the Rue de Maistre was tall and slim when all the others dispatched by Moncin had been short and plump; somewhat ironically the same shape as the two women in his office.

Maigret provocatively suggests they are unwilling to accept that every time he killed, in his mind he was killing them. Maigret says Moncin was trying to separate himself from his wife and mother so that he could have some kind of freedom and existence away from them. Maigret taunts them by demanding to know if they really think it is worth risking their necks on the guillotine to save such a man. But perhaps it is a simple matter of them wanting to preserve and protect what they consider to be their property. Moncin's mother is the first to crack under the pressure. His wife, Yvonne, remains silent while her mother-in-law says she is perfectly willing to die for her son because he is her child. She has no concern about what he has done and equally she is not interested in the fate of women she describes as 'little tarts' who dare to walk the streets of Montmartre at night.

Maigret presses her to confirm that she killed Jeanine Laurent. When she says she did not know her name, Maigret rephrases the question and asks if she is responsible for last night's murder in the Rue de Maistre. Yes, replies Moncin's mother, but then Maigret says she can surely tell him the colour of the victim's dress. The mother stalls again. It was dark, she says. Oh no it was not, replies Maigret, for she was killed less than 5 yards from a street lamp:

MOTHER: I didn't pay attention.
MAIGRET: But when you slashed the material? The colour Madame?
YVONNE MONCIN: The dress was blue.

(Woods/BBC, 1976)

'The Deadly Attachment' is the title of an episode from the *Dad's Army* sitcom series, but it is not as famous as one comedic line which it contains and has become legendary in British comedy and for any fan of the series produced for television and radio between 1968 and 1977. It was episode 1 of season 6 on television and episode 49 of the BBC radio drama series. The Home Guard platoon is tasked with looking after a surly and menacing U-Boat captain and his crew. Captain Mainwaring and his part-time soldiers mock Adolf Hitler. The German Captain is keeping a list of people who will have to meet their just deserts when the Germans win the war. Private Pike spurts out a 'Hitler half barmy, so's his army' ditty which provokes the Nazi submariner to demand his name so it is added to those who will face future arrest and retribution. Captain Mainwaring cries out 'Don't tell him Pike'.

In the build-up to this famous moment in British comedy, Captain Mainwaring had been dismissing the German submariners as a nation of 'ignorant automatons' led by a madman who has made himself look like Charlie Chaplin. Captain Muller is outraged the Home Guard officer should dare to compare Hitler to Charlie Chaplin described by Muller as a 'non-Aryan clown'. He brings out his notebook to announce he is going to keep a list of all the insults he and his men are confronted with. Mainwaring's name will be in it and when they win the war, he will be brought to account.

The scene then reverts to the classic pantomime ritual of Mainwaring saying they are not going to win the war followed by 'Oh yes we are', Oh no you're not,' and 'Oh yes we are'. This is when Pike intervenes with his Hitler jerk and half barmy ditty while sitting at the top of the ladder nearby while holding the platoon's Tommy Gun:

CAPTAIN MULLER: (*Interrupting Pike*) You boy. Your name will also go on the list. What is it?
CAPTAIN MAIN: Don't tell him Pike!

(Croft & Perry, 2002, p. 167 Adjusted to match radio adaptation)

Again this line and dramatic moment is not even the climax and resolution of the episode, but it is a key turning point in revealing ironic characterisation and developing conflict. The Home Guard platoon consists of civilians volunteering in a home defence militia with no pay, and they are frequently accused of playing at soldiers; particularly by the Head Air Raid Warden Hodges. Mainwaring's gaffe is a combination of sheer incompetence and amateurism and well-intentioned defiance and goodwill. He is as stupid as the teenage boy he is often dismissing publicly for being 'stupid'. Co-writer Jimmy Perry based the character Pike on recollections of his young teenage self actually serving in the Home Guard during WWII and being called a 'stupid boy' by his father when he said his ambition in life was to be a film star.

The exchange also raises the threat level and menace presented by the U-boat prisoners. The British part-timers appear to have all the guns and power over their German prisoners, but the Germans appear to have so much more guile and intelligence. Giving Pike's name away so carelessly is an indication of perhaps worse things to come.

My next selection of ironic resonance and transposition is from cinema, but I have previously defined it as pure audio drama which happens to just be on the screen (Crook, 2013, pp. 1–2). In this sequence from Frank Darabont's *Shawshank Redemption* (1994), Andy Dufresne's campaign of writing begging letters to improve the prison library bears fruit. He has been imprisoned for a murder he did not commit. While in the penitentiary, he has become enthralled by the potential of the donation of a gramophone and 78 rpm records. The film uses the power of the sound in a record of the opera singers and Dufresne's subversive playing of it on the prison's public address system to use sound poetically and with an expression of exquisite dramatic irony.

It is also poignant characterisation of Andy Dufresne's friend 'Red' who articulates how the music liberates the inmates spiritually even though they remain physical prisoners:

SOUND OF A RECORD PLAYER NEEDLE SCRATCHING ON AN OLD 78 RPM RECORD AND BEING PLAYED OUT OF THE PRISON'S PUBLIC ADDRESS SYSTEM
    BEGINS PLAYING THE LETTER DUET FROM THE MARRIAGE OF FIGARO.

PRISON OFFICER: (*Doing his business on the toilet, with his trousers around his ankles*) Andy do you hear that?
MUSIC CONTINUES. SOUND OF ANDY LOCKING THE PRISON OFFICER IN THE TOILET FROM THE OUTSIDE AND LOCKING HIMSELF INSIDE THE PRISON'S PA SYSTEM CONTROL ROOM.
FEEDBACK SEGUES INTO HOW THE OPERA SOUNDS THROUGH THE SPEAKERS BLARING OUT INTO THE OPEN YARD OUTSIDE WHERE HUNDREDS OF PRISONERS BEGIN TO LISTEN AND STOP WHAT THEY ARE DOING.
PRISON OFFICER: (*Struggling to open the locked door of the toilet.*) Dufresne! Dufresne! Andy let me out! (*Banging on the door.*) Andy? Andy?

RED IN NARRATION: I have no idea to this day what those two Italian ladies were singing about. The truth is, I don't want to know. Some things are best left unsaid. I like to think they were singing about something so beautiful it can't be expressed in words, and makes your heart ache because of it. I tell you those voices soared higher and farther than anybody in a grey place dares to dream. It was like some beautiful bird flapped into our drab little cage and made those walls dissolve away. And for the briefest of moments every last man at Shawshank felt free. It pissed the Warden off something awful.

(Crook, 2011, p. 2; Darabont, 1994)

This moment is again a dramatic revelation of hope and possibility for a situation that is so depressing, unfair, and heart-breaking for many of the inmates of Shawshank including Andy Dufresne himself. Sound conveys a tremendous paradox that people can remain free on the inside whatever the constraints and injustices denying them freedom, liberty, and art.

In *The Battle of the Warsaw Ghetto*, Morton Wishengrad manages to evoke devastating truths about the Nazi persecution of the Jews during the Second World War. It is through the experiences of the fictional family Isaac, Dvora, and Samuel Davidson that he dramatises the diminishing value and dignity of human beings. I would argue there are significant, revealing, ironic, and dramatic turning points on every page. Dvora has to quickly come to terms with all the sadness attending the day-by-day humiliation and stripping away of human pride and self-respect. She is being shown the way to their living quarters. A woman takes them into one room where she is also living. But you live here, says Dvora. The woman explains that is in one corner. The other corner is for her Dvora's family. Dvora thought it would never come to this, but the woman does not give much time to dwell on this because they really should appreciate how lucky they are to have a window.

Bourgeois middle-class politeness takes over momentarily. Dvora says they really shouldn't trouble the woman any further. Perhaps there is some other place? The woman laughs bitterly. Any illusions Dvora has dissolved into despair when the woman says before the Ghetto was walled 50,000 people lived in these slums. Now there are half a million. The woman leaves Dvora and the listeners with this desolating advice: 'I know a man who sleeps in a vault in the cemetery. Don't be a fool, come in. It's still better than the cemetery' (Barnouw/Wishengrad, 1945, pp. 35–36). For home to be better than the cemetery has an appalling implication for the Jews of the Warsaw Ghetto and the writing of this dramatic and ironic resonance is a credit to Morton Wishengrad's achievement as a radio dramatist.

Companion Website Resources

Additions and Updates for Chapter 8 Sustaining the Sound Story: Techniques and Devices https://kulturapress.com/2022/08/12/updates-for-chapter-8-sustaining-the-sound-story/

Roy Williams and Radio Drama https://kulturapress.com/2022/08/29/roy-williams-and-radio-drama/

Sir Lenny Henry and Radio Drama https://kulturapress.com/2022/08/29/sir-lenny-henry-and-radio-drama/

Tanika Gupta and Radio Plays https://kulturapress.com/2022/08/29/tanika-gupta-and-radio-plays/

Mabel Constanduros and Radio Drama https://kulturapress.com/2022/08/29/mabel-constanduros-and-radio-drama/

Martin Esslin Radio Drama and National Theatre of the Air https://kulturapress.com/2022/08/29/martin-esslin-radio-drama-and-national-theatre-of-the-air/

9

PLOTTING THE SOUND STORY

Techniques and Devices

The Mechanics

Plotting audio drama is the equivalent of engineering the sound play with words, music, sound effects, and silence. The script is the equivalent of the architect's technical drawing and artistic design for a building. Keith Richards talked about the mechanics of radio drama with structuring, planning transitions, paying attention to the opening sequence, holding the listener's attention throughout, and excising surplus writing or the cutting of scenes. He said: 'a radio piece, like poetry, can have a musical structure where you might explore a theme with variations, or run two or more themes together like a fugue, or write a solo piece with some accompaniment' (Richards, 1991, pp. 21–22). Felix Felton was a polymath of the BBC during the 1930s, 40s, and 50s and as an accomplished actor, radio dramatist, composer, and director/producer he was able to provide an influential fusion of all these arts in his 1949 book *The Radio Play*. He was a key figure in BBC training, and newly appointed producers at the BBC, including George Orwell, would have to attend induction courses in programme production conceived and instructed by him.

Felton saw the structuring of sound programmes very much like the rhythm and movements of music and explained how he applied the method of the Rondo form:

> This consists of a principal tune 'A', followed by another tune 'B', 'A' is then repeated; then comes a third tune 'C'; then 'A: again; then a fourth tune "D", and so on'.
>
> *(Felton, 1949, p. 105)*

He talked about when a change of key was desirable, he would introduce a new light section of the programme 'like a musical scherzo' (Felton, 1949, p. 107).

DOI: 10.4324/9780203838181-9

Tom Stoppard discloses his structural planning for his radio play *Artist Descending a Staircase* in the publication of his *Plays for Radio 1964–1991*. There are three main male characters: Martello, Beauchamp, and Donner in their senior years and correspondingly their younger selves and relationship with the blind woman character Sophie. It is a murder mystery about one of them, Donner, dying by falling down a flight of stairs. But was he pushed and who killed him? The title references the 1912 painting by Marcel Duchamp 'Nude Descending a Staircase, No. 2'. A tape recording of Donner's death constitutes sonic evidence and is part of the radiophonic tapestry of the mystery and investigation because Beauchamp is a soundscape artist fascinated by recording the sound of everyday life. The plot is a process of flashback and flashforward; something Keith Richards could describe as prospective exposition and retrospective exposition. Stoppard set out his plan in the following way:

There are 11 scenes. The play begins in the here-and now; the next five scenes are each a flashback from the previous scene; the seventh, eighth, ninth, tenth, and eleventh scenes are, respectively, continuations of the fifth, fourth, third, second, and first. So the play is set temporally in six parts, in the sequence ABCDEFEDCBA

    A = here and now
    B = a couple of hours ago
    C = Last week
    D = 1922
    E = 1920
    F = 1914

(Stoppard, 1994, p. 111)

Keith Richards creatively set out a diagram of the play's scenic structure (Richards, 1991, 21) which gives clarity to the Stoppard scheme in the form of a descending staircase and then an ascending staircase:

Plot descending through time: 1 – The present, 2 – A few hours previously, 3 – A week earlier, 4 – 1922, 5 – 1920, 6 – 1914 – The war begins.

Plot ascending through time: 7 – 1920, 8 – 1922, 9 – A week earlier, 10 – A few hours previously, 11 – The present.

Richards' diagram is an amusing appreciation of the intellectual and artistic genre of Stoppard's writing, which is to explore with some Beckettian style humour the meaning and purpose of art with some delightful mocking of modernism. And if you will forgive my potential plot spoiler, it could be said it would not be a Tom Stoppard play if Martello and Beauchamp were ever to solve the mystery of their friend's apparent murder.

Audio Drama Plot Peculiarities

I have always subscribed to the view that audio drama has much in common with literary prose and poetry, and at the same time it is a very different form of story-telling and requires its own technique:

> The active audience in the line of communication is one person. Radio's fifth dimension of narrative communication, the listener's imagination, is central to the cognitive, metaphysical and subconscious experience of the reader of written poetry and prose. However, listening to radio plays, like watching live stage theatre performances, involves a limited time frame. The listener's imagination may not be the contained space of the theatre, but the commitment in time is contained in the same way. The reader of literature can stop and resume, can vary the pace of imaginative interaction, which in radio drama and stage drama is controlled by the performance. In this regard, audio drama has a strong similarity to music. The composition depends for its expression on interpretation and performance. This is not so with literature. This means that radio plays can apply some narrative elements with great effect in the construction of plot, but because of the exigencies of contained time and the fact that radio drama is performed rather than read silently, the emphasis in structuring radio plays must be on the dramatic rather than the narrative.
>
> *(Crook, 1999, p. 162)*

One of the most memorable recommendations in Shaun MacLoughlin's *Writing for Radio* is that words should be used as flying sculptures (MacLoughlin, 1998, pp. 55–56). He was referencing the French poet Paul Claudel who conjured this vivid image when defining the tangible power of spoken language where words are made by inspired and expired breathing with the exercise of mind, life, lips, tongue, and teeth in the articulation of consonants, vowels, and words. Audio drama can be seen and indeed heard as audiogenic sculpture.

Moving from poetry to practicality, Vincent McInerney reminds radio drama-tists that most effective plotting follows what he described as the ODARE scheme:

> ...the unfolding of a play's plot will present the listener with the same five elements necessary to maintain the classical structure of any play in any dramatic medium. That is Opening, Development, Argument, Resolution, Ending. There will always be experimental works in which characters on Hampstead Heath stand up to their necks in giant jam-jars full of sand talking about Jean-Paul Sartre; but true drama demands a rigid structure.
>
> *(McInerney, 2001, p. 92)*

McInerney also argues that there are three basic types of dramatic plots: simple spiral plot which he described as the equivalent of starting at the top of the stairs and falling down; simple plot with complications; and plot plus subplot (McInerney,

2001, pp. 93, 96). In constructing and sequencing scene Pamela Brooke advises writers to always ensure that every scene advances the plot, each scene should be as simple as possible and be part of the balance and unity of the whole play by carrying the plot forward and sustaining 'interest in what's going to happen next' (Brooke, 1995, 117). She advised varying the pace in each scene 'Dramatic pacing is achieved in each scene by gradually increasing the listener's sense that something new is just about to happen' (Brooke, 1995, p. 118).

In the end, there can be only one main overriding purpose in the plotting of a radio play – the listener stays listening to what you started:

> The purpose of plot in radio playwriting is to create a dramatic and narrative structure which can convey aesthetic meaning. It should be able to accommodate characterisation and subtext, establish a firm hold on the listener's attention through a 'trussing' of question marks which swell the listener's anticipation and interest in accompanying the story to the climax. Plot in radio playwriting has to achieve the objective of warding off the enemy which includes the heat and cold of distraction from outside stimuli. The temperature of human communication from within the radio play has to be pleasing and sensuous. The gravitational pull of internal emotions which can 'switch off' the listener's imagination has to be 'buttressed' through an ascending and accelerating structure of dramatic storytelling. The gravity of conscious concentration has to be harnessed through a coherence of dramatic narrative. The rising of each scene's upward momentum secures the listener's direction of understanding.
>
> *(Crook, 1999, pp. 162–163)*

Analysing Plot Structure in *The Wasted Years* (1984) by Caryl Phillips

BBC radio drama production during the first half of the 20th century favoured the common plot structure of the microphone or wireless play having the characteristics of the one-act play for theatre – small casts, one plot storyline and usually situated in one setting. One-act plays were a staple cultural form in school-teaching, amateur dramatics, and repertory theatre and a significant royalty income for playwrights. *One Act Plays of Today*, edited by J.W. Marriott, was published in six editions between 1924 and 1934. In the third edition, Marriott quoted from a conference in America where one-act plays were a key form in the Little Theatre industry of the USA from which writers such as Eugene O'Neill had emerged to national and international significance (Marriott, 1926, p. 5). Of the 12 plays included in the 1926 volume, *The Dumb and the Blind* by Harold Chapin, *The Golden Doom* by Lord Dunsany, *Rory Aforesaid* by John Brandane, *The Master of the House* by Stanley Houghton, *Friends* by Herbert Farjeon, *The Bishop's Candlesticks* by Norman McKinnel, *Between the soup and the savoury* by Gertrude Jennings, *Master Wayfarer* by J.E. Harold Terry, *The Pot of Broth* by W.B. Yeats, and *A King's Hard Bargain* by Lt.-Col. W.P. Drury were all produced for broadcast by the BBC. There was a similar uptake by the BBC in relation to the plays selected for the other five volumes in the series.

By 1984, Giles Cooper award-winning plays are much more sophisticated and have the fluidity, scope, and ambition of full-length feature films. This is certainly true of *The Wasted Years* by Caryl Phillips. Here is the play's plot and scene structure for a listening time of 87 minutes 50 seconds:

Scene 1. Present Classroom scene. Confrontation and tension between Solly Daniels and his teacher Mr Teale.

Scene 2. Past. BBC television news archive of West Indian migrants being interviewed on their arrival in Britain in the 1950s.

Scene 3. Street scene between Solly and his friend Tagger. They discuss what they hope to do as they are both leaving school.

Scene 4. Daniels' home. Mother Cynthia asks her son Chris (Solly's younger brother) where his brother is. He doesn't know.

Scene 5. Past. Cynthia and her husband Roy are on the train to London after arriving in Britain by ship. They discuss their hopes and their ambitions for the children they hope to have.

Scene 6. Present. Cynthia interior speech to Roy – gives a report on their sons Solly and Chris as though Roy is no longer with them. Interrupted by Chris who is worried about her health because she is working too hard. They talk about Solly and Chris says they are not getting on so well.

Scene 7. Present. Discotheque with Solly and friend Tagger. They talk about girlfriends. It emerges that Solly likes a girl called Jenny. They are joined by Tagger's girlfriend Tracey. Tagger teases Solly over Jenny and they argue. Solly leaves. Tracey scolds Tagger.

Scene 8. Present. Daniels' home. Solly returns home and is met by his mother Cynthia. Solly complains she is always criticising him. They argue. Solly tries to explain his feelings about being different. He wants to talk about his father. Cynthia is reluctant.

Scene 9. Present. In the bedroom Solly and Chris share. They share anxiety about their mother, but then argue about school. Solly is trying to write a letter.

Scene 10. Past. Archive newsreel interview with white Britons expressing racist attitudes about Black people from the West Indies.

Scene 11. Past. 1966. Cynthia and Roy in their bedroom. Argument develops when Roy describes being discriminated against at work and struggling to get his share of overtime. Cynthia wants to work, but Roy refuses because it challenges his pride.

Scene 12. Present. Classroom scene. Tagger plays a prank by carving 'Jenny' on Solly's desk. Teale enters, calls them a wasted generation, announces there's a disco to celebrate those leaving school and finds the carving on Solly's desk. He suspects Solly, asks him to stay behind, Solly denies doing it and refuses to say who did. Teale tries reaching out to him, but Solly is angered and says he does not want to talk to him. Teale sends him to the Headteacher.

Scene 13. Present. Headteacher's office. He refuses to help Teale get to the bottom of what is troubling Solly and Solly waiting outside is sent on his way.

Scene 14. Present. Girls' Toilet. Tracey and Jenny talk about Solly. Jenny has received a letter from him asking her if she will go out with him.

Scene moves to playground with Tagger and Solly. They are friendly and share a cigarette. Solly describes what happened with Mr Teale and how he did not 'split on him'. Solly agrees to do Tagger's maths test. While these are two separate and sequential dialogues, I have considered these as one scene in terms of the parallel purpose of their respective friendships coinciding with each other in decisions and action.

Scene 15. Past 1969. Bedsitter. Cynthia and Roy. Terrible row between them. Solly is an infant child of 18 months and crying. Roy has had enough of the racism and discrimination in England. Cynthia reveals she is pregnant with another child. Roy says he is going home to the Caribbean if she has another child.

Scene 16. Present. Changing room after game of soccer. Tagger gives Solly a letter Jenny has given to Tracey to pass onto Solly. In the letter she agrees to meet Solly at the Odeon cinema that evening at seven.

Scene 17. Present. On the football pitch. Jenny's brother 'Bates' fouls Solly badly, and bruises his ankle.

Scene 18. Present. Daniels' home. Solly finds out from his brother Chris that their mother is in bed ill. The doctor had been round and it seems she is suffering from exhaustion. They argue after Chris accuses Solly of shouting at her and not helping their mother. Solly cannot go to the Odeon to meet Jenny.

Scene 19. Present. Daniels home. Brothers talk about their worry for their mother who is a single parent and does everything for them.

Scene 20. Present. Cynthia's bedroom. Solly checks in to find out how she is. She says they can both be good boys and says her exhaustion is nothing for them to worry about.

Scene 21. Past. Bedsitter. Final row between Cynthia and Roy. She refuses to have an abortion. She says she is ashamed of him. He says she can keep the children because he is going to reclaim sunshine and real life.

Scene 22. Present. Daniels' home. Solly and Chris arrange to take turns to stay from school to look after their mother. They talk about their father and the surname they should have.

Scene 23. Present. Classroom. Teale announces investigation into theft of money from other boys and everyone will have to stay behind until the culprit owns up. Solly says he can't because his mother is ill, but Teale says he cannot be an exception.

Scene 24. Present. Playground behind toilets. Tracey and Jenny talk and Jenny explains Solly did not turn up for their date. Tracey is critical, but Jenny said he did not have her number and thinks there must have been a good reason for him not being there. Solly arrives to apologise and explain. They talk about their families and agree to see each other again.

Scene 25. Present. Classroom. Teale has the class back for detention but Solly is not there.

Scene 26. Present. Daniels' home. Teale has visited and is in the front room. He explains why people think Solly took the money, which Solly continues to deny. He tries to find out what is worrying Solly, even asking him about his girlfriend. Solly refuses to let him talk to his mother because she is ill, and sends him packing even with the final words: 'get stuffed'.

Scene 27. Present. Daniels' home. Boys' bedroom. Emotional scene between them. Chris says he has noticed Solly crying after Teale left and Solly notices Chris crying over the effect of their arguments and tension between them.

Scene 28. Present. Headteacher's office. Awkward meeting with Mr Teale. Headmaster refuses to help him with Solly and questions Mr Teale's ability to work at their comprehensive.

Scene 29. Past. Train station. Cynthia says goodbye to her husband Roy who is returning to the Caribbean. They part on bad terms after Roy says she should tell their children 'their father was going mad in England and he left before he killed somebody'.

Scene 30. Present. Daniels' home. Solly catches his mother Cynthia talking to his father though because this is in the recollection of their last meeting she is shouting. Solly wants to talk about him. He explains today is his last day at school. She cries when describing why his father left her. Solly says he is so proud of her and what she has achieved and she in turn expresses how proud she is of her boys.

Scene 31. Present. School playground. Tracey and Jenny. Solly has sent Jenny a poem. Jenny is having second thoughts about going out with Solly because of the attitude of her parents. It is implied they would not approve of her going out with a Black boy.

Scene 32. Present. Daniels' home. Teale has given Chris a letter to take home to give to his mother about Solly. Solly has confirmed he is going out with Jenny but asks his brother not to tell their mum. Chris promises not to 'split on' him.

Scene 33. Present. School. Leaving disco. Tagger reveals to Solly he stole the money. Teale greets Solly and says he hopes he will give his mother his letter. Teale tries to reach an understanding and communication with Solly, references identity, and offers to help by giving him his telephone number. For the first time Solly indicates that it would be alright if he saw him again.

Tagger and Tracey join Solly. Tracey explains Jenny will not be coming because of her parents but will be ringing him tomorrow. Jenny's brother appears and tells him he will not be going out with his sister. He racially abuses Solly and when Solly insists his relationship with Jenny is none of his business, Bates tries to beat him up. Teale breaks up the fight. Tagger and Tracey stand up for Solly and explain that Bates started the fight. Solly leaves for home bruised.

Scene 34. Present. Daniels' home. Cynthia attends to Solly's bruise. He tells his mother what has happened doesn't matter and it's all over with. Solly learns they are going on a holiday. The brothers show respect and love for their mother by agreeing to have an early night so they can get up early in the morning.

Scene 35. Present. Boys' bedroom. Solly admits to Chris that he is still going to go out with Jenny Bates.

Scene 36. Present. Cynthia interior to Roy. She says he was right that England was not for them, but she was right to stay and fight for her sons.

Scene 37. Present. Boys' bedroom. Exchange between Solly and Chris indicating that they are now back to being friends as well as brothers.

Scene 38. Present. Cynthia interior to Roy. She says her boys will find their father if they want to. She regrets nothing because they can have a better future in England far away from the demeaning work of 'cutting cane' or 'herding scrawny goats in the West Indies'.

Scene 39. Present. Boys' bedroom. Further exchange between Solly and Chris of brotherly affection. Chris wants to know if Solly's face is still hurting. Solly says 'In the morning, man'.

Scene 40. Present. Cynthia interior to Roy. She ends by affirming that her boys have now got a life and coming to England has given them a chance.
    End.

(Phillips, 1984, pp. 87–141)

I would strongly argue this is one of the finest radio plays ever written for the sound medium. And similar close textual analysis of the structure and language of other Giles Cooper award-winning scripts is more than capable of eliciting a similar conclusion. *The Wasted Years* is technically and creatively strong writing on all fronts. The action remains focused on what happens next. The story is true to the characters and the ideas and themes at the core of the drama.

Phillips has skilfully crafted parallel journeys of conflict between characters who coincide and interact with each other. This impacts and changes relationships and characters. Mr. Teale's struggle to understand Solly's sense of alienation dominates scenes 1, 12, 13, 23, 25, 26, 28, and 33. Their relationship is strained when Teale suspects him of vandalising his desk with graffiti and then stealing money from other students, but his friend Tagger is actually responsible. Teale's efforts to garner support for Solly from his headmaster are met with hostility and the undermining threat that he should move to another school in scenes 13 and 28. Solly and Mr. Teale eventually begin to connect when they both adjust their attitude and approach to each other in scene 33.

The narrative speeches from Cynthia are in character and dramatically intrinsic to the story of her marriage with Roy and what went wrong. This is developed in flashback scenes of newsreel archive, arguments, and imaginative interior speeches to Roy even though he is not there to hear her in scenes 2, 5, 10, 11, 15, 21, 29, and from scene 30 when Cynthia's speaking to Roy morphs into dialogue with Solly and later addresses to him in the present here and now in scenes 36, 38, and

40. All the dialogue is natural speech and easy to listen to. All the dialogue is in character. It is not possible to mistake a line as belonging to somebody else in the play. The speech rhythm in each scene is varied and interesting.

Solly's friendship with Tagger appears to be to Tagger's advantage where his pranks and stealing isolate Solly and target him because of his difference and the prejudice against him in being one of only two Black boys in the school. By the end of the play Tagger and his girlfriend Tracey stand up for him after the racist abuse and attack by Bates over Solly's romantic liaison with Bates' sister Jenny. This is developed through scenes 1, 3, 7, 12, 14, 16, and 33.

Sound effects, setting, atmosphere, and transitions support the plot. Every scene has a point of interest and dramatic purpose. There is no excess of description through dialogue. Character entrances and exits are clear and all changes in time and place through flashback are clear and easy to follow. There is cohesion between main plot and subplots. Resolution is achieved for all directions and imperatives of tension and conflict. The play's opening hooks the listener and the end is inspiring and thought-provoking. Solly's aspiration for a relationship with Jenny undergoes twists and turns through scenes 7, 12, 14, 16, 18, 24, 31, and 33.

The main characters are changed by the action and development of the story. There is a richness in the contrast and balance of character and conflict development. It is entertaining and enlightening with subtlety and elegant writing which also respects the dignity of the characters; particularly the Daniels family. This is represented in the scenes charting the ups and downs in the relationship between Solly and his brother Chris and their relationship with their mother Cynthia through scenes 4, 8, 9, 18, 19, 20, 22, 27, 30, 32, 35, 37, and 39. The characters live and breathe through their dialogue and speak for themselves. Not one scene is superfluous to the dramatic purpose of the story. The most resolving scene for Teale's struggle to reach an understanding with Solly, Solly and Jenny's wish to pursue a relationship despite the racism directed towards him by her family and brother, and the emergence of loyal friendship and support from Tagger and Tracey takes place at the leaving disco in scene 33. The resolution of Solly's tensions within his own family and an understanding and explanation of why his father is not with them takes place in scene 30 and continues through scenes 34–40. The play does not need a preface or introductory explanation. It is self-contained with brilliant exposition.

Checklists for the Audio Drama Writer

I finish with an outline of some checklists that could be applied to the draft or, indeed intended finished script of audio playwriting. I have selected some of the key advice provided in *So You Want to Write Radio Drama* by Claire Grove and Stephen Wyatt. They cite these excellent objectives:

1. You are writing what is to be heard and not seen;
2. Decide well on the point where you intend to start;
3. Think in sound when you are writing; better still speak what you write;

4. Don't tell the listener everything – a reminder of the showing not telling in dramatic exposition and with restraint;
5. Ask yourself 'is this the right point to start the scene'?
6. Raise your stakes by making your play bigger, bolder, funnier, and more exciting;
7. Leave time before you rewrite, listen to your instincts and those of others whose advice you have sought;
8. Is the right voice at the centre of the play in terms of point of view?
9. Do you have the right number of characters to tell the story?
10. Are you clear about the core idea of the play and has it been explored and expressed effectively through the dramatic action?

(Grove & Wyatt, 2013, pp. 7–62)

Pamela Brooke hopes that audio dramatists have been reading their dialogue aloud, picturing the action as they write it, feeling for pacing rhythm in the scenes and have smoothly integrated sound effects and music with dramatic purpose. She suggests adherence to five basic scriptwriting rules:

> Action is better than description
> Characterisation is better than preaching
> Short is better than long
> Simple is better than complex
> Less is better than more

(Brooke, 1995, p. 125)

In *Radio Drama Theory and Practice* in the 'Writing Agenda for Radio Drama' I set out analysis and identification of the building blocks for sound drama along with an analytical template which can obviously be added to or subtracted from. I believe these are the useful tools in the audio dramatist's toolbox, but not all of them have to be used for any project:

Plotting Tools:

1. Central Character
Main character force and focus providing the point of view for the play.

2. Secondary Characters
Character forces who create disruption in the original equilibrium of the central character's life, offer the conflict resistance which strikes the play's essential tension, or generate the developing crises of experience for the central character.

3. Main Plot
It is the deliberately constructed architecture of storytelling which drives the central character from the opening crisis or issue to eventual climax and change/resolution.

4. Secondary/Subsidiary Plot
A related and relevant storyline contributing to tension and conflict.

5. Crisis
This is the dilemma or problem that should be immediately apparent from the beginning of the play

6. Sub-Climax
This is a significant device which builds tension and increases the grade of suspense and excitement for the listener.

7. Main Climax
An exploding and dramatic reaction of conflicting forces that have the effect of resolving and displaying the consequences of the plot's human imperatives. The climax can also disclose the play's essential enigma.

8. Linear and Lateral Time Frames
A linear time frame unfolds a story chronologically. A lateral time frame unfolds the story through flashback or begins a narrative at the end and proceeds to explain the enigma and mystery of the end as a narrative that then switches to the beginning.

9. Narrative Cohesion
This means telling a story with narrative passages interspersed with dramatic scenes.

10. Dramatic Cohesion
This is the presentation of the play's story through dramatic action where character is established and communicated by dialogue and interior monologue communicated in present time.

11. Time Transitional Lintel
This is a sound symbolism or musical bridge which facilitates the lateral transference of the listener's understanding backwards or forwards in time, or in some instances on to a parallel time narrative line.

12. Interior to Exterior Consciousness Transepts
These transepts can be a simple cross-fade or sound effect and design.

13. Fifth Dimensional Dome Narrative and Drama
The dome narrative on the fifth dimension involves characterisation and plot line substantially in the imaginative spectacle of the listener.

14. Conscious and Subconscious Transepts
The conscious and subconscious transepts represent the elegance and style of moving from scene to scene in the unfolding play. They tend to be punctuating words,

expressions, thoughts through words or sounds which blend or echo the beginning of the following scene.

15. Long Scene Pacing
This is the pacing of scenes in long and involved interaction between characters.

16. Short Scene Pacing
This has a more exhilarating drive of narrative and dramatic cohesion.

17. Long/Short Scene Pacing
A varied rhythm of scene construction is advisable. There is a danger of repetitive and predictable patterns of structure and euphony having a hypnotic or mesmerising effect on radio audiences.

18. Pyramid Narrative
Plot structure beginning with at least two and sometimes several subplot origin points, building as parallel storylines, occasionally crossing through the common strand of characterisation and conflicting relationships into a climactic point of resolution.

19. Inverse Pyramid Narrative
The inverse pyramid has a multi-strand subplot development that arises out of one incident or one original storyline event and builds into a range of differing experiences and parallel consequences, intertwining irony, and significant points of tension. The resolution has a lateral rather than linear line of coincidence.

20. Arch Narrative
This is a process of providing the exposition of the story after the event. The listener begins the play with the event or crisis which is the source of the story's drama.

21. Arcaded Narrative
Arcaded narrative is a process of story exposition using traditional techniques of story revelation on a progressive timeline.

22. Ironic Framing
This is a narrative structure embedded and woven with ironic lines of information for the listener.

23. Contrapuntal Multi-Track
This is a narrative structure with paralleled main plot and subplots which contrapuntally combine at key points and with a gathering momentum of excitement combine at the end in a climax of contrapuntal harmony.

24. Time Frame Overlap
This narrative structure shuffles timelines like moving sheets of mica. The time dimensions can be past, present, and future.

25. Spiral Staircase Progression
The spiral narrative progression towards climax involves a spiral oscillation with interruption and delay before the story's tension is ultimately resolved.

26. Direct Staircase Progression
This generates the conceit of the listener already knowing the end of the apparent story. The plot line is therefore direct, transparent, and incontrovertible. But the tension and conflict in the play lies in more subtle and ironic nuances of characterisation, internalisation, and exposition.

Analysing the Plot
An analysis of plot will require the identification of the following building blocks:

    a. *The beginning*
    b. *Conflict and attack*
    c. *Rising and balanced action through plot*
    d. *Tension and humour*
    e. *Emotion and ambience*
    f. *Dialogue and purpose*
    g. *The main character*

The listener must be able to identify and experience empathy or sympathy with the main character.

h. *Turning point and climax*
The developing plot and rising crisis need to have changed the main character and/or audience in a fundamental way. This has to arise as a result of the battle between the polarising forces inherent in the plot.

i. *Issue and theme*
There has to be a euphonic balance between the stating of the play's issue and its clarity

j. *Structuring a radio play – the scenes*
Every scene has to have an introduction whether by word, sound effect, atmosphere or music. It should be underpinned by the conflict of two character forces each with an aim and objective. Every scene leaves the listener with tantalising and resonating questions that future scenes are expected to answer.
(Crook, 1999, pp. 163–173)

Companion Website Resources

Additions and Updates for Chapter 9. Plotting the Sound Story: Techniques and Devices https://kulturapress.com/2022/08/12/updates-for-chapter-9-plotting-the-sound-story/

Samuel Beckett and Radio Drama https://kulturapress.com/2022/08/29/samuel-beckett-and-radio-drama/

Tom Stoppard and Radio Plays https://kulturapress.com/2022/08/29/tom-stoppard-and-radio-plays/

Harold Pinter and Radio plays https://kulturapress.com/2022/08/30/harold-pinter-and-radio-plays/

One Act Plays and Radio Drama https://kulturapress.com/2022/08/29/one-act-plays-and-radio-drama/

R C Scriven Radio Playwright https://kulturapress.com/2022/08/29/r-c-scriven-radio-playwright/

10

ENDING THE SOUND STORY

Techniques and Devices

One of the most ungenerous observations that could be made of some radio plays and productions is that they have a tendency to often end as badly as they began. Some end worse than they began. Is it any wonder that anyone bothered to listen to them in the first place? The cold truth is that listeners will not tolerate this situation, and then radio services when looking at the listening surveys will decide not to schedule audio drama at all.

What is meant by the bad ending? The concept of a good ending is arguably a cultural construction. Aesthetically good or bad endings will often depend on the motivation and purpose of the production institution, i.e., is the purpose to provide entertainment and emotional gratification? Is the purpose to provoke a political, philosophical, or social reaction? Certainly, in the playwriting craft, entertainment should be the abiding and crowning objective of a good end.

If we accept the rather controversial proposition that in general the endings of radio plays are rather poor, what is the problem, and why is this the case? It could be argued that the better writers are attracted to the more ruthless and better remunerated production arenas of film, television, and now streaming services such as Netflix and Amazon Prime. Production companies will sack writers if their drafts lack promise. They have the financial resources and executive brutality to keep bringing in somebody who they think can write better. The reputation and fame of an original writer is utterly irrelevant. Consequently, it is not unknown for famous dramatists and experienced, indeed award-winning screen-writers, to have their credits on films when what they wrote originally bears no resemblance to the finished production and any success and real credit is sometimes denied to the effective 'ghost writers' who have been brought in at great expense to deploy surgery, creativity, and brilliance to turn the scripts round.

DOI: 10.4324/9780203838181-10

The audio/radio drama industry does not usually have any such power and range of options. The success of the production is usually dependent on the one writer and ability of the producer/director to cajole and encourage rewrites. It may well be a subjective perception that radio drama has a tendency to lack the intrigue and plot sophistication of the film/screen writing art. It is possible that radio dramatists are persuaded to play it simple by an over-reliance on the idea of the listener's promiscuous and easily distracted commitment to radio consumption. Most radio plays are one-act plot constructions because of the half hour, 45 minute, and 1 hour time frames, and this means endings will have a limited range of resolutions. On the other hand, there should be no handicap to tantalising and intensifying a sense of imaginative suspense in any kind of sound play.

The individual writer and/or the cultural production environment can influence endings. Four factors can be taken into account:

1. Social and political ideology, i.e., the representation of figures and forces that need to win or lose. Who wins the moral battle and confrontation?
2. The purpose of entertainment context, i.e., the audience needs to be left happy, reassured, inspired by ideological purpose, or disturbed by the construction of threat and menace.
3. Desire to be avant-garde, rebellious, and poised against the mainstream culture, i.e., striking an effect that is shocking and fundamentally undermines cultural, political, and social expectations.
4. Symmetry and Gestalt finality through beginning and ending echoes. This is a device often used in radio drama. The opening narrator is in the same position or location, but the situation has changed either in time or fortune. The central character has been changed by the action of the play. This device is exemplified in the 1999 HBO war film directed by John Irvin *When Trumpets Fade*.

The purposes of factor 3 can be subsumed into factors 1 and 2 by encapsulated sub-climatic 'hanging staircases' and 'fire escape' devices of narrative. In other words, the writer can weave a sophisticated process of multiple endings that are scored into a movement of interrupted closures or false resolutions. The audience is at various points led to believe this is the end, but then something happens to make it clear this is not the case. The crisis and tension move up another flight of escalation in suspense and anticipation. A straightforward pattern would be an exploitation of the reversal of the happy/feel good expectation by the process of advance-reversal-final recovery.

A happy goal could be fully established in relation to the plot structure and the audience would emotionally be lulled into a false sense of closure and end. This could be disrupted by a dangerous change of mind by the central character that generates additional struggles, and the end is only achieved where there has to be a sacrifice of one hero(oine) over the other. In other words: One wins, and the other is defeated.

There could also be a contrast between temporal and spiritual victories and defeats or winners and losers, i.e., the central character is defeated in the temporal/mortal frame but victorious in the spiritual/ethical frame. The alcoholic character Ben played by Nicholas Cage in *Leaving Las Vegas* (Lumiere Pictures, 1995, directed by Mike Figgis) performs this function. Ben wins through the enjoyment of human dignity and appreciation of love by the second lead character Sera played by Elisabeth Shue. She is a woman working in the sex industry. Drunk man and prostitute represent the full debasement of bourgeois middle-class respectability. The plot is a narrative that subverts the cultural expectation that everybody should live happily ever after. This is a story that elevates the moral dignity of the alcoholic and the prostitute. Mainstream moral values are being challenged by the ending. Ben dies, and Sera is heartbroken but something spiritual has triumphed. These are essential truths about human nature and relationships that transcend values constructed as social deviancy and the end of the dramatic narrative is consequently thought-provoking and potentially liminal in changing general public opinion and views on notions of goodness, badness, social value, and alienation.

Concentric rings of character development combined with sub-plot intersection can be resolved with a struggle and battle at the end through varying resolutions. The overall effect on the audience is a grand closure or resolution. This technique is offered in the films *Heat* (Warner Bros 1995 written and directed by Michael Mann) and *The Bridges of Madison County* (Warner Bros 1995 directed by Clint Eastwood).

In *Heat* Al Pacino plays Lt. Vincent Hanna and Robert De Niro plays a master criminal Neil McCauley. They are rivals in law and order but develop a mutual respect for each other that even involves a 'pow wow' over coffee. McCauley wants to carry out the final big heist of his career. He has fallen in love with a middle-class designer called Eady. But his 'crew' is disrupted by a psychopath and paedophile called Waingro who slaughters security guards in a robbery and then informs on McCauley's gang after being kicked out. In a police ambush two of McCauley's gang members die. A third, Chris is injured in the neck and the FBI plan to lure him into an arrest after 'turning' his wife Charlene. But will she allow him to be caught in this snare? Vincent Hanna has a chaotic private life that is resolved positively through the attempted suicide of his stepdaughter and her rescue, justice for a serial killer and 'grass' of the criminal underworld, and the death of and ultimate defeat of the ruthless armed robber McCauley. Hanna and McCauley are constructed as hero and anti-hero. McCauley's eventual arrest or death is an ideological necessity but death is constructed as the only pathway of honour. Even though his end is to be regretted, the original Los Angeles Police Department enquiry has to be successful. To this extent, the ideological frame is no different to the plots in the US Golden Age radio cop series 'Gangbusters'.

McCauley's girlfriend is not to be rewarded with the romantic resolution. She is left abandoned by the tragic twists and turns of the interrupted end sequence that follow the logical consistencies of McCauley's character. His 'character flaw' has been seeded by previous dialogue, and it is essential that he abandons his personal duties in relationships for the 'professionalism' of survival: 'Walk away. I will kill you if I have to'.

Complicating and Enhancing Conflict Struggles

Heat has in fact around six endings. The first ending is resolving the Chris and Charlene story. At the FBI stake-out, Charlene gives a surreptitious signal. Chris escapes, but will she and their child ever see him again? In the second ending, we wonder if the film will end with Hanna losing the chase, because it is apparently clear that Neil McCauley must have escaped. Hanna hears the Charlene snare has produced nothing, and another stake out, this time of Waingro's hotel in the hope that McCauley might go after him for revenge, has produced nothing. Hanna exclaims to his team: 'You know what? Neil has gone. Bang! Flying like a bird'.

This is the apparent victory of McCauley in getting away with all the money, with his NPR listening, university educated and cultured girlfriend, his survival against the odds, and the prospect of living in the paradise of sun and sand as a rich fugitive. In the third ending, even though Hanna has been defeated in the struggle of investigation and detection, he does enjoy the compensation of his personal crisis involving the overdose of his teenage stepdaughter, interrupting her death, and delivering her survival (folkloric rebirth, or rescue by his intervention) and the reconciliation and realisation of present and future love with his partner. Both hero and anti-hero are rewarded with an equilibrium in their private and emotional worlds.

The fourth ending is generated when McCauley is given an opportunity of interrupting his escape to apply justice to the unadulterated evil character who has betrayed the lives of his comrades, serially murdered the innocent and raped underage girls. The 'execution' is achieved by apparently outmanoeuvring the surveillance maintained by the police. He uses subterfuge, nerve, and disguise to achieve the triumph of retribution on the apogee of evil representation.

The fifth ending involves the intervention of misfortune on McCauley, or the accident of luck for Hanna who is able to reconvene the chase and struggle with McCauley. Hanna is bleeped. An alert has been activated at Waingro's hotel. Will McCauley get away having killed him? Hanna is rushed by helicopter to the scene. In the chaos of the hotel's evacuation by fire-alarm, he succeeds in finding and seeing McCauley before he can get to the car with the waiting Eady. McCauley's hope of romance is dashed as he has to walk past his waiting girlfriend in the getaway car.

The sixth ending is the final chase/struggle in a machismo duel in a container park adjacent to the airport runway that would have conveyed McCauley and the woman he loves to freedom. This end is invested with greater power of irony and paradox. The building of audience sympathy for the hero(ine) and anti-hero(ine) has been predicated with equivalence. This has the advantage of deepening the paradoxical nature of the ultimate conflict. The audience wants both Hanna and McCauley to succeed, but one has to be defeated. The basic values of law and order are resolved ideologically with the death of McCauley, but a separate spiritual value of 'warrior's dignity' is upheld as Hanna holds McCauley's hand when he dies from his fatal gunshot wound. McCauley's defeat in the gun battle is brought about by misfortune, a tripping on rough ground rather than any intrinsic weakness in marksmanship. Whereas the forces of law and order succeed in the temporal struggle, both men are brothers at the end with Hanna holding McCauley's hand in comfort as he dies.

Locations of Ironic Effect

The film *When Trumpets Fade* is the story of Private David Manning, a soldier in the US Army's 28th Infantry Division fighting against the Germans in North West Europe towards the end of 1944 during the high casualty Battle of the Hürtgen Forest. The film ends with profound irony, and this is symmetrical with the beginning. The film starts with Private Manning stumbling through the forest carrying a critically wounded comrade who begs him to shoot him to be put out of his pain and misery. We hear the diegetic sound of a shot, but only see the forest they have been stumbling through. In the end, it is clear that Manning has become the sole survivor of his platoon. As so many officers and non-commissioned officers have been killed, Manning is assigned to lead a squad of reinforcements who are just out of training and have no combat experience. Manning is appalled to find that he has been given a field promotion to sergeant. He tries everything to avoid the responsibility even claiming to be medically unfit through battle stress, but his company commander is having none of this and gives him no choice but to carry on. Manning is the reluctant hero who finds that his actions are attenuated by an innate respect and response to other people's humanity. In the ensuing bloody and traumatic frontline action, he gradually shows qualities of leadership which further leads to promotion to second lieutenant and the eventual respect of his soldiers. At the end of the film the audience is presented with one of the raw recruits Manning had to lead into battle carrying him back through the forest from the frontline. This time it is Manning's body that is broken and bleeding. He is the person begging to be dropped to the ground so he can die or be killed off with a bullet from one of his own comrades. The film ends with him losing consciousness as his sole surviving recruit Private Sanderson continues carrying him back to their lines. We have to imagine his fate. The only information offered is the text on the screen which explains that the Allies eventually took Hürtgen Forest on the border with Germany after 3 months of heavy fighting, though this battle was overshadowed and became lost to history by the Battle of the Bulge which took place soon afterwards.

In *The Bridges of Madison County*, the location of ironic effect at the end is an assertion of the moral force of duty and the cowardice of individual determination/freewill triumphing over the selfish pursuit of happiness. The film has two time settings: 1965 and the present. In the past, an Italian war bride, Francesca Johnson, meets a National Geographic photojournalist, Robert Kincaid who comes to Madison County on a project to take pictures of its bridges. Francesca lives on a farm there with her husband and two children, but her family is away on a trip and over the four-day period she and Kincaid have an affair. In the present time,

Francesca's two adult children, Michael and Carolyn, travel to her Iowa farm to settle her estate and are perplexed by her request to be cremated with her ashes scattered from Roseman Covered Bridge, rather than buried with her late husband and their father. The discovery of notebooks, love letters, and photographs takes them back to the story of their mother's love affair and the impact of that on the lives of those who are no longer alive and what this means for their own present lives and relationships.

Loyalty to husband and primarily children are paradigmatic moral values and given precedence over the truth and passion of individual love and fulfilment. The film is enveloped through an alternative ending played out vicariously through the potential change in the expectations and attitudes of the central characters' adult children. Here, we have an ending that depends on the flashback/generational concentric ring of narrative frame rippling significant emotional influences through the characters. The resolution is profoundly moral by setting up the triumph of Platonic/spiritual love over moral love.

The lesson of story construction is that across the timeline and boundary of cultures there is very little that is prescriptive. Undoubtedly, there are consensual conventions that can be subverted in order to establish a surprise presence in the arena of storytelling entertainment. Religious and philosophical imperatives are often at work. An end may be determined by the Judeo-Christian belief of life after death, the Buddhist belief in reincarnation, an agnostic or atheistic/existential attitude that finalises a story through the taste of nothingness, the absurdity of life, or the banal denial of justice and righteousness.

Beau Travail (Pathé TV/SM Films (1999) directed by Claire Denis) is an example of a French film that subverts storytelling conventions in resolving narrative and action. Sergeant-Major Galoup, played by Denis Lavant, has undergone a crushing defeat when he is forced to leave his beloved Foreign Legion because he was unable to control his homoerotic jealousy for the heroic new recruit Sentain.

Beau Travail was inspired by Herman Melville's Billy Budd. Foreign Legion Sergeant Major Galoup finds his position and power threatened when the bravery and heroism of a young recruit Sentain attracts the admiration of the platoon's commander. Galoup plots Sentain's downfall but is discovered and kicked out of the world and family that he has depended on all his adult life.

Psychological and cultural expectations are that he cannot survive in the outside world of 'civvy street' in Marsailles. Yet Denis (also the co-writer) reverses the nihilistic road of suicide in the hotel room. The audience is drawn to a false resolution with the slow, disciplined, and silent military making of his bed, the 'lying down on parade' and the positioning of the pistol against his body. Is he preparing for death? The film could end here. But it does not. Galoup reinvents himself through a beautiful expression of modern/break dancing movements in the café/club that appear to be a natural evolution of the choreography of military training that he had commanded in the barren desert outside Djibouti. The symmetrical frame of beginning and end is exquisitely achieved as the play began with filmic sequences showing the almost balletic dance ritual of Foreign Legion soldiers carrying out their physical exercise and training, and this being juxtaposed with their recreation in the discotheque. At the beginning of the film Galoup's preoccupation is in looking on jealously at how the young Sentain is popular with his fellow soldiers in that environment. At the end Galoup has found himself in the very environment which tortured him with what Shakespeare described as 'the green-eyed monster', but he is now liberated from the hierarchical constraints and rituals of his past regimental existence.

In an article for *Frieze* in 2019, Erika Balsam argued: 'This is, perhaps, the best ending of any film, ever' (Balsam, 2019). She explained:

> Galoup's obsession with the young legionnaire Gilles Sentain (Grégoire Colin) has degenerated into cruelty, violence, sabotage. Whether undertaken out of envy, unspeakable desire or some combination thereof, the pock-marked officer's actions have led to the pretty Sentain lying salt-crusted in the Djiboutian desert, a near-corpse to be found by a passing family; Galoup himself has been expelled from the Foreign Legion for his transgressions, cast out of its motley family of men and into dishonour.
>
> Back in Marseille, gun in hand, his pulse is visible in the vein of his bicep as the house beat of Corona's 'Rhythm of the Night' (1993) fades in on the soundtrack […]
>
> Alone amidst mirrored tiles and twinkling lights, Galoup finds a rhythm of life that follows none of the patterns of colonial, patriarchal power the film so skilfully traces and complicates. On this impossible dancefloor, he inhabits a utopia of movement without rules.
>
> *(Balsam, 2019)*

Ken Loach's iconic television film *Cathy Come Home* (BBC, 1966, directed by Ken Loach) written by Jeremy Sandford, was a political drama based on a radio documentary about homelessness in Britain. It begins with Scene 1 titled 'New Home' showing the happiness of the love story between Cathy and Reg and their being so thrilled in exploring the interior of their new home. This is opening with so much hope and optimism and becomes powerfully and emotionally contrasted with the end of Scene 12 titled 'The Snatch'. By this time Cathy has been forced by economic circumstances to live apart from him because of the homelessness that descended on them. He had lost his job following a road traffic accident which was not his fault. Cathy is at Liverpool Street Station with her children. Social Services arrive to take them away from her. We witness the indifference of authority and the cruelty of social poverty tearing the children away from the mother who loves them. The screaming and distress in a public place is heart-rending. The political and emotional impact of this film led to the national campaign against Homelessness and the setting up of the charity Shelter.

Audio and Radio Dramatic Endings

Audio drama can certainly take its inspiration from these impressive cinematic endings; and an analysis of various examples from radio drama history suggests the sound medium can complete the storytelling experience with as much impact and resonance. Some inspiration can be taken from African radio plays produced by the BBC World Service in 1972 and selected for the BBC African Service radio play competition.

Make Like Slaves by Richard Rive was selected by one of the judges Wole Soyinka because:

> It's a study of relationships, not only between the two characters, but between each character and the social reality each thought He or She understood. And the process of the continuous shifting of this relationship I think was very subtly handled. I think that it is a very finely written play.
>
> *(Henderson, 1973, p. 2)*

Rive's play ends with the line: 'SHE: Now then, all of you, spread out more…I want you to…to make like slaves'. This last line is ironic in providing the title and showing that one of the main characters 'She', a supposedly liberal white South African woman, has learned and understands nothing about how she patronises the black South Africans when she 'charitably' goes into townships to teach drama. This 50-year-old play is instructive about the phenomenon of white saviourism in race relations where people of white ethnicity approach issues of racial equality with confused and selfish motivation.

The potential problems in the relationship between 'He', a black man, and 'She' are given foreground in the opening scene. She patronises him by implying he does not know and has not read Robert Hayden's *Middle Passage*. When she talks about the drama school slang she picked up in London, 'They make like slaves', he quotes Countee Cullen to her with the words 'Yet do I marvel at this curious thing, to make black and bid him sing', and it is clear She has no understanding of what he is trying to say to her (Henderson, 1973, pp. 4–5).

The chasm in education, knowledge, and understanding between the two characters is deeply ironic and subtextual throughout. HE has already said 'Suit yourself' after SHE has related and asked: 'One of the consulates in town has asked me to put on an indigenous play for their staff. They want black since they also have their own Negroes back home. Does one say blacks or Africans? I'm never sure' (Henderson, 1973).

Richard Rive (1931–1989) was a prominent South African sportsman, writer, and academic and recognised in 2013 for his contributions to the fight against apartheid through literature. In the apartheid era, he was given the racial classification 'Coloured'. He was stabbed to death in Cape Town in 1989 two weeks after completing his fourth novel *Emergency Continued*.

Some endings are so resonant that their power in subtext stands on its own. They resolve the difficult and visceral decisions that characters in conflict with members of their own family and diverging cultural imperatives on their identity and hopes and aspirations. This is certainly the case with Elvania Namukwaya Zirimu's *Family Spear* also from 1972. Wole Soyinka said, this was the work of a very accomplished playwright charting the battle 'of the old versus the new' (Henderson, 1973, p. 110) and Lewis Nkosi praised how it so successfully dramatised the conflict between the traditional and the modern Africa and 'in personal terms' (Henderson, 1973).

The central character Muweesi has decided to leave his family and community even when his father Seekisa is taken ill. The leaving and parting is painful, but the courage to walk is also noble and affirming:

MUWEESI: We must go.

BIRUNGI: He may be dying.

MUWEESI: He's been dying a long time.

BIRUNGI: Do you love him?

MUWEESI: The way to walk is long. Don't let's waste energy with talk. (*Very hesitantly and thoughtfully*) Let's go.

FX: *Thunder louder – then fade out slowly.*

(Henderson, 1973, p. 129)

Elvania Namukwaya Zirimu (1938–1979) was a Ugandan poet and dramatist who formed the Kampala drama group the Ngoma Players which also first produced the stage version of *Family Spear*. She is best known for her plays *Keeping up with the Mukasas* and *When the Hunchback Made Rain*. She helped found Uganda's National Choir and National Theatre, but her promising life was cut short in 1979 after her appointment to be Uganda's High Commissioner to Ghana when she was killed in a car crash as she was preparing to leave Uganda to take up her post.

Khalid Almubarak Mustafa in his radio play *Station Street* crafted an end demonstrating how the unsaid, the misunderstood and twists of irony can be so impactful in sound drama. The delicate register of human utterance and engagement of sound design is uniquely radiophonic and audiogenic – suited so well to radio production and reception, and creative in representing characters, feelings, and ideas through sound alone.

Martin Esslin said that this is a play which is particularly subtle because of a central character 'who doesn't even appear, namely, the son who has won a scholarship in England' (Henderson, 1973, p. 20) and becomes 'extremely vivid and sympathetic, simply through the way in which the impact of his success and his letter impinges on the other people' (Henderson, 1973). Esslin is referring to Dr. Salim Abdallah who has written to his mother to explain he will not be coming back from England where he has accepted a well-paid research post. He has also apparently married a German woman in England despite the fact he had been promised to the daughter of one of his father's best friends, Nour back in his home country. His father had been killed in a rebellion against British colonial occupation. Salim's younger brother Osman is developing a relationship with the daughter of another of their father's best friends. He is called 'Sergeant' and Osman is looking forward to leaving to study at university.

The father is another character heavily present in the play but only speaking through memories and documents, one to be read only after his sons had finished their studies and before they embark on their careers, and another to only be made public after independence. Mother has insisted everything is revealed and read out now after receiving her older son's letter which she will be sending back to him. The first letter reveals that her husband wants Salim to have his sword and Osman his dagger (Henderson, 1973, pp. 31–32).

The second document reveals that the founding group of independence fighters included his close friends Uncle Sergeant and Uncle Nour. It is not clear if Sergeant and Nour have already left and are not around to hear this. The subtlety of this play is in concatenating emotionally the postcolonial ironies of an Arabic speaking and Muslim African country that is now independent, but where its promising children have aspirations to study and pursue lives perhaps in the very country which previously oppressed them.

The past no longer matters in terms of heritage, customs, and obligations. The present is not something Osman feels he needs to stay for. He has the dagger his father has left him, but it is not clear if he will take it with him. His brother Salim will receive the sword left to him and his Mother says: '…he may hang it in his English house'. The end of the play is rueful, sad, poignant, and thought-provoking with every listener left to imagine what the future will hold for Osman, his mother, the rest of his family and father's friends and indeed his country. These thoughts are imaginatively wafted through the cross-fading of Mother's weak coughing and the rising and falling of the train whistle:

OSMAN: All members of the first Independence Group. Thanks to father's document, they are both being honoured as heroes now. (*Low voice*) Allah sometimes likes to have a good laugh.
MOTHER: I can't hear you. What is it you are muttering?
OSMAN: (*Still low voice*) I can't help wondering, if he, too, survived the mutiny –
MOTHER: What was that?
OSMAN: Nothing, Mother, nothing.
FX: *Mother starts to cough. Loud, clear, train whistles drown cough. Fade out.*
(Henderson, 1973, pp. 32–33)

Wole Soyinka admired how Khalid Almubarak Mustafa's *Station Street* had created 'an atmosphere, a mood … through language, and through a very quiet dignified portrayal of the various characters … It has a very gentle lyrical quality' (Henderson, 1973, p. 20). The author was born in Kosti, Sudan, in 1937. He obtained PhD and M. Litt degrees at the University of Bristol and became an academic authority on Northeast African drama and literature.

The Haunting Ends of Lucille Fletcher's *The Hitch Hiker* and *Sorry, Wrong Number*

Lucille Fletcher's skill at crafting a 20th century story of the supernatural about a man driving across America on Route 66 and being haunted by a hitch hiker continually appearing in front of him on the road reached the heights of brilliance in the climax to her suspense classic *The Hitch Hiker*, which was such a great favourite of Orson Welles. Ronald Adams has pulled up in a deserted auto camp in Gallup, New Mexico. Time to ring mother who had sent him on his way with love and bon voyage. He finds a Mrs. Whitney answering. Mrs. Adams is not at home because she is still in the hospital with a nervous breakdown (Mackey, 1951, p. 284).

All this is disturbing and alienating enough, but what follows does not fail to stir the hairs on my spine whenever I read the script or hear it performed. Adams says he has never known his mother to be nervous. He cannot understand why she has had a breakdown. It is then Mrs. Whitney informs him this has happened since the death of her oldest son, Ronald, killed just six days ago in an automobile accident on the Brooklyn Bridge. The operator breaks in with the repeated message 'Your three minutes are up, sir' (Mackey, 1951, p. 285).

Suddenly, the play with all its mysterious events, characters, and atmosphere is spiralled chillingly into the realm of the modern ghost story. The repetitive and fading operator's message: 'Your three minutes are up, sir' are symbolic of the hopelessness and meaninglessness of human life in the context of all time and the wider universe and everything we do not know. Ronald Adams is finding out that he has already died and how. What is the nature of his existence? The listener and perhaps even Adams are offered an intriguing and chilling unravelling of the mystery of the identity of the mysterious hallooing hitch-hiker Adams has been trying to run down throughout the foregoing journey. Perhaps it has been the ghost of Adams all the while. His journey now seems to be endless. He needs to continue searching for the hitch-hiker and perhaps, most importantly answer the question 'Who am I?' He leaves the listener with a deep sense of loneliness, a true lost soul of the radio age on America's Route 66: 'Ahead of me stretch a thousand miles of empty mesa, mountains, prairies—desert. Somewhere among them, he is waiting for me, Somewhere I shall know who he is, and who …I…am…' (Mackey, 1951, p. 286).

The end of *The Hitch Hiker* is also symmetrical with its beginning. Essentially Lucille Fletcher has taken the listener back to the beginning which was in fact the end though that was not at all clear to the listener: 'I am in an auto camp on Route 66 just west of Gallup, New Mexico. If I tell it perhaps it will help me. It will keep me from going mad. But I must tell this quickly' (Mackey, 1951, p. 271).

Lucille Fletcher's resolution of *Sorry, Wrong Number* remains one of the most terrifying finalities of crime fiction. The horror chills most effectively in the sound medium. A woman all alone is beginning to realise that the call she was wrongly switched into was in reality the exchange of men plotting her assassination in less than the half an hour of the listening provided by the play's duration. All of the advantages of telephone communications turn out to be most disadvantageous. It is impossible to reach her husband for help because his business number is permanently engaged. The police are busy with other emergencies and somewhat sceptical of her tone and perspicacity. Again, Fletcher strips the telephone system of its humanity. The operators are like robots. They are merely indifferent machines that route messages and calls, stripped of any vestiges of human kindness and sympathy. They cannot rescue and provide any agency of justice.

Leona Stevenson is being asked to speak louder, but she knows there is an intruder in the house coming to kill her. Clicks on the telephone mean he has put down the extension phone. He's coming up the stairs. She demands to be put through to the police department (Fletcher, 1980, p. 21).

The approaching murderer is syncopated by the mere sound of clicks on the telephone and the appalling reality that the speed of sound cannot be matched by the time it will take for an officer to get to her intensifies the terror. It does not matter how many times she cries 'Help me!' Everyone knows she is doomed and that she knows what is coming her way. Listeners feel it and identify with it and Mrs. Stevenson's screams are like streaks of lightning in their imagination. The cross-fade with the whistle of the train as it roars across the bridge is reminiscent of how Alfred Hitchcock in the film *Thirty Nine Steps* (1935) juxtaposed silent film showing a cleaner screaming when discovering a murdered body of a woman in a London mansion flat with the screech of a steam engine whistle at the head of a train hurtling north towards Scotland with the fugitive Richard Hannay on board being pursued by police and enemy agents. The imagination of the audience hears the scream of the cleaner woman although the actual screen shot of her is silent. The sound of the train whistle heard provides the register and tone of the emotion and then represents the transition to speed and escape.

Lucille Fletcher has also deployed exquisite dramatic irony by dramatising Mrs. Stevenson's successful connection with the police department only a second or two after her wretched demise, and the last words we hear are those of her murderer George approximately articulating the words of the play's title *Sorry, wrong number*, followed by improvisation in the 1943 radio production 'Don't worry. Everything's OK' – the very words and homily Mrs. Stevenson longed and prayed for (Fletcher 1980 & Fletcher 1943).

The Filmic Sophistication of the Ending of Caryl Phillips' First Radio Play *The Wasted Years*

Caryl Phillips wrote the equivalent of a feature film in his first play produced by the BBC in 1984. At nearly 90 minutes, the complexity of the themes and interaction of characters justified multiple directions of narrative. The central plot concerning the main character Solly is all about his future as listeners join his story when he faces the cliff-edge venture of leaving school early with no career plan nor any decision on what he is going to do. This is combined with his grave sense of alienation and feeling of being so different; primarily because he is one of only two Black boys in his school.

This is a multi-stranded story with several equivalent sub-plots and together they could be said to amount to a whole. Solly's mother Cynthia through flashback recalls how all the hopes and ambitions of immigration with her husband Roy to Britain from the Caribbean were challenged by the ugliness and injustice of racial discrimination and their separation when he decided this betrayal of promise meant he had to return home, leaving her in the cold and unwelcoming Mother

Country with infant son and pregnant with another child. At the very end of the play, Phillips gives Cynthia a triumph of dignity and steadfastness. She is going to stay the course because she has full faith in her sons and their future. They have a life now and at least making the tremendously challenging journey to England has 'given them a chance' (Phillips, 1985, p. 141).

All of the social and personal burdens on Solly have taken their toll on his relationship with his younger brother Chris with whom he has been continually compared because whereas his apparently resentful and rebellious attitude has singled him out as a trouble-maker, Chris has been excelling academically. Phillips again resolves this conflict between the characters with subtlety of writing, compassion, and understated love. Chris asks his brother if his face is still hurting from the earlier fight at the school-leaving disco with the racist brother of Jenny Solly wants to go out with. Solly is not hurting. He is falling asleep and everything will be fine in the morning (Phillips, 1985, pp. 140–141).

Again, Phillips has presented an integrity and logic to the development of his play's characters in the context of a single parent mother's relationship with her teenage sons against the background of being a first generation immigrant heroically struggling to work and give them a secure home with the discipline and parental guidance which will encourage their commitment to education, hard work, good behaviour, and bettering themselves. She has had to negotiate and explain to Solly why his father is not with them. The play resolves the conflict and tension with love and dignity. She is taking them on trip in the morning together as a family and they have to get up early. She will wake them up and everyone wishes each other a good night (Phillips, 1985, p. 140).

The other conflict to be resolved is between Solly and his teacher Mr. Teale. This is set out dramatically in a tense classroom scene at the very beginning of the play. Teale has to deal with Solly's difficulties and throughout seeks to reconcile his duty to maintain discipline and respect for authority with care and welfare for the boy in his charge and educational care. But Solly is leaving. Teale knows he should not. He knows he has so much promise. He wants to find out and solve something which is most likely a much bigger problem way beyond anything he could do in a professional situation where he has no support from his head teacher. Essentially, Solly is no longer a child, he has had to grow up faster and with more risk than the boys staying on at school. This is also the case with those of his friends who are also leaving. Again with subtlety Phillips delineates the resolution of this conflict with quiet understanding and respect between the two of them, a dimension of equality and a prospect of help and support in the future. It seems Mr. Teale has written his phone number on a piece of paper for Solly to put in his pocket before his friends come back. Solly takes it and says it is all right if he sees Mr. Teale again (Phillips, 1985, pp. 136–137).

The other significant story and issue in Solly's life is the inter-racial relationship developing with Jenny where there is more than just mutual attraction. But this is acutely threatened by the racism of her parents and her brother who will eventually racially abuse and attack him. Phillips resolves this dimension of the play with statements of intent from Solly to his brother Chris. He will be going out with Jenny Bates now he has left school (Phillips, 1985, p. 140).

In the earlier dialogue between Jenny and her friend Tracey – even though Jenny has to stand him up at the school's leaving disco, she makes it clear that she is going out with him. She says she has to stand up to her parents some time and this is certainly a good reason to. She is who she is; otherwise she says 'I wouldn't have Solly' (Phillips, 1985, p. 134).

Phillips was 25 years old, when he wrote this realistic and socially conscious play with so much profound affection and understanding of the people his characters represent, the struggles of their community and the first generation of Windrush African-Caribbean immigrants coming to Britain after 1948 and their children. *The Wasted Years* is an outstanding model of the sophistication of radio playwriting in the long form which I would argue is more than equal to what can be achieved in the feature and television film industries in terms of significant storytelling, quality, and impact.

Endings in Richard Durham's *Destination Freedom* Plays

Richard Durham is a genius at using the ends of the 91 half-hour plays he wrote for the *Destination Freedom* series to surprise and generate political and philosophical reflection and thought-provoking resonances. Logic and symmetry are the hallmarks for most of them. The beginnings work back from the ends and the creativity is enduring. In *The Heart of George Cotton* (1948), we hear how the pioneering surgeons save the very heart that Durham characterised and gave voice to at the beginning. We are reminded so imaginatively and poetically that 'these are indeed the men who first healed me' (Durham and MacDonald, 1989, pp. 128–129).

In *The Trumpet Talks* (1949), the story of Louis Armstrong, Durham morphs the sound and spirit of the characterisation of 'The Trumpet', given the narrative and musical voice at the very beginning, with the heart and soul of Louis Armstrong himself:

(RECORD: *Prelude of 'West End Blues' up and then as it ends, shift*)
TRUMPET: Yes, he was the one who could make me talk—and he did. I'd spoken
    for the angel Gabriel and had blown taps for the Romans. My voice had been
    heard in high and low places. But he got out of me tones…
(RECORD: *Out*)
TRUMPET: …I'd never knew were my own. He made the trumpet tell the truth.
(MUSIC: *'West End Blues' curtain*)

(Durham and MacDonald, 1989, pp. 228–229)

In *Anatomy of an Ordinance* (1949) Durham seems to give the last word to the menacing and malignant voice of the Slums, but the surprise in this dramatic production is its transgression to documentary when the voice of Archibald Carey himself is presented in transcription. We have heard that at Chicago City Hall Alderman

Carey's Ordinance to deal with Slums has been defeated 31–13. But Slums is not happy. Because the Alderman has gone back to his Woodlawn AME Church and preached another sermon. Slums knows his enemy has renewed energy. Now he's campaigning all over the country. San Francisco has adopted the same Ordnance Chicago turned away.

All the same, Slums says he is still spreading and growing. He has 26 acres of dark stairways, dirty alleys, and rundown shacks covering Chicago. He is segregating the Blacks away from the Whites and the rich away from the poor. But there is still something nagging. What if Carey teams up with a lot of other people like him and they aim to do away with all Slums everywhere. That's certainly something to think about: 'I don't know what would happen to a poor slum like me. What in the world would happen?' (Durham, 1949b).

This is an indication that Richard Durham was creating political drama in the late 1940s which not only entertained and informed but also operated as social activism and attracted close surveillance by the FBI since Durham had been identified in their files as a Marxist and Communist. Durham dramatised past and present injustice and social struggles which were relevant and pressing in the politics of his time. This radio play broadcast on Chicago's NBC WMAQ radio station on 5 June 1949 segued into a platform for Alderman Carey's continuing campaign where he said he was neither worthy of the time nor characterisation, but 'to summon such talents and energies as we have to create in America shelter, clean and honourable; not only for the families of our citizens, but for the ideals of fair play and equal opportunity which nourish the Republic' (Durham, 1949b).

Trust in the Listener's Imagination. Bertolt Brecht's *The Trial of Lucullus*

Social activism and political epiphany is certainly a central part of the purpose of Bertolt Brecht's theory of theatre. It is not widely known that he was also a radio playwright. In *The Trial of Lucullus* written in 1940 in a didactic verse style, Lucullus, the great Roman general, is in the underworld and stands trial before a judge and jury drawn from members of the lower classes. Should he be allowed into the Elysian Fields or despatched to languish in the hell that is Hades? He is allowed to summon witnesses portrayed on a triumphal frieze that he had commissioned. His defence is trivial, superficial, and shallow – introducing a cherry tree to Europe, caring about books, and appreciating and promoting fine cooking. Compared to all the true grief and suffering he has caused in wars judge and jury are traumatised and exhausted by the evidence of his infamy and the responsibility for the verdict that they must read. A decision is made to adjourn.

But the listener never hears them return. It is left to their imagination to provide their own verdict on Lucullus. This is a classic example of the radio playwright engaging the listener's participation in the trial format. The listener decides if Lucullus may enter the Elysian Fields – the final resting place of the souls of the heroic and the virtuous in Greek mythology and religion, or face something much worse in Hades.

Conclusions

It is now clear that audio drama contains both narrative and dramatic elements and the writer can effectively write forwards and backwards for the listener. The dramatic purpose of the end of a play and, indeed any standalone sequence of audio drama whether complete or episodic is that all the key elements driving towards the end convergence have heightened tension, revelation, resolution, or indeed frustration. Any character or scene that does not serve this purpose needs to be removed. As has been shown in the analysis of examples, all forms of play can have a variety of explicit and implicit conflicts, but there needs to be clarity in the writer's mind about the central theme and subject. Caryl Phillips was supremely skilful in combining multiple conflicts in the life of Solly that came together at the end to say something essential about where Solly is going and his situation as a Black British youngster, a second-generation Windrush person at the crossroads of his life and as the play's title implied somebody who is trying to move on from *The Wasted Years* which had driven his father back to the Caribbean.

In 1940, Barnouw was analysing a radio drama topography with mainly short-form fifteen-minute and half-hour sequences. His advice on the radio drama climax was, therefore, rather simple: 'A climax scene is, most frequently, one in which the two sides of a conflict face each other to win or lose. It is the scene in which we finally "find out what happens"' (Barnouw, 1940, p. 95). Barnouw felt that with all the competing distractions of radio drama listening there should be 'a constant awareness of conflicting forces, simultaneously. Here, if ever, we cannot let an important character "die"' (Barnouw, 1940). Hence, the importance of shorter and shorter speeches. He thought rising tension between characters and rising conflict benefit from even 'chopped speeches ... dovetailed into a rapid machine-gunning pattern' (Barnouw, 1940, p. 96) so that the conflicted forces in the drama have an almost spontaneous spotlight. He said the writers should be aiming for 'constant electric aliveness in the listener's mind-world' (Barnouw, 1940).

William Ash's advice on working back from the climax at the end enables writers to 'consider ways of imparting or withholding information so as to create little surprises along the slope of rising tension leading to the big surprise' (Ash, 1985, p. 53). We are always reminded of the teaching of writing shibboleths: Showing and not telling; people, action, and events which change and transform characters; conflict and struggle; and the advantages of epiphany and ironic revelation or transposition.

One-act or shorter plays usually work better with one-plot strands leading to climax and resolution. However, in series and serials and in longer forms two or more streams of plotting can intertwine, parallel, counterpoint, and then converge at the final point, clashing, frustrating, helping or accelerating the journey to the endpoint; and Keith Richards argues quite convincingly that 'Because radio drama is generally much shorter than other dramatic forms writers are inclined to believe there is insufficient time to develop a sub-plot. But a play without a sub-plot is emotionally bereft' (Richards, 1991, p. 54). The cyclical nature of dramatic storylines, the ability of audio drama to compress and journey through time, the streams of consciousness dimension of the dramatic sound medium with the potential to juxtapose exterior and interior consciousness means that the relationship between a play's beginning and end can be counter-cultural, reverse expectations and surprise the listener. There is though the caveat that any enigma in dramatic storytelling is limited by the audience's patience and willingness to appreciate it. There is a pivot which needs to work in favour of intelligibility and appreciation over confusion and disappointment.

Pamela Brooke advises that the climax of a radio play happens 'at the instant the conflicting forces meet head on and a change occurs in at least one of them. Either one force wins and the other loses or a compromise occurs that allows the crisis to pass' (Brooke, 1995, p. 69). She explains that the story of a sound play can be complete at the dramatisation of the climax or it is possible to continue into a final scene of resolution to sort out 'loose ends left to wrap, mysteries left to explain or reflections needed for events to jell' (Brooke, 1995). However, it is most advisable that the logical imperatives of the end following from what has happened before are respected. Otherwise, the finish of the drama could be a rather risible *deus ex machina* arriving to unravel everything that is wrong with plot structure, characterisation, the essential idea or core of the play, and the proper identification of voice and point of listening. The solution to the listener's question what is going to happen and what is this about cannot come out of nowhere. As Brooke insists: 'It must be the inevitable result of the actions and decisions of the leading characters and entirely consistent with the motives and characteristics you've attributed to them' (Brooke, 1995).

Claire Grove and Stephen Wyatt wisely advise audio dramatists to get to the end as soon as they can because 'The only way you'll learn where you're going is by travelling the whole journey' (Grove & Wyatt, 2013, p. 118). This provides the opportunity to reflect, ruminate, and rewrite. The trajectory between beginning, middle, and end will be clear and the opportunity and need for restructuring and improvement equally revealing.

Rosemary Horstmann says at the end of the radio play the listening audience:

> must be left with a sense of "rightness." Whether the conclusion is happy or sad, the audience must not feel cheated. The ending should tidy up any unfinished business left hanging in the plot and return us to the level of everyday life from the heightened tensions of dramatic experience.
>
> *(Horstmann, 1991, p. 33)*

She discussed the emotions and concepts of catharsis, adjustment, balance and well-being and quoted Jean Louis Barrault from his *Reflections on the Theatre*:

> In fact, at the theatre, we are always assisting at a vast settling of accounts. From all the opposing rights, from the Rugby scrum of rights, there should by degrees emerge a Sentence. Justice. And the spectator isn't satisfied unless

the sentence is just. Just, not in relation to the individuals participating in the conflict, but in relation to Life, in the universal sense of the word. Always make sure that the universal spirit of justice has been respected in a play. If not: beware of the mood of the audience.

(Barrault, 1951, p. 137)

Shaun MacLoughlin believes audio dramatists need to apply their minds to the end of the play 'as you might to the end of a pilgrimage, to give shape and meaning to your journey, to your narrative' (MacLoughlin, 1998, p. 36). He advised keeping in mind the questions: 'Why am I writing this play? What do I want to say? What thoughts and feelings do I want to leave the listener with at the end of the play?' (MacLoughlin, 1998).

The connection between beginning and end needs to be there. It helps if the end of the play needs to have been promised in some way by the beginning (MacLoughlin, 1998, p. 40).

Vincent McInerney provides a clear reminder that:

[W]hatever happens in the opening and middle sections of a play, all things must come to an end. And as the ending of a play is the last immediate memory a listener will carry of your work – make it memorable.

(McInerney, 2001, p. 107)

He explains that satisfaction will only be achieved by clarity and a sense that the listener has had value for money. This means that radio plays need to have a closed plot with central argument and resolution provided and no unanswered questions. He argues that open-plotted plays with deliberately missing information and unresolved strands are not appreciated by listeners. He insists: 'In radio drama the listener deserves, and should have, absolute clarity of purpose in the main body of the play and a firm, self-explanatory ending' (McInerney, 2001, p. 108).

I finish with the ending of Morton Wishengrad's play *The Battle of the Warsaw Ghetto*, written in the very same year, 1943, when the terrible event it dramatises took place. I would argue this sequence embodies many of the foregoing ideas and suggestions on what constitutes the end of a significant radio play. The narrator has been an active participant character in the action of the play, but he is also framing for the listener the context of what has happened as a surviving witness to history.

At the height of the battle, Isaac hears the voice of one of his son's teachers who is lying in a trench. His right arm has been blown off at the elbow and he tries to tie a tourniquet around his arm. But the teacher doesn't want him to waste his bandage. He only wants to know how it is going. Isaac tells him, they are still fighting. The teacher is so proud that after 37 days, a few Jews with guns have been fighting an entire Nazi army for all this time. He smiles even though his blood runs from his shattered stump to soak the ground. He smiles at the folly of the Nazis who should have known that the Ghetto would explode. Isaac reassures him that they know now.

The teacher is dying as his eyes begin to glaze. 'How many did we kill?' he asks of his friend and Isaac is able to say 1,000, some even say 1,200. Isaac Davidson says the teacher's last words are an epitaph for the Warsaw Ghetto fighters: 'It is not for thee to complete the work, but neither art thou free to desist from it. Tell them to mark that on our graves' (Barnouw & Wishengrad, 1945, p. 44.) The play ends with a symmetry of its beginning. We hear the Cantor again singing the unaccompanied solo, 'El Mole Rachamim' which fades under the Voice's narration.

We are asked to listen to the Cantor with reverence for he is singing a prayer for the dead. No ordinary prayer for the 25,000 who will never be the ordinary dead. Those dead of the Warsaw Ghetto are sleeping in their last trench in the year of 1943. Their clothes have been dispersed into ashes, holy books sodden in rain, and deep rubble all over the entrances to their houses. The Voice wants the listener to know they were the Jews with guns who fought the Nazis. The Voice demands that everyone understands that defiance and to continue hearing the Cantor chanting the prayer for their dead. The Voice says the fighting Jews of the Warsaw Ghetto wrote a sentence that shall be an atonement: 'Give me grace and give me dignity and teach me to die; and let my person be a fortress and my wailing wall a stockade, for I have been to Egypt and I am not departed' (Barnouw & Wishengrad, 1945, p. 45).

Companion Website Resources

Additions and Updates for Chapter 10 Ending the Sound Story https://kulturapress. com/2022/08/12/updates-for-chapter-10-ending-the-sound-story/

BBC World Service Radio Drama – Play Publications https://kulturapress.com/ 2022/08/30/bbc-world-service-radio-drama-play-publications/

Benjamin Zephaniah Radio Plays https://kulturapress.com/2022/08/30/benjamin-zephaniah-radio-plays/

Cecil Lewis and Radio Plays https://kulturapress.com/2022/08/30/cecil-lewis-and-radio-plays/

BBC World Service African Plays 1973 https://kulturapress.com/2022/08/30/ bbc-world-service-african-plays-1973-2/

German Radio Plays hörspiel and the Avant Garde https://kulturapress. com/2022/08/30/german-radio-plays-ho%cc%88rspiel-and-the-avant-garde/

Columbia Workshop and Radio Drama https://kulturapress.com/2022/08/30/ columbia-workshop-and-radio-drama/

D G Bridson and Radio Plays https://kulturapress.com/2022/08/30/d-g-bridson-and-radio-plays/

Dylan Thomas Under Milk Wood and Radio Drama https://kulturapress. com/2022/08/30/dylan-thomas-under-milk-wood-and-radio-drama/

European Radio Drama https://kulturapress.com/2022/08/30/european-radio-drama/

11
FILM, INTERNET, AND STAGE DIMENSIONS TO SOUND STORYTELLING

Techniques and Devices

Cross-Media Projects

One summer's day in 1994, I sat in a stage manager's control room of the Cottesloe Theatre in Britain's National Theatre complex as the director of a two-hour live performance of four productions of new plays demonstrating their expression as pure sound drama with the theatre in darkness, traditional stage theatre with design, props, physical performance on the stage and lighting, and the curious experience of each play having sequences performed as if they were in the radio drama studio and the actors performing before microphones mixed with spot effects and sound atmospheres. The plays as radio drama had been rehearsed, performed, and produced first. The plays as live theatre were next rehearsed, set designed and produced for the stage, and then merged in the exploration of the different application of the dramatic arts to new writing. Each play switched between the forms usually according to when the script promised more in live theatre production, audio drama listening, or indeed performance in the sound studio which listeners never usually experience.

For several years, I and my colleagues in Independent Radio Drama Productions and its stage arm On Air Theatre originated and produced new dramatic writing in cross-media projects between theatre and radio. In 1996, I had the privilege to produce a virtual sound design with several surround sound and stereo fields for a theatre production of Samuel Beckett's *All That Fall* directed by Tom Morris at the BAC, in Battersea London. The performances were live and in darkness for the actors and audience (Crook, 1999, p. 67). Through these ventures, writers, directors, and audiences gained significant knowledge about the strengths and weaknesses of sound storytelling in the different dramatic forms and how some techniques, artifices, and methodologies do not transfer so well from one to the other.

DOI: 10.4324/9780203838181-11

These were not unique experiences. In the 1920s, Reginald Berkeley success-fully transliterated and transferred his anti-war play, *The White Château*, originally written for BBC Radio for Armistice Night 1925, to West End theatre production. The length of the play was extended by another half hour. It was the first radio drama script published and sold in book form. In 1938, the BBC produced the play for early television drama from Alexandra Palace and even deployed actual artillery in the grounds of the Palace to generate the realistic sounds of war and in the process caused some alarm and consternation to local residents already anxious about the Munich crisis in Europe and fears for the outbreak of another world war.

Berkeley had his 1926 BBC radio play *The Quest for Elizabeth* produced for the-atre immediately after the BBC had censored the end of it without his permission. The excised scene of the central character of the young girl dying on the hospital operating table was performed in the theatre in complete darkness, thus seeking to reproduce a near equivalent of the social psychology of radio listening for the live theatre audience. Two of the modern classic radio plays referenced in this book, Anthony Minghella's *Cigarettes and Chocolate* and Tom Stoppard's *Artist Descending a Staircase* have been adapted successfully for live theatre.

In 2010, Theatre503 in London presented a season of 'Auricular – Fresh Audio Drama Live'. The directors Faith Collingwood and Jacqui Honess-Martin said at the time the work:

> ...promises to immerse a live theatre audience in more audio adventures, thrilling theatricality and an innovative fusion of audio and stage drama. Emerging and experienced radio and theatre writers cross form and style to create an evening of groundbreaking, funny and moving short pieces for a unique audio theatric form.
>
> *(Crook, 2011, p. 163 & Theatre 503, 2010)*

In 2008, the BBC embarked on an ambitious innovative audio drama and film project called *The City Speaks*. It was described as a foray into film-making by BBC Radio 4 and Radio Drama. The multi-platform project was a collaboration between BBC Radio Drama and Film London and experimented with the concept of visual radio by producing two BBC radio plays, an entire feature film, and six collaborations between sound drama directors, scriptwriters, filmmakers, composer David Pickvance, and sound designer Peter Ringrose. Project originator and direc-tor was Conor Lennon. The film was premiered at BFI Southbank and the audio dramas and their visualisation were broadcast by BBC Radio 4 and the BBC's dig-ital television system via remote red button access in March 2008.

Sound drama and film were fused in the exploration of his blindness by film-maker and artist Derek Jarman in 1993 with *Blue* – a film and a radio drama. When broadcast by the UK's Channel 4, it was simultaneously transmitted in sound by BBC Radio 3. BBC R3 later broadcast *Blue* as a standalone radio play with cross-media distribution in CD, DVD, and book publication. I have described the work as 'a beautiful fusion of sound expression across the media of poetic literatures, radio, film and television' (Crook, 2011, p. 75).

Audio drama has a powerful and dynamic cross-media interface between radio, theatre, music, film, animation and games, art exhibition and installation, and Internet and podcasting. The audiogenic storytelling imperatives work in different ways in each context (Crook, 2011, pp. 82–83). For example, Hand & Traynor have explained how the listen-again opportunity to pause, rewind, and listen again changes the potential for appreciating sound and non-word audio plays such as *Revenge* by Andrew Sachs (BBC, 1978) and *A Pot Calling the Kettle Black* by Andreas Bick (SilenceRadio, 2010). Hand & Traynor compared and contrasted as 'a close study of sound alone; its vocabulary in radio drama, its scenography and how these elements synthesize with the imagination of the listener to construct meaning' (Hand & Traynor, 2011, pp. 58–68).

The Internet has expanded audio drama's interactivity and provides listeners as cross-media participants to influence plot developments rather like immersion in computer and online gaming. In the late 1980s, Independent Radio Drama Productions provided LBC phone-in listeners the opportunity to vote on the outcome of moral dilemma short story dramas after broadcast discussion of the themes in phone-in debates. Hand & Traynor discuss BBC radio drama interactive projects, including *The Wheel of Fortune* by Nick Fisher (2001) with three simultaneous versions of the same play on radio and online, and *The Dark House* by Mike Walker (2003) where listener voting could construct a live direction of plot from character options (Hand & Traynor, 2011, p. 72). The dramatisation of *The Unfortunates* by Graham White on BBC Radio 3 in 2010 used the online dimension to replicate B.S. Johnson's rather modernist experiment of having 25 chapters randomly retrievable from a box (Hand & Traynor, 2011). Lance Dann's creative, interactive, and hugely imaginative transmedia *Flickerman* (2009–2010) project is representative of the scale and inventiveness that is possible when experimenting and developing storytelling narrative through dramatic writing augmenting with notions of reality. The series was broadcast on ABC National Radio (Australia), VPRO (Holland), and WFMU (New York). Dann is the author and producer of one of the most original drama-documentaries in British broadcasting, *Ho! Ho! The Clown is Dead* (1994) which traverses dramatic narrative monologue in the characterisation of a clown juxtaposed with authentic documentary reminiscences of real clowns. The texture, emotions, and dramaturgy combine for a unique impact. The programme merits re-broadcasting by the BBC.

It is possible to rewind the history of BBC radio as far back as 1926 on the subject of listener interactivity. The first director of drama productions R.E. Jeffrey originated radio drama competitions under the title *What Would You Do?* He devised four short dramatic sketches enacted in the studio with each sketch terminating in an ambiguous situation. Listeners writing in for the best solutions to the dilemmas received prizes totalling £100 from the editor of *Pearson's Weekly*.

Jeffrey also developed the concept further in respect of the mystery play he had written called *Wolf! Wolf!* Listeners were invited to write in with their account of how the play should have ended. The actual 150-word script was kept secret for a week until the day of the live broadcast with the end included. The version sent which was the closest match to R.E. Jeffrey's secret ending won a top cash prize of £50, worth nearly £3,400 in 2022.

The podcast revolution, which I have described as audio drama's 'platinum age', provides so many more creative concepts in exploring online and digital technology where surround sound software extends binaural, stereo, and 360° listening into so many kinds of immersive intensities.

Dad's Army Ten Seconds from Now

An entertaining and instructive example of cross-media production between television and radio was achieved by *Dad's Army* cowriters David Croft and Jimmy Perry in a storyline about the Home Guard platoon being asked to take part in a live outside BBC broadcast. This was actually produced as a 14 minute Christmas sketch titled *Broadcast To Empire*. Television was done first and radio later. The sound version titled *Ten Seconds from Now* was adapted by Harold Snoad and Michael Knowles as the last and 67th episode of the radio drama series in 1976. Quite apart from being an entertaining lampoon on how not to write and produce radio drama, it exemplified through further comedy what will and will not work so well in each medium. The Home Guard soldiers are to perform a drama script written for them by the BBC producer in London who communicates to them via a large talkback speaker placed behind them in the Church Hall where they usually meet to do their drill and training. The 1940s style BBC microphone is set up in front of them. There is a clear visual comedy in the bungling Captain Mainwaring replying to the producer's questions coming out of the speaker walking over to the speaker to reply. This does not work in radio. The over-enthusiastic and slapstick Lance Corporal Jones repeatedly hits and bangs the microphone for emphasis, but this is always a violent explosion of sound in the ears of the BBC outside broadcast engineer Bert who is monitoring on location. In television, the character looks traumatised and frozen in pain. This is the way the comedy is visualised. However, in the radio production, every time Jones smashes the microphone the sound is amplified in howling feedback and a yelling scream of agony from the engineer. Is the sound version funnier? I have to say I am inevitably biased as the writer of a book on audio drama and say the radio interpretation is so much more impactful.

The parody on bad radio scripting works equally in both media:

MAIN: I decide it's time to go out on patrol. I speak to my sergeant. Sergeant it's
    time for us to go out on patrol.
WILSON: Cor, blimey sir. So it is 'an all.
MAIN: Corporal, it's time for us to go out on patrol.
JONES: Men, it's time for us to go out on patrol.

(Croft & Perry adapted by Snoad & Knowles 1976)

The soldiers are asked to simulate the sounds of sea and seagulls with Private Walker's offer 'shall I make wind, sir' understandably being declined. The writing demonstrates how the presence of bird sounds can be fatal in a sound mix. The young Private Pike, frequently dismissed as a 'Stupid Boy' by Captain Mainwaring, overdoes the seagull squalling and when told to lower the noise he is making, he drops to the floor; comedy again more visual and sonic. Although as the radio version is performed before a loud audience, we hear the laughter first followed by Mainwaring shouting 'Get off the floor, you stupid boy'.

Sorry, Wrong Number – Radio, Film, Radio

Lucille Fletcher's outstanding thriller began as an original radio play with first broadcast on 25th May 1943. It was then made into a film in Hollywood in 1948. Its fame as a radio play in the CBS *Suspense series* preceded the production for the screen and the film's promotion relied on publicity reminding the public that the original sound version had thrilled 40 million people. It was also called the 'most famous radio drama of all time' (Solomon, 1998, p. 25). It then had a reverse trans-ference back into another form of radio with a 1 hour sound version of the film for Lux Radio Theater in January 1950. It also had a live television drama con-version for CBS in November 1954. Fletcher had the opportunity of co-writing the crime novel of the film enjoying global success in Germany as *Falsch verbunden* and in France as *Raccrochez C'est Une Erreur*. Comparing the different versions is a fascinating exercise.

The original sound programme can justifiably be called the perfect radio play. In theoretical language it is mimetic and not diegetic. Everything is shown, the structure is self-contained with no narration, no interior speeches, and the drama equivocates to real time. Listeners join Leona Stevenson's telephone world and that is the point of listening and where the microphone remains throughout. In the 1948 film version so much more back and parallel story is added with flashback. It is ironic that the structure deploys classic radio drama narrative conventions with the points of view of the additional characters joined – most of whom had no voice in the original radio version.

Certainly, the sophistication of multiple strands of narrative and sub-plotting means that the screenplay has a force of ironic tragedy at the end which offers an additional powerful surprise for fans familiar with the original. The villain of the piece, Leona's husband Henry, realises too late that his contract to kill her is no longer necessary and in a reverberation of the panic and helplessness experienced by Leona in the radio version, he cannot stop the murder he no longer needs, nor wants. The Lux Radio Theater 1950 adaptation of the film repeats the narrative conventions and Solomon observes quite rightly this indicates:

> [J]ust how radio-genic the narrative structures of Fletcher's screenplay were to begin with. For, although the character-narrators presumably relate their stories to Leona (or to the doctor, in Henry's case), they also serve a narrative function analogous to that of the radio play announcer or narrator.
>
> *(Solomon 37)*

Citizen Kane – Radio Play on the Screen?

Radio drama teachers can always have fun workshopping the Orson Welles classic film. This is because it has been canonised as the greatest film ever made, or at least one of the greatest, and it has been made by a radio drama practitioner par excellence who brought positive and negative sound play influences and techniques to his first feature length film.

Welles and his *Mercury Theatre on the Air* production culture at CBS had developed the use of detailed and accurate sound effects to enhance the spatial sense of action and atmosphere in their radio dramas. The CBS sound effects studio engineer Ora Nichols deserves significant credit for this qualitative dimension to the sound texture of their output in an age when most people listened to radio on monophonic medium wave. This aspect of *Citizen Kane* revolutionised cinematic sound design. Another aural positive from radio drama in the film was the elevated level of effective and realistic dialogue. Distinct voices matched their characters. The natural cadence of speech with ungrammatical sentences and overlapping and interrupted conversation charged the sound track with verisimilitude.

Although appreciated by radio drama aficionados, filmmakers can properly argue that character-narrators as transitions to flashbacks overload the pace and texture of cinema with a surfeit of telling rather than showing. The deployment of uninterrupted synchronous sound to bridge visual time transitions is something that again might bring joy to the sound dramatist because sound appears to win and dominates the audio–visual relationship. The visual paradigm of cinema is reversed. In reality, this can be judged to cause confusion and distraction. Evan William Cameron argues: 'Accustomed to the sounds of radio but not the sights of cinema, Welles attempted to treat visuals as sounds and subject them to sound techniques. The results were counterproductive...' (Cameron, 1977, p. 96). Cameron explained ears and hearing lack the facility of lenses present in vision. Eyes can focus on objects one at a time. Ears cannot. Hearing perceives aural mixes and sorts them out. The perception is different.

Consequently, when Welles 'attempted to use visual mixes and superpositions to effect time transitions (or to unify disparate events), the results were unnatural and hence emotionally vacuous' (Cameron, 1977, p. 97).

Radio and Film – Oluwale by Jeremy Sandford

Jeremy Sandford discovered that his visceral radio documentary on homelessness in Britain for the BBC Radio Home Service had no social or political impact. He took the subject to Ken Loach at BBC television drama and they reconceived it as the film *Cathy Come Home* (1966). To use a word from social anthropology, this was liminal. The campaigning charity Shelter was conceived. Every main political party in Britain became committed to confronting homelessness and poor housing as an urgent social problem. In 1972, Jeremy Sandford wrote a radio drama on the life of Nigerian migrant David Oluwale who was found dead in the River Aire in

Leeds in suspicious circumstances in 1969. Two police officers were acquitted of his manslaughter but found guilty of repeatedly assaulting him beforehand and jailed for 3 years and 2 years and 3 months. This was the first successful prosecution of British police officers for involvement in the death of a Black person in the United Kingdom.

Jeremy Sandford's BBC Radio play *Oluwale*, produced at BBC Radio Brighton, and then broadcast by BBC Radio 3 in 1972 and 1973 sought to give voice to David Oluwale and expose the scandal of his physical and psychological humiliation when homeless, and the brutal and systematic harassment he was subjected to by the Leeds City Police. Sandford uses classic audio dramatic narrative and dialogic scene sequencing. He begins with the narrator simply informing listeners they are about to hear a dramatisation of the life and death of David Oluwale, a Nigerian who came to Britain in 1949 full of hope and who died tragically in a river in northern England in 1969 just 20 years later. The sound of song, water noise, and ships' hooters is then brought up and faded as the narration explaining that it was on the 16th of August of 1949 that David stowed away on the ship Temple Star sailing to London from Lagos in Nigeria. This is the start of the story. A short bridge of the bedded sound crossfades to a Black man saying that they were a crowd all coming in on boats then and they were on the 'Empire Windrush' (Sandford, 1972, p. 1). The *Guardian*'s then radio critic, Gillian Reynolds said of the radio play:

> A marvellous piece of radio by any standards using the reconstructed docu-
> mentary technique, it employed the fluidity of sound to a remarkable effect.
> The listener was told something, then heard voices expressing shades of opin-
> ion on the same thing so that all statements of fact achieved a dramatized
> depth of opinion, was reminded always of when this man's life was going
> to end, was brought to consider the manner of that death in a way which
> evoked concern and humanity beyond telling…Must mark one of the year's
> landmarks in the use of radio.
>
> *(Sandford, 1974, p. 1)*

Perhaps mindful of his *Cathy Come Home* experience, Sandford wrote the screen-play *Smiling David: The Story of David Oluwale*, published in book form in 1974, optioned by Harlech television, but unfortunately never produced and broadcast as a television film. Sandford artistically respects the different demands between the radio and film media with his screenplay reverting to the mimetic paradigm of showing rather than telling.

In vision there is Lagos shown with seascape, a wide sweeping bay, the dog barking, then dissolved or cut to townscape, Nigerian music, various shots showing the lively street life in Lagos with music. This is then dissolved or cut to the view of a mountain with a boy sitting there. He is David when 6 years old with two or three other boys in the mid-1930s. This is followed by cutting to or dissolving to a Catholic Mission School with children sitting in class and David, now 8 years old, among them. As we see this, we hear the voice of his mother addressing him personally and saying they know he will be somebody they can be proud of. She talks of the sacrifice they have made for him which includes saving up for him to go the Catholic school (Sandford, 1974, p. 13).

In 2007, with access to confidential files released under the 30-year restriction rule, Kester Aspden was able to write and publish a new book investigating David Oluwale's life and the racist hounding he was subjected to. The legacy of what happened to him has been reframed and commemorated through the anthology, *Remembering Oluwale*, published in 2016, a new stage play based on Aspden's book, the formation of the David Oluwale Memorial Association, and the installation of a blue plaque remembering him along with the naming of a new bridge over the River Aire.

Audio drama had an important role as an art form in initiating the necessary political, cultural, and social interrogation of David Oluwale's life journey and experiences in British society.

The playwright Harold Pinter once said 'I like writing for sound radio because of the freedom...' (Pinter, 1977, p. 12). I would like to conclude by saying nearly 100 years after the sound drama form began to be produced for broadcasting, it exponentially fulfils this promise. I sincerely hope all your talents and ambitions as a writer can share in the privilege and fun of writing for it too.

Companion Website Resources

Additions and updates for Chapter 11 Film, Internet and Stage dimensions to Sound Storytelling https://kulturapress.com/2022/08/12/updates-for-chapter-11-film-internet-and-stage-dimensions-to-sound-story-telling/

Orson Welles and Radio Plays https://kulturapress.com/2022/08/29/orson-welles-and-radio-plays/

Oluwale Jeremy Sandford and Radio Drama https://kulturapress.com/2022/08/29/oluwale-jeremy-sandford-and-radio-drama/

Caryl Churchill and Radio Plays https://kulturapress.com/2022/08/30/caryl-churchill-and-radio-plays/

Cinema Television and Audio Drama https://kulturapress.com/2022/08/30/cinema-television-and-audio-drama/

Audio Crime Drama and Radio Detectives https://kulturapress.com/2022/08/30/audio-crime-drama-and-radio-detectives/

Radio Drama and Stage Theatre https://kulturapress.com/2022/08/30/radio-drama-and-stage-theatre/

BIBLIOGRAPHY

Books and Journals

Abbott, W. (1941) *Handbook of Broadcasting (How to Broadcast Effectively)*, New York: McGraw-Hill Book Co.

Achebe, C. (1988) 'An image of Africa: Racism in Conrad's *Heart of Darkness*'. *Massachusetts Review*, 18 (1977). Rpt. in: ed. R. Kimbrough (1961) *Heart of Darkness*, An Authoritative Text, Background and Sources Criticism, 3rd edition. London: W.W Norton and Co., pp. 251–261.

Adams, D. (1985) *The Hitch-Hiker's Guide to the Galaxy: The Original Radio Scripts*, ed. and int. G. Perkins, London: Pan.

Adorno, T. (2000) *The Psychological Technique of Martin Luther Thomas' Radio Addresses*, Stanford, California: Stanford California Press.

Allan, A (1987) *All the Bright Company: Radio Drama Produced by Andrew Allen*, eds H. Fink and J. Jackson, Kingston, Ont.: Quarry Press.

Allan, E., Allan, D., et al. (1951) *Good Listening: A Survey of Broadcasting*, London: Hutchinson & Co. Ltd.

Arden, J. & D'Arcy, M. (1988) *Whose Is the Kingdom: Nine Part Radio Series*, London: Methuen.

Aronson, L. (2001) *Screenwriting Updated: New (and Conventional) Ways of Writing for the Screen*, Los Angeles: Silman-James Press.

Ash, W. (1985) *The Way to Write Radio Drama*, London: Elm Tree.

Ashton, P. (2011) *The Calling Card Script: A Writer's Toolbox for Screen, Stage and Radio*, London: A & C Black.

Balsam, E. (2019) The Closing Sequence of Claire Denis's *Beau Travail*, *Frieze*, (200), 8 Jan 2019. https://www.frieze.com/article/closing-sequence-claire-deniss-beau-travail

Bannerman, R. L. (1986) *Norman Corwin and Radio: The Golden Years*, Tuscaloosa, Alabama: University of Alabama Press.

Barnouw, E. (1940) *Handbook of Radio Writing: An Outline of Techniques and Markets in Radio Writing in the United States*, Boston: Little, Brown and Company.

Barnouw, E., ed. (1945) *Radio Drama in Action: 25 Plays of a Changing World*, London & Toronto: Farrar & Rinehart, Inc. incorporating the plays: *Columbus Day* by O. Welles, in collaboration with R. Meltzer and N. Houghton, *Will This Earth Hold?* By P.S. Buck, *The Battle of the Warsaw Ghetto* by M. Wishengrad, *Mister Ledford and the Tva* by A. Lomax, *Open Letter on Race Hatred* by W. N. Robson, *Bretton Woods* by P. Lyon, *The Last Day of the War*, by Sgt. A. Laurents, *A Child Is Born*, S. V. Benet, *The Halls of Congress* by J. Gottlieb, *Radioman Jack Cooper*, H. Chevigny, *Concerning The Red Army* by N. Rosten, *Inside a Kid's Head* by J. Lawrence and R. E. Lee, *London by Clipper* by N. Corwin, *Japanese-Americans* by H. Kleiner, *The Lonesome Train* by M. Lampell, *The 'Boise'* by R. MacDougall, *Grandpa and the Statue* by A. Miller, *Booker T. Washington In Atlanta* by L. Hughes, *North Atlantic Testament* by Father T. J. Mulvey, *Typhus* by B. V. Dryer, *Pacific Task Force*, by T/Sgt. L. Lader, *Against the Storm* by S. Michael, *The Negro Domestic* by R. Ottley, *Japan's Advance Base: The Bonin Islands* by A. Marquis, *The House I Live in* by A. Oboler.

Barrault, J.-L. (1951) *Reflections on the Theatre*, London: Rockliff.

Beck, A. (1997) *Radio Acting*, London: A. and C. Black.

Beck, A. (2000) *The Invisible Play*, Canterbury: Kent University CD-Rom.

Beckett, S. (1989) *Collected Shorter Plays of Samuel Beckett* (includes radio plays: *All That Fall, Embers, Rough for Radio I, Rough for Radio II, Words and Music, Cascando*), London: Faber and Faber.

Bennett, A. (1988) *Talking Heads*, London: BBC Books, incorporating 6 monologues written for television: *A Chip in the Sugar, Bed Among the Lentils, A Lady of Letters, Her Big Chance, Soldiering On, A Cream Cracker Under the Settee.*

Berkeley, R. (1925) *The White Chateau: The Play Broadcasted by the B.B.C. Armistice Night, 1925*, London: Williams and Norgate Ltd.

Berkeley, R. (1926a) *The World's End The Quest of Elizabeth and Other Plays*, London: Williams & Norgate Ltd, incorporating *The World's End, Eight O'Clock, Mango Island, The Quest of Elizabeth.*

Berkeley, R. (1926b) *The Dweller in the Darkness: A Play of the Unknown in One Act*, London: H.F.W. Deane & Sons, The Year Book Press Ltd.

Berkeley, R. (1927a) *Machines: A Symphony of Modern Life*, London: Robert Holden & Co., Ltd.

Bernaerts, L. & Midlorf, J., eds. (2021) *Audionarratology: Lessons from Radio Drama*, Columbus, USA: The Ohio State University Press.

Birney, E. & Fink, H., introd. (1985) *Words on Waves: Selected Radio Plays of Earle Birney*, Kingston, Ont: Quarry Press, incorporation: *Beowulf, Gawain & The Green Knight, The Griffin & The Minor Canon, Piers Plowman, The Third 'Shepherds' Play', The Duel, Court Martial, Damnation of Vancouver.*

Boardman-Jacobs, S., ed. (2004) *Radio Scriptwriting*, Bridgend, Wales: Seren.

Booker, C. (2004) *The Seven Basic Plots: Why We Tell Stories*, New York: Continuum.

Bradley, A., ed. (1967) *Worth a Hearing*, London & Glasgow: Blackie, incorporating *The Mating Season* by A. Plater, *The Dock Brief* by J. Mortimer, *Don't Wait for Me* by D. Campton, *She'll Make Trouble* by B. Naughton, *The Day Dumbfounded Got His Pylon* by H. Livings.

Bradley, A., ed. (1978) *Out of the Air*, London: Longman Group Ltd, incorporating *We Could Always Fit a Sidecar* by S. Barstow, *There's No Point in Arguing the Toss* by D. Haworth, *Relics* by D. Campton, *Jump!* By K. Whitmore, *Take Any Day* by I. Wilson.

Bradley, S. J. (2016) *Remembering Oluwale*, Scarborough: Valley Press.

Bridson, D. G. (1943) *Aaron's Field*, London: Pendock Press.

Bridson, D. G. (1971) *Prospero and Ariel: The Rise and Fall of Radio, A Personal Recollection*, London: Victor Gollancz Ltd.

British Broadcasting Corporation (1932) *Broadcasting House*, London: B.B.C.

Brooke, P. (1995) *Radio Social Drama: Communicating through Story Characters*, New York: University Press of America.

Brooks, C. (1983) *The Case of the Stolen Dinosaur: A Play in 2 Versions – Stage and Radio*, Claremont, CA, USA: Belnice Books.

Burrows, A. R. (1924) *The Story Of Broadcasting*, London: Cassell and Company Ltd.

Busfield, R. M. (1971) *The Playwright's Art: Stage, Radio, Television, Motion Pictures*, Westport, CT: Greenwood.

Cameron, E. W. (1977) Citizen Kane: The Influence of Radio Drama on Cinematic Design. in: Lewis, P. ed., *Papers of the Radio Literature Conference 1977*, Durham: Durham University.

Cantril, H., Gaudet, H. & Herzog, H. (1966) *The Invasion from Mars: A Study in the Psychology of Panic with the Complete Script of the Famous Orson Welles Broadcast*, Princeton, NJ: Princeton University Press.

Carlile, J. S. (1939) *Production and Direction of Radio Programs*, New York: Prentice-Hall Inc.

Carter, A. & Clapp, S., introd. (1997) *The Curious Room: Angela Carter, Collected Dramatic Works*, London: Vintage incorporating the radio plays *Vampirella (Radio Play)*, *Come unto These Yellow Sands*, *The Company of Wolves*, *Puss in Boots*, *A Self-Made Man*.

Carter, A. (1985) *Come Unto These Yellow Sands: Four Radio Plays*, Newcastle upon Tyne: Bloodaxe Books.

Caulfield, A. (2009) *Writing for Radio: A Practical Guide*, Marlborough, Wiltshire: The Crowood Press Ltd.

Chignell, H. (2017) British radio drama and the avant-garde in the 1950s. *Historical Journal of Film, Radio and Television*, 37(4): 649–664.

Chignell, H. (2019) *British Radio Drama, 1945-63*, London: Bloomsbury.

Chothia, J. (1996) *English Drama of the Early Modern Period 1890–1940 (Longman Literature in English Series)*, London: Routledge.

Churchill, C. (1990) *Churchill Shorts: Short Plays by Caryl Churchill*, London: Nick Hern.

Cooper, G. (1966) *Giles Cooper: Six Plays for Radio*, London: British Broadcasting Corporation, incorporating the plays *Mathry Beacon*, *The Disagreeable Oyster*, *Without the Grail*, *Under The Loofah Tree*, *Unman, Wittering and Zigo*, & *Before the Monday*.

Corwin, N. & Fadiman, C., introd. (1944) *More by Corwin: 16 Radio Dramas by Norman Corwin*, New York: Henry Holt and Company.

Corwin, N. & Roosevelt, F. D. (1942) *We Hold These Truths: A Dramatic Celebration of the American Bill of Rights*, including an address by Franklin D. Roosevelt. New York: Howell, Soskin, Publishers.

Corwin, N. (1942) *Thirteen by Corwin*, New York: Henry Holt and Company.

Corwin, N. (1945) *They Fly Through the Air With the Greatest of Ease*, Vermont: Vrest Orton.

Corwin, N. (1947) *Untitled and Other Radio Dramas by Norman Corwin*, New York: Henry Holt & Company.

Coulter, D., ed. (1939) *Columbia Workshop Plays: Fourteen Radio Dramas*, New York: Whittesley House, McGraw-Hill Book Company, Inc.

Coulton, B. (1980) *Louis MacNeice in the BBC*, London: Faber and Faber.

Crews, A., et al. (1944) *Radio Production Directing*, Boston, New York: Houghton Mifflin Company, The Riverside Press Cambridge.

Croft, D. & Perry, J. (2001) *Dad's Army: The Complete Scripts of Series 1–4*, London: Orion.

Croft, D. & Perry, J. (2002) *Dad's Army: The Complete Scripts of Series 5–9*, London: Orion.

Crofts, C. (2003) *Anagrams of Desire: Angela Carter's Writing for Radio, Film and Television*, Manchester: Manchester University Press.

Crook, T. & Shannon, R. (1991) *Radio Drama, Writing, Acting and Production*, Manningtree, Essex: IRDP/Woolwich Building Society (booklet with cassette pack).

Crook, T. (1997) *International Radio Journalism: History, Theory and Practice*, London & New York: Routledge.

Crook, T. (1999) *Radio Drama: Theory and Practice*, London & New York: Routledge.

Crook, T. (2011) *The Sound Handbook*, London & New York: Routledge.

Crook, T. (2012) George Orwell: Cold War Radio Warrior?' in: *Orwell Today*, Keeble, R.L. ed., Bury St Edmunds: Abramis Academic.

Crook, T. (2014) Norman Corwin's the Lonesome Train (Live Broadcast) CBS 1944: A critical reflection. *RadioDoc Review*, *1*(1). doi:10.14453/rdr.v1i1.5

Crook, T. (2016) Transatlantic or Ango-American Corwin? in: *Anatomy of Sound: Norman Corwin and Media Authorship*, Smith, J. & Verma, N., eds., Oakland, California USA: University of California Press.

Crook, T. (2018) *Devils On Horseback*, unpublished stage play performed in Deptford Town Hall, Lewisham, London, and taken on national tour to Cambridge, Dover, Leeds and Middlesborough by the Creative Vortex Company with performances at the Tristan Bates Theatre, London, and Sands Film Studios, Rotherhithe.

Crook, T. (2020) *Audio Drama Modernism: The Missing Link between Descriptive Phonograph Sketches and Microphone Plays on the Radio*, Singapore: Palgrave Macmillan.

Crook, T. (2021) The Audio Dramatist's Critical Vocabulary in Great Britain. in: *Audionarratology: Lessons from Radio Drama*, Bernaerts, L. & Midlorf, J. eds., Columbus USA: The Ohio State University Press.

Cusy, P. & Germinet, G. (1926, 1949) *Théâtre radiophonique, Mode nouveau d'expression artistique*, Paris: Etienne Chiron.

Daley, B. (1994) *The National Public Star Wars Radio Dramatization*, NewYork: Ballantine.

Dancyger, K. (1991) *Broadcast Writing: Dramas, Comedies, and Documentaries*, (Electronic Media Guides), Boston, MA: Focal Press.

Dancyger, K. & Rush, J. (1995) *Alternative Scriptwriting: Writing Beyond the Rules*, 2nd edition, Boston, MA: Focal Press.

Dane, C., (1942) *The Saviours: Seven Plays on One Theme*, London: William Heinemann Ltd, incorporating the radio plays: *Merlin, The Hope of Britain, England's Darling, The May King, The Light of Britain, Remember Nelson, The Unknown Soldier*.

Dann, L. (2015) *Only Half the Story: Radio Drama, Online Audio and Transmedia Storytelling*, Brighton: University of Brighton at https://cris.brighton.ac.uk/ws/files/376126/Dann%20-%20Only%20Half%20the%20Story.pdf

Dann, L. & Spinelli, M. (2021) *Podcasting: The Audio Media Revolution*, London: Bloomsbury.

De Bernières, L. (2001) *Sunday Morning at the Centre of the World: A Play for Voices*, London: Vintage.

De Fossard, E., et al. (2005) *Writing and Producing Radio Dramas: Communication for Behavior Change, Vol. 1*, Thousand Oaks: Sage Publications.

Dixon, P. (1936) *Radio Sketches and How to Write Them*, New York: Frederick A. Stokes Company.

Drakakis, J., ed. (1981) *British Radio Drama*, Cambridge: Cambridge University Press.

Douglas, S. J. (1999) *Listening in: Radio and the American Imagination, from Amos'n' Andy and Edward R. Murrow to Wolfman Jack and Howard Stern*, New York: Times Books, Random House.

du Garde Peach, L. (1931) *Radio Plays: The Path of Glory, The Mary Celeste, Love One Another, La Bastille, Ingredient X*, London: George Newnes Ltd.

Dunlap Jr., O. E. (1936) *Talking on the Radio: A Practical Guide for Writing and Broadcasting a Speech*, New York: Greenberg.

Durham, R. & MacDonald, F. J., eds. (1989) *Destination Freedom: Scripts from Radio's Black Legacy, 1948–50*, Westport, CT: Praeger.

Edgar, D. (2009) *How Plays Work*, London: Nick Hern Books.

Egri, L. (1942) *How to Write a Play*, New York: Simon and Schuster.

Eliot, T. S. (1975) *Collected Poems, 1909–1962*, London: Faber and Faber.

Eliot, T. S. & Haywood, J., eds. (1955) *Selected Prose*, Harmondsworth, England: Penguin.

Ellis, K. M. (1931) *The Trial of Vivienne Ware: A Radio Drama*, New York: Grosset & Dunlap.

Esslin, M. (1961) *Brecht: The Man and His Work*, New York: Doubleday & Company, Anchor Books.

Esslin, M. (1987) *The Field of Drama: How the Signs of Drama Create Meaning on Stage and Screen*, London: Methuen.

Esslin, M., ed. (1966) *New Radio Drama*, London: The British Broadcasting Corporation, incorporating *Tonight Is Friday* by C. Finbow, *A Voice Like Thunder* by I. Rodger, *A Nice Clean Sheet* by R. Adrian, *Sixteen Lives of the Drunken Dreamer* by S. Grenfell, *The Ruffian on the Stair* by J. Orton, *The Sconcing Stoup* by S. Raven.

Ewens, E. & Bakewell, M., eds. (1961) *From the Fifties: BBC Sound Radio Drama Series*, London: British Broadcasting Corporation.

Felton, F. (1949) *The Radio Play: Its Technique and Possibilities*, London: Sylvan Press.

Fink, H. (1981) Beyond Naturalism: Tyrone Guthrie's Radio Theatre and the Stage Production of Shakespeare. *Theatre Research in Canada/Recherches théâtrales Au Canada*, 2(1): 19–32, Retrieved from https://journals.lib.unb.ca/index.php/TRIC/article/view/7519

Fletcher, L. (1980) *Sorry, Wrong Number* and *The Hitch-Hiker*, New York USA: Dramatists Play Service Inc.

Fountain, T. (2007) *So You Want to Be a Playwright? How to Write a Play and Get It Produced*, London: Nick Hern Books.

Freeman, B. P. (2001) *The Superman Radio Scripts: Volume 1: Superman vs. The Atom Man, the Original Scripts from the 1940s Radio Series: The Adventures of Superman*, compiled and edited by DC Comics, New York: Watson-Guptill Publications.

French, F. F. (1946) *The Birth of the Song, 'Silent Night': An Original Historical Radio Drama for School Public Address Systems*, Boston, Massachussetts: Baker's Plays.

Frick, N. A. (1987) *Image in the Mind: CBC Radio Drama 1944 to 1954*, Toronto, Ontario: Canadian Stage and Arts Publications Ltd.

Frost, E. C., ed. (1991) *Radio Drama, Theatre Journal*, Vol. 43(3), Baltimore, USA: John Hopkins University Press.

Frost, E.C., & Herzfeld-Sander, M., eds. (1991) *German Radio Plays: Jurgen Becker, Gunter Eich, Peter Handke, and Others*, Vol. 86, New York: Continuum, The German Library.

Fryer, P. (1984) *Staying Power: The History of Black People in Britain*, London: Pluto Press.

Gamlin, L. (1947) *You're on the Air: A Book About Broadcasting*, London: Chapman & Hall Ltd.

Gielgud, V. (1932) *How to Write Broadcast Plays*, London: Hurst & Blackett, Ltd, incorporating *Friday Morning, Red Tabs*, and *Exiles*.

Gielgud, V. (1946) *Radio Theatre: Plays Specially Written for Broadcasting*, London: MacDonald & Co.

Gielgud, V. (1948) *The Right Way to Radio Playwriting*, Kingswood, Surrey: Right Way Books Andrew George Elliot.

Gielgud, V. (1949) *Years of the Locust*, London & Brussels: Nicholson & Watson.

Gielgud, V. & Marvell, H. (1934) *Death at Broadcasting House*, London: Rich & Cowan Ltd.

Gielgud, V., et al. (1957) *British Radio Drama 1922–1956*, London: George G. Harrap & Co. Ltd.

Gilliam, L., ed. (1950) *B.B.C. Features*, London: Evans Brothers Ltd, by arrangement with the British Broadcasting Corporation.

Gooch, S. (2004) *Writing a Play (Writing Handbooks)*, London: A & C Black Publishers Ltd.

Graves, R. P. (1994) *Richard Hughes: A Biography*, London: André Deutsch.

Grove, C. & Wyatt, S. (2013) *So You Want To Write Radio Drama?* London: Nick Hern Books.

Guralnick, S. E. (1996) *Sight Unseen: Beckett, Pinter, Stoppard and Other Contemporary Dramatists on Radio*, Athens, Ohio: Ohio University Press.

Guthrie, T. (1931) *'Squirrel's Cage' and Two Other Microphone Plays*, London: Cobden and Sanderson. [Incorporating the scripts *Squirrel's Cage, Matrimonial News, & The Flowers Are Not for You to Pick*.]

Guthrie, T. (1934) Radio drama in *B.B.C. Annual 1935*, London: BBC.

Guthrie, T. (1935) 'Radio drama in *B.B.C. Annual 1935*, London: The british Broadcasting Corporation, pp. 179–183.

Haddon, A. (1924) *Hullo Playgoers: Wireless Theatre Talks: Broadcast to the British Iles from 2LO*, London: Cecil Palmer.

Hall, L. (1997) *Spoonface Steinberg and Other Plays*, London: BBC Books.

Hand, R. J. & Traynor, M. (2011) *The Radio Drama Handbook*, New York: Continuum.

Harrison, C. (1982) *A Suffolk Trilogy: Three Plays for Radio by Carey Harrison*, Cambridge: Oleander Press, incorporating *I Never Killed My German, The Anatolian Head, Of The Levitation At St. Michael's*.

Hatton, C. (1948) *Radio Plays and How to Write Them*, St. Ives, Huntingdon: Matson's Publications.

Haworth, D. (1972) *We All Come to it in the End and Other Plays for Radio*, London: British Broadcasting Corporation.

Henderson, G. & Pieterse, C., eds. (1973) *Nine African Plays for Radio* incorporating the plays: *Sunil's Dilemma* by K. Sondhi, *The Soldiers* by R. White, *The Trial of Busumbala* by G. J. Roberts, *The Prisoner, the Judge and the Jailer* by D. Clems, *Oh, How Dearly I Detest Thee* by J. N. Libondo, *Lagos, Yes, Lagos* by Y. Ajibade, *Beyond the Line* by L. Erapu, *Full-Cycle* by G. Tialobi, *Addo: Company Pot* by P. Henaku, London: Heinemann.

Henderson, G., ed. (1973) *African Theatre: Eight Prize-Winning Plays Chosen by Wole Soyinka, Martin Esslin, Lewis Nkosi*, incorporating the plays: *More Like Slaves* by R. Rive, *Station Street* by K. A. Mustafa, *Sweet Scum of Freedom* by J. Singh, *Double Attack* by C. C. Umeh, *Scholarship Woman* by D. Clems, *The Transister Radio* by K. Tsaro-Wiwa, *Family Spear* by E. N. Zirimu, & *Sign of the Rainbow*, by W. Ogunyemi, London: Heinemann.

Heppenstall, R., ed. & introd. (1948) *Imaginary Conversations: Eight Radio Scripts by Michael Innes, Rose McAulay, Sean O'Faolain, V.S.Pritchett, Herbert Read, G.W.Stonier, C.V. Wedgwood*, London: Secker & Warburg.

Hill, S. (1975) *The Cold Country and Other Plays for Radio*, London: British Broadcasting Corporation.

Horstmann, R. (1991) *Writing For Radio*. 2nd edition, London: A&C Black.

Hughes, J. C. (1990) *Dismal Man Two Radio Plays*, Cincinnati, Ohio: Cincinnati Poetry Review Press, incorporating *The Tanyard Murder* and *The Night Creeper*.

Hughes, R. (1924 & 1928) *Plays: The Sisters Tragedy, A Comedy of Good and Evil, The Man Born to Be Hanged, Danger*, London; The Phoenix Library, Chatto & Windus.

Hulke, M. (1980) *Writing for Television*, London: A. and C. Black.

Huwiler, E. (2005) Storytelling by Sound: A Theoretical Frame for Radio drama analysis. *Radio Journal: International Studies in Broadcast & Audio Media*, 3(1):45–59.

Jarman, D. (1994) *Blue: Text of a Film*, Woodstock, New York: Overlook Press.

Jennings, G. E. (1915) *Five Birds In A Cage: A Play in One Act*, London: Samuel French Ltd. Also in Marriott, J. W. (1928) *One-Act Plays of To-Day Fourth Series*, London: The Harrap Library, pp. 193–215.

Johnson, P. H. (1958) *Proust Recaptured: Six Radio Sketches Based on the Author's Characters*, Chicago: The University of Chicago Press.

Jones, P. A., ed. (1976) *Imagist Poetry (The Penguin poets)*, Harmondsworth: Penguin.

Jonsson, J. (1949) *Writing For Broadcasting: A Complete Guide to the Requirements of All Departments of the B.B.C.*, St Ives, Huntingdon: Matson's Publications.

Kamerman, S. E., ed. (1975) *A Treasury of Christmas Plays: One-Act, Royalty-Free Plays for Stage or Microphone Performance and Round-the-Table Reading*, Boston: Plays, Inc.

Kaplan, M. A. (1949) *Radio and Poetry*, New York: Columbia University Press.

Keillor, G. (1991) *A Radio Romance*, London: Faber and Faber. Other titles by the same author and publisher include *Happy to Be Here* (1982), *Lake Wobegon Days* (1985), *Leaving Home* (1987) and *We Are Still Married* (1989).

Keith, A. (1944) *How to Speak and Write for Radio*, New York: Harper & Brothers.

Keller, E. L. (1944) *The Script Shop Presents Eleven Radio Plays*, Sharon, PA, USA: Sharon Herald Broadcasting Co.

Kester, M. & Collier, E. (1937) *Writing for the B.B.C. Practical Hints on How to Write Successfully for the Light Entertainment Department of the B.B.C.*, London: Sir Isaac Pitman & Sons, Ltd.

Kisner, D. (2004) *Theatre of the Mind: Writing & Producing Radio Dramas in the Classroom*, Sangar, CA, USA: Balance Publishing Company.

Koch, H. (1971) *The Panic Broadcast: Portrait of an Event by Howard Koch*, New York City: Avon.

Krulevitch Walter, K. & Cowgill, R. (1954) *Radio Drama Acting and Production: A Handbook*. [1st edition, 1946], CA, USA: Rinehart Radio and Television Series.

Lawton, S. P. (1938) *Radio Drama*, Boston, Massachusetts: Expression Company.

Lea, G. (1926) *Radio Drama and How to Write It*, London: George Allen & Unwin Ltd.

Lea, G. (1949) *Modern Stagecraft for the Amateur*, London: Sir Isaac Pitman & Sons, Ltd.

Lewis, C. A. (1924) *Broadcasting from Within*, London: George Newnes Limited.

Lewis, P. M. (1991) Referable words in radio drama. in: P. Scannell (ed.) *Broadcast Talk*, London: Sage.

Lewis, P., ed. (1977) *Papers of the Radio Literature Conference 1977*, Durham: Durham University.

Lewis, P., ed. (1981) *Radio Drama*, Harlow, Essex: Longman Group Ltd.

Lloyd, A. L. & Vinogradoff, I. (1940) *Shadow of the Swastika*, London: John Lane the Bodley Head.

Mackey, D. R. (1951) *Drama on the Air*, New York: Prentice-Hall, Inc.

MacLeish, A. (1937) *The Fall of the City: A Verse Play for Radio*, New York & Toronto: Farrar & Rinehart, Inc.

MacLeish, A. (1941) *Air Raid: A Verse Play for Radio*, New York: Harcourt, Brace and Company.

Macleish, A. (1944) *The American Story: Ten Broadcasts*, New York: Duell, Sloan and Pearce.

MacLoughlin, S. (1998) *Successful Writing for Radio: How to Create Successful Radio Plays, Features, and Short Stories*, Oxford: How to Books.

MacNeice, L. & Auden, W.H., introd. (1969) *Persons from Porlock and Other Plays for Radio*, London: British Broadcasting Corporation, incorporating the scripts *Enter Caesar, East of the Sun and West of the Moon, They Met on Good Friday, Persons from Porlock*.

MacNeice, L. (1944) *Christopher Columbus: A Radio Play*, London: Faber & Faber.

MacNeice, L. (1946) *The Dark Tower and Other Radio Scripts*, London: Faber and Faber Limited.

MacQueen-Pope, W. (1959) *The Footlights Flickered: The Story of the Theatre of the 1920s*, London: Herbert Jenkins.

Marriott, J. W. (1926) *One-Act Plays of To-Day: Third Series*, London: George G. Harrap & Co.

Marriott, J. W. (1928) *One-Act Plays of Today: Fourth Series*, London: George G. Harrap & Co., incorporating *Five Birds In A Cage* by Gertrude E Jennings, pp. 193–215.

Matheson, H. (1933) *Broadcasting*, London: Thornton Butterworth.

McGill, E. (1940) *Radio Directing*, New York and London: McGraw-Hill Book Company, Inc.

McInerney, V. (2001) *Writing for Radio*, Manchester & New York: Manchester University Press.

McMurtry, L. (2019 *Revolution in the Echo Chamber: Audio Drama's Past, Present, and Future*, Bristol: Intellect Books.

McMurtry, L. (2021) Special Section: Radio Drama Takeover. *RadioDoc Review*, Online at https://ro.uow.edu.au/cgi/viewcontent.cgi?article=1111&context=rdr

McWhinnie, D. (1959) *The Art Of Radio*, London: Faber and Faber.

Mestrovic, J., ed. (1999) *Croatian Radio Plays in the 1990s*, Zagreb, Croatia: Croatian Radio Library.

Minghella, A. (1989) 'Cigarettes and Chocolate' in *Best Radio Plays of 1988*, London: Methuen/BBC Publications, pp. 123–148.

Minghella, A. (1997) *Anthony Minghella Plays: 2*, London: Methuen, incorporating *Cigarettes and Chocolate, Hang Up, What If It's Raining, Truly, Madly, Deeply, Mosaic, & Days Like These*.

Moffatt, N.D. (1988) 'Lifetime' in *Best Radio Plays of 1987*, London: Methuen/BBC Publications, pp. 71–82.

Napier, F. (1948) *Noises Off: A Handbook of Sound Effects*. 3rd Edition, London: Frederick Muller Ltd.

Nesbitt, C. (1975) *A Little Love & Good Company*, London: Faber & Faber.

Ney, D., Hitchinson, D., et al. ed. (1995) *Radio Plays for the World: BBC World Service Drama*, London: British Broadcasting Corporation.

Nicholson, N., Read, H., et al., introd. (1964) *Writers on Themselves*, London: British Broadcasting Corporation.

Oboler, A. & Longstreet, S., ed. (1944) *Free World Theatre: Nineteen New Radio Plays*, New York: Random House.

Oboler, A. (1940) *Ivory Tower and Other Radio Plays*, Chicago: William Targ.

Oboler, A. (1942) *This Freedom: Thirteen New Radio Plays*, New York: Random House.

Oboler, A. (1945) *Oboler Omnibus; Radio Plays and Personalities*, New York: Duell, Sloan & Pearce.

Oboler, A., Stone, I., introd. (1940) *Fourteen Radio Plays*, New York: Random House.

Olfson, L. (1958) *Radio Plays from Shakespeare: Ten Plays by William Shakespeare Adapted for Royalty-Free Performance*, Boston, USA: Plays, Inc.

Perry, J. & Croft, D. (1998) *Dad's Army: The Lost Episodes*, London: Virgin Publishing Ltd, including the episode 'The Loneliness of the Long Distance Walker" pp. 59–84.

Pietropaolo, D., ed. (2005) *Where Is Here? The Drama of Immigration*, Vol. II, Winnipeg: Scirocco Drama, incorporating the plays: *Novena* by Marie-Beath Badian, *The Clothesline* by Donna Caruso, *Spring Arrival*, by Marjorie Chan, *The Gift*, by Marty Chan, *Say Ginger Ale*, by Marcia Johnson, *One Officer's Experiences*, by Arthur J. Vaughan.

Phillips, C. (1985) 'The Wasted Years' in *Best Radio Plays of 1984*, London: Methuen/BBC Productions, pp. 85–141.

Pinter, H. (1977) *Pinter Plays Two: The Caretaker, The Collection, The Lover, Night School, The Dwarfs*, London: Methuen.

Pope, T. (1998) *Good Scripts: Learning the Craft of Screenwriting through 25 of the Best and Worst Films in History*, New York: Three Rivers Press.

Pownall, D. (1998) *Radio Plays: An Epiphanous Use of the Microphone, Beef, Ploughboy Monday, Flos, Kitty Wilkinson, Under the Table*, London: Oberon.

Pownall, D. (2010) *Sound Theatre: Thoughts on the Radio Play*, London: Oberon Books.

Putt Jr, B. M. (2023) *Stories Told through Sound: The Craft of Writing Audio Dramas for Podcasts, Streaming, and Radio*, Montclair, New Jersey, USA: Applause Books.

Reed, H. (1971) *The Streets of Pompeii and Other Plays for Radio*, London: British Broadcasting Corporation.

Reed, H. (1976) *Hilda Tablet and Others: Four Pieces for Radio*, London: British Broadcasting Corporation.

Reith, J. C. W. (1924) *Broadcast over Britain*, London: Hodder and Stoughton Ltd.

Richards, K. (1991) *Writing Radio Drama*, Sydney: Currency Press.

Rodger, I. (1982) *Radio Drama*, London and Basingstoke: The Macmillan Press Ltd.

Rogers, R. (1937) *Do's and Don'ts of Radio Writing*, Boston: Associated Radio Writers.

Sackville-West, E. (1945) *The Rescue: A Melodrama for Broadcasting Based on Homer's Odyssey*, London: Secker and Warburg.

Sandford, J. (1974) *Smiling David: Story of David Oluwale*, London: Calder & Boyars.

Sayers, D. L. (1943) *The Man Born to be King*, New York: Harper.

Scarpa, T. (1997) *Popcorn*, Rome: RAI and Prix Italia.

Schafer, R. M. (1977, 1994) *Our Sonic Environment and the Soundscape: The Tuning of the World*, New York: Alfred Knopf/Random House.

Scriven, R.C. (1974) *The Seasons of the Blind: And Other Radio Plays In Verse*, London: British Broadcasting Corporation.

Seymour, K. & Martin, J. T.W., et al. (1938) *Practical Radio Writing: The Technique of Writing for Broadcasting Simply and Thoroughly Explained*, London: Longmans, Green and Co.

Sher, E. (1998) *Making Waves: Three Radio Plays: Mourning Dove, Denial Is a River, Past Imperfect*, Toronto & Oxford: Simon & Pierre, a member of the Dundurn Group.

Sheriff, R.C., et al., (1929) *Famous Plays of To-Day*, London: Victor Gollancz Ltd.

Sherman, J. and 29 Other Playwrights (1996) *Instant Applause II: 30 Very Short Complete Plays*, Winnipeg, Man: Blizzard.

Shields, C. and 25 Other Playwrights (1994) *Instant Applause: 26 Very Short Complete Plays*, Winnipeg, Man: Blizzard.

Shirazi, S. F. (2020) *Radio/Body: Phenomenology and Dramaturgies of Radio*, Manchester: Manchester University Press.

Sieveking, L. (1934) *The Stuff of Radio*, London: Cassell, incorporating the plays *Arrest in Africa, The Sea in a Shell, The Wings of the Morning, The Seven Ages of Mechanical Music, Money for Nothing, Victoria, Intimate Snapshots, Human Nature*, and 'Extracts from Plays too purely Radio to be printed for reading' including: *Kaleidoscope I, Kaleidoscope II, The End of Savoy Hill, The Pursuit of Pleasure & Love*.

Smith, I. (1976) *The Death of a Wombat*, Melbourne, Australia: Sun.

Solomon, M. (1998) Adapting 'Radio's Perfect Script': 'Sorry Wrong Number' and *Sorry, Wrong Number, Quar. Rev. of Film & Video*, 16(1): 23–40.

Spencer, S. (2004) *The Playwright's Guidebook*, London: Faber & Faber.

Stoppard, T. (1994) *Stoppard: The Plays for Radio 1964–1991*, London: Faber and Faber, incorporating *The Dissolution of Dominic Boot, 'M' is for Moon Among Other Things, If You're Glad I'll be Frank, Albert's Bridge, Where Are They Now? Artist Descending a Staircase, The Dog It Was That Died, in the Native State*.

Straczynski, M. J. (1996) *The Complete Book of Scriptwriting*, 2nd edition, Cincinnati, Ohio: Writer's Digest.

Sykes, A., ed. & introd. (1975) *Five Plays for Radio: Nightmares of the Old Obscenity Master and Other Plays by Maslen, Free, Marshall, Nowra*, Sydney, Australia: Currency Press.

Teller, N. (2018) *Audio Drama: 10 Plays for Radio and Podcast*, Kindle at: https://www.amazon.co.uk/Audio-Drama-Plays-Radio-Podcast-ebook/dp/B07NCYRZX9/

Teller, N. (2021) *More Audio Drama: 10 More Plays for Radio and Podcasts*, Kindle at: https://www.amazon.co.uk/More-Audio-Drama-Plays-Podcast-ebook/dp/B097Q8MLPW/

Thomas, D. (1985) [Jones, D. prefaces 1954, 1974] *Under Milk Wood: A Play for Voices*, London and Melbourne: Dent, Everyman's Library.

Thomas, H. & Watt, J., introd. (1940) *How to Write for Broadcasting*, London: George Allen and Unwin Ltd.

Thompson, K. (1999) *Storytelling in the New Hollywood: Understanding Classical Narrative Technique*, Cambridge, Massachusetts, London, England: Harvard University Press.

Turner, A. (1944) *Australian Stages: A Play in Verse for Radio*, Sydney, Australia: Mulga Publications.

Verma, N. (2012) *Theater of the Mind; Imagination, Aesthetics, and American Radio Drama*, Chicago & London: The University of Chicago Press.

Wade, P. (1936) *Wedding Group and Other Plays*, London: Stanley Smiths (Publishers) Ltd.

Watt, J. (1940) *How to Write for Broadcasting*, London: George Allen and Unwin Ltd.

Watts, E. (2018) *Drama Podcasts: An overview of the US and UK Drama Podcast Market*, London: BBC Sounds and published at: http://downloads.bbc.co.uk/radio/commissioning/Drama-Podcast-Research-Dec2018.pdf

Weaver, L. (1948) *The Technique of Radio Writing*, New York: Prentice-Hall, Inc.

Weiser, N. (1941) *Writer's Radio Theatre*, New York: Harper & Brothers.

Whipple, J. (1938) *How to Write for Radio*, New York: McGraw-Hill Books Co.

Whitaker-Wilson, C. (1935) *Writing for Broadcasting*, London: A. & C. Black, Ltd.

Wyatt, S. (2008) *Memorials to the Missing*, Milton Keynes: Amazon/Lightning Source.

Wylie, M. & Titterton, L., introd. (1939) *Radio Writing*, New York & Toronto: Rinehart & Company, Inc.

Zephaniah, B. (1988) 'Hurricane Dub' in *Young Radio Playwrihts' Festival 1988*, London: BBC Books, pp. 11–31.

Academic Theses

Johnstone, P. (2022) *Independent Local Radio Drama: A cultural, historical and regulatory examination of British Commercial Radio Drama*, Bournemouth: Bournemouth University.

Knight, P. (2007) *Radio Drama: Sound, Text, Word; Bakhtin and the Aural Dialogue of Radio Drama*, London: Goldsmiths: University of London.

Pepler, C. S. L. (1988) *Discovering the Art of Wireless: A Critical History of Radio Drama at the BBC, 1922–1928*, Bristol: University of Bristol. online at https://research-information.bris.ac.uk/ws/portalfiles/portal/34496537/381402.pdf (Accessed 3 September 2022).

Smith, A. (2022) *'Look With Thine Ears': A Century of Shakespeare's Plays on BBC Radio*, Nortwich: University of East Anglia.

Wood, R. (2008) *Radio Drama at the Crossroads: The History and Contemporary Context of Radio Drama at the BBC*, Leicester: De Montfort University.

A series, Methuen/BBC publication from 1978, including the radio scripts of the winning writers for each year. Methuen pulled out when the sales were too poor and there has been a hiatus in publication apart from years when the BBC was willing to fund the full cost. This was the BBC selection of scripts it considered to be 'Best Radio Plays' that particular year.

Rather than list each author alphabetically in the bibliography I have set out this special section which gives year of publication and names and authors of plays.

In an appendix to J. Drakakis (ed.) (1981) *British Radio Drama*, Cambridge: Cambridge University Press (pp. 256–62), there is a very helpful attempt to list play scripts published between 1924 and 1979. Drakakis modestly qualifies the list by saying that it cannot claim to be complete. However, I would say that for this period it is the most comprehensive.

Giles Cooper Award winners

Best Radio Plays of 1978
Richard Harris: *Is it Something I Said?*
Don Haworth: *Episode on a Thursday Evening*
Jill Hyem: *Remember Me*
Tom Mallin: *Halt! Who Goes There?*
Jennifer Phillips: *Daughters of Men*
Fay Weldon: *Polaris*

Best Radio Plays of 1979
Shirley Gee: *Typhoid Mary*
Carey Harrison: *I Never Killed My German*
Barrie Keeffe: *Heaven Scent*
John Kirkmorris: *Coxcomb*
John Peacock: *Attard in Retirement*
Olwen Wymark: *The Child*

Best Radio Plays of 1980
Steward Parkeer: *The Kamikaze Ground staff Reunion Dinner*
Martyn Read: *Waving to a Train*
Peter Redgrove: *Martyr of the Hives*
William Trevor: *Beyond the Pale*

Best Radio Plays of 1981
Peter Barnes: *The Jumping Mimuses of Byzantium*
Don Haworth: *Talk of Love and War*
Harold Pinter: *Family Voices*
David Pownall: *Beef*
J. P. Rooney: *The Dead Image*
Paul Thain: *The Biggest Sandcastle in the World*

Best Radio Plays of 1982
Rhys Adrian: *Watching the Plays Together*
John Arden: *The Old Man Sleeps Alone*

Harry Barton: *Hoopoe Day*
Donald Chapman: *Invisible Writing*
Tom Stoppard: *The Dog it Was That Died*
William Trevor: *Autumn Sunshine*

Best Radio Plays of 1983
Wally K. Daly: *Time Slip*
Shirley Gee: *Never in My Lifetime*
Gerry Jones: *The Angels They Grow Lonely*
Steve May: *No Exceptions*
Martyn Read: *Scouting for Boys*

Best Radio Plays of 1984
Stephen Dunstone: *Who Is Sylvia?*
Robert Ferguson: *Transfigured Night*
Don Haworth: *Daybreak*
Caryl Phillips: *The Wasted Years*
Christopher Russell: *Swimmer*
Rose Tremain: *Temporary Shelter*

Best Radio Plays of 1985
Rhys Adrian: *Outpatient*
Barry Collins: *King Canute*
Martin Crimp: *Three Attempted Acts*
David Pownall: *Ploughboy Monday*
James Saunders: *Menocchio*
Michael Wall: *Hiroshima: The Movie*

Best Radio Plays of 1986
Robert Ferguson: *Dreams, Secrets, Beautiful Lies*
Christina Reid: *The Last of a Dyin' Race*
Andrew Rissik: *A Man Alone: Anthony*
Ken Whitmore: *The Gingerbread House*
Valerie Windsor: *Myths and Legacies*

Best Radio Plays of 1987
Wally K. Daly: *Mary's*

Frank Dunne: *Dreams of Dublin Bay*
Anna Fox: *Nobby's Day*
Nigel D.Moffat: *Lifetime*
Richard Nelson: *Languages Spoken Here*
Peter Tinniswood: *The Village Fete*

Best Radio Plays of 1988
Ken Blakeson: *Excess Baggage*
Terence Frisby: *Just Remembeer Two Things: It's Not Fair and Don't Be Late*
Anthony Minghella: *Cigarettes and Chocolate*
Rona Munro: *The Dirt Under the Carpet*
Dave Sheasby: *Apple Blossom Afternoons*

Best Radio Plays of 1989
Elizabeth Baines: *The Baby Buggy*
Jennifer Johnston: *O Ananias, Azarias and Misael*
David Zane Mairowitz: *The Stalin Sonata*
Richard Nelson: *Eating Words*
Craig Warner: *By Where the Old Shed Used to Be*

Best Radio Plays of 1990
Tony Bagley: *The Machine*
David Cregan: *A butler Did It*
John Fletcher:*Death and the Tango*
Tina Pepler: *Song of the Forest*
Steve Walker: *The Pope's Brother*

Best Radio Plays of 1991
Robin Glendinning: *The Words Are Strange*
John Purser: *Carver*
Tom Stoppard: *In the Native State*
Steve Walker: *Mickey Mookey*
Craig Warner: *Figure with Meat*

Giles Cooper: Six Plays for Radio 1966
Introduction by Donald McWhinnie

Mathry Beacon (1956)

The Disagreeable Oyster (1957)

Without the Grail (1958)

Under the Loofah Tree (1958)

Unman, Wittering and Zigo (1958)

Before the Monday (1959)

BBC Radio Drama Young Playwrights Festival 1988

Benjamin Zephaniah: *Hurricane Dub*

Hattie Naylor: *The Box*

Jeanette Winterson: *Static*

Richard Hayton: *One Friday Not a Million Miles Past*

Abigail Docherty: *Listen to My Inside Mind*

Ann Ogidi: *Ragamuffin*

BBC World Service Radio Plays for the World (published 1996)

Diane Ney: *Truckin' Maggie* (1989)

Andrew Verster: *You May Leave, the Show is Over* (1992)

Katy Parisi: *Puzzles* (1995)

Herbert Kaufman: *Last Supper* (1995)

Margaret Bhatty: *My Enemy My Friend* (1995)

Morningside was a mainstream morning sequence programme on CBC in Canada and in 1991 two compilations of radio plays were published bearing the title *The Morningside Dramas*.

Take Five edited by Dave Carley

Mary Burns: *Yukon Quintette*

Timothy Findley: *Love and Deception: Three by Chekhov*

Richardo Keens-Douglas: *Once Upon an Island*

Thomas Lackey: *The Skid*

Arthur Milner: *The City*

Airborne: Radio Plays by Women, edited by Ann Jansen

Judith Thompson: *White Sand*

Renee: *Te Pouaka Karaehe* [*The Glass Box*]

Anne Chislett: *Venus Sucked in: A Post-feminist Comedy*

Dacia Maraini: *Mussomeli-Dusseldorf*
Sharon Pollock: *The Making of Warriors*
Diana Raznovich: *That's Extraordinary!*

New Radio Drama by the BBC 1966
Colin Finbow: *Tonight is Friday*
Ian Rodger: *A Voice like Thunder*
Rhys Adrian: *A Nice Clean Sheet of Paper*
Stephen Grenfell: *Sixteen Lives of the Drunken Dreamer*
Joe Orton: *The Ruffian on the Stair*
Simon Raven: *The Sconcing Stoup*

Worth A Hearing: A Collection of Radio Plays edited by Alfred Bradley published
by Blackie in 1967
Alan Plater: *The Mating Season*
John Mortimer: *The Dock Brief*
David Campton: *Don't Wait for Me*
Bill Naughton: She'll Make Trouble
Henry Livings: *The Day Dumbfounded Got His Pylon*

New English Dramatists Radio Plays published by Penguin in 1968
Introduction by Irving Wardle
Giles Cooper: *The Object*
Barry Bermange: *No Quarter*
Caryl Churchill: *The Ants*
Jeremy Sandford: *The Whelks and the Chromium*
Alan Sharp: *The Long-distance Piano-player*
Cecil P. Taylor: *Happy Days Are Here Again*

Out of the Air: Five plays for radio, selected and edited by Alfred Bradley for
Longman in 1978
Stan Barstow: *We Could Always Fit a Sidecar*
Don Haworth: *There's No Point in Arguing the Toss*
David Campton: *Relics*
Ken Whitmore: *Jump!*
Ivor Wilson: *Take Any Day*

Newspaper, Magazine and Online Articles

Anon, (20 March 1923) 'Romeo and Juliet: British Empire Society Reading', *The Times*, p. 10.

Anon, (16 January 1924a) 'Drama Thrills by Wireless' *Daily Mail*, p. 7.

Anon, (10 April 1924b) 'New radio drama', *The Radio Times*, p. 100.

Anon, (4 January 1926) '"The Dweller In The Darkness" A Play of the Unknown in One Act', *The Radio Times*, p. 59.

Anon, (1 November 1929) 'And at 9.15 tonight "Carnival" A Story of London before the War', *The Radio Times*, p. 331.

Anon, (5 December 1930) 'Both Sides of the Microphone: Amos n Andy Next Month', *The Radio Times*, p. 655.

Anon, (1 May 1931) 'The Mary Celeste: A Mystery of the Sea', *The Radio Times*, p. 291.

Anon, (14 December 1933a) 'Tonight at 8.0 A ★★★★★★ Minstrel Show, produced by Harry S. P. The Kentucky Minstrels', *The Radio Times*, p. 852.

Anon, (24 October 1933b) 'Wireless Programmes: A Play About The Black Watch', *The Scotsman*, p. 16.

Anon, (26 July 1934) 'The Theatres'. *Times*, p. 10.

Anon, (2 November 1956) 'The Mystery of the Mary Celeste', *The Radio Times*, p. 26.

Anon, (1 June 1978) 'The Revenge: A play for radio without words by Andrew Sachs' *Radio Times*, Issue 2846, online archive at https://genome.ch.bbc.co.uk/731c3868560546f1ab8369520c0297fe

Archer, W. (29 August 1924) 'The Future of Wireless Drama', London: *The Radio Times*,

Berkeley, R. (27 May 1927b) 'Broadcasting and the Theatre', London: *The Radio Times*, p. 374.

Bland, A. (13 March 1929) 'Squirrel's Cage', *The Listener*, p. 333.

Devlin, P. (14 August 1980) 'Writing a radio play: "Radio makes no map to hinder the imagination"', London: *The Listener*.

Drinkwater, J. (12 September 1924) 'Reflections on Radio and Art', London: *The Radio Times*, p. 485.

Gielgud, V. (Weekly in six parts between 24 May and 28 June 1929a) guidance on writing for the microphone play, *The Radio Times*.

'The Wireless Play – I. For The Aspiring Dramatist', 24 May, p. 397,

'The Wireless Play – II. Choice of Subject', 31 May, pp. 449–50,

'The Wireless Play – III. Length And Method', 7 June, pp. 502, 513,

'The Wireless Play – IV. "How Many Studios?"', 14 June, p. 555,

'The Wireless Play – V. People of the Play', 21 June, p. 608,

'The Wireless Play – VI. A Practical Example', 28 June, pp. 605, 668.

Gielgud, Val, (1 November 1929b) 'The Broadcast plays—Are they getting worse'? *The Radio Times*, pp. 314, 357.

'What The Listener Thinks' – letters likely written by Val Gielgud to provoke debate.

31 May 1929, *The Radio Times*, p 487.

28 June 1929, *The Radio Times*, p. 670.

Jacobs-Jenkins, B. (2022) An Octoroon. Interview with Branden Jacobs-Jenkins, playwright, *National Theatre Blog*. https://www.nationaltheatre.org.uk/blog/octoroon-interview-branden-jacobs-jenkins-playwright. visited 13th August 2022.

Jeffrey, R.E. (17 July 1925) The Need for a Radio Drama; Plays That Spell Success,' London: The Radio Times, p 151–2.

Jeffrey, R.E. (2 April 1926a) 'What Happened in the Third Act? The Result of Our Radio Drama Competition,' London: *The Radio Times*, p. 58.

Jeffrey, R.E. (5 November 1926b) 'Seeing With the Mind's Eye', London: *The Radio Times*, p. 325.

Jeffrey, R.E. (28 September 1928) 'Technique or Dramatist?', London: *The Radio Times*, p. 617.

Knowles, J. (1 May 1931) 'Mystery Ship Of This Week's Radio Play', London: The Radio Times, pp. 263 & 276.

Lewis, C. (11 February 1927a) '"Lord Jim": A Romantic Radio Story-Play', London: *The Radio Times*, p. 333.

Lewis, C. (30 December 1927b) 'St Augustine and the Cucumber', London: *The Radio Times*, p. 711.

Postgate, R. W. (25 September 1929) Expressionism and Radio Drama, *The Listener*, Issue 37, p. 405.

Shaw, F. H. (2 April 1926) 'Secrets of the Radio Drama,' London: *The Radio Times*, p. 50.

Smythe, V. (29 February 1924) 'The Play in the Studio' London: *The Radio Times*, p. 391.

Thorndike, S. (3 July 1925) 'Where Radio Drama Excels,' London: *The Radio Times*, pp. 49–50.

Witty, M. (23 June 1923) 'The B.B.C. Plays,' London: *Popular Wireless*, p. 688.

Wright, W., Murdoch, M., Bloch, A., Hark, M., McQueen, N. 'Some Form Grows Perfect', 'The Cuckoo', 'The Champ', 'A Reasonable Facsimile', *One Act Play Magazine and Radio Drama Review*, March–April, 1942, Boston, Massachussetts, USA.

Radio and Audio Programmes referenced in the text

Bick, Andreas (1 May 2010) *A Pot Calling the Kettle Black!* SilenceRadio.org, Available at: https://soundcloud.com/andreas-bick/a-pot-calling-the-kettle-black (Accessed 31 August 2022).

Brecht, B. (1963) *The Trial of Lucullus*. KPFA Readers' Theatre, technical production by John Whiting. Translation HR Hays. Broadcast March 18, 1963 on KPFA, Berkeley, California, Available at: https://www.ubu.com/media/sound/brecht_bertolt/Brecht-Bertolt_The-Trial-of-Lucullus_KPFA_1963.mp3

Cooper, G. (1984) Under *The Loofah Tree* & The Disagreeable Oyster [Audio Cassette] Giles Cooper, Audio Cassette, Publisher: BBC Plays On Tape (1984) 'Two comedies written by Giles Cooper and performed by the BBC Radiophonic Workshop'. Cassette contains both original BBC broadcasts in full.

Cooper, G. (2018) *The Disagreeable Oyster*, 21:15 06/08/2018, BBC Radio 4 Extra, 45 minutes. Available at: https://learningonscreen.ac.uk/ondemand/index.php/prog/00525703?bcast=127238309 (Accessed 31 Aug 2022).

Corwin, N. (1995) *Thirteen By Corwin: Thirteen of Radio Pioneer Norman Corwin's Most Celebrated Radio Plays*, cassette pack, [Including 'The Undecided Molecule'] Bloomington, Indiana: The Lodestone Catalog.

Dann, L. (5 August 1995) *Ho! Ho! The Clown is Dead*, BBC R3, by Noiseless Blackboard Eraser, A Festival Radio Production.

Dann, L. (2009–2010) *Flickerman*, Variously broadcast ABC National Radio (Australia), VPRO (Holland), and WFMU (New York).

Durham, R. (15 May 1949a) *The Ballad of Satchel Paige*, NBC/WMAQ in the series *Destination Freedom*. Available at: https://www.youtube.com/watch?v=pSyaU7BcZSc (Accessed 19 August 2022).

Durham, R. (5 June 1949b) *Anatomy of an Ordinance*, NBC/WMAQ in the series *Destination Freedom*. Available at: https://www.youtube.com/watch?v=pnUQT4HA6ck, (Accessed 19 August 2022).

Fisher, N. (19 and 20 September 2001) *The Wheel of Fortune*, BBC R3 with interaction on BBC R4 and online. 'In BBC Radio's first interactive drama, you have the chance to play the wheel of fortune by switching between simultaneous broadcasts on Radio 4 and Radio 3.'

Fletcher, L. (17 November 1941) *Suspense – The Hitch-hiker*, CBS Radio production from 1942, Available at: https://archive.org/details/Suspense-TheHitchhiker, (Accessed 25 Aug 2022).

Fletcher, L. (25 May 1943) *Suspense – Sorry, Wrong Number*, CBS Radio production, Available at: https://archive.org/details/Episode31SorryWrongNumberEastCoast/Episode+31+-+Sorry+Wrong+Number+East+Coast.mp3, (Accessed 25 Aug 2022)

Phillips, C. (2017) *The Wasted Years*, 20:30 27/08/2017, BBC Radio 4 Extra, 90 minutes. https://learningonscreen.ac.uk/ondemand/index.php/prog/008934EA?bcast=124931667 (Accessed 31 Aug 2022).

Sachs, A. (1978) *Revenge*, BBC Radio Four, 'Pioneering thriller featuring sound effects and eleven actors, but no written dialogue,' rebroadcast on BBC 7 and BBC Radio 4 Extra. Produced and directed by Glyn Dearman.

Smith, Al (2021) *Life Lines*, 'Episode 1 of 6, Series 5, BBC Radio 4, 15 September 2021, available online 30 July 2022 at: https://www.bbc.co.uk/programmes/p09w05mj

Snoad, H. & Knowles, M. (7 September 1976) 'Ten Seconds From Now', *Dad's Army*, BBC Radio Drama Series, adapted from television script by David Croft and Jimmy Perry. Available on *Dad's Army: The Complete Radio Series, Series Three*, CD collection, London: BBC Worldwide, 2015.

Stoppard, T. (2017) *Artist Descending A Staircase*, Drama on 3, 21:00 08/10/2017, BBC Radio 3, 80 minutes. Available at: https://learningonscreen.ac.uk/ondemand/index.php/prog/0BA9EF4E?bcast=125283656 (Accessed 31 Aug 2022).

Walker, M. (23 September 2003) *The Dark House*, BBC Radio 4. Available at: https://learningonscreen.ac.uk/ondemand/index.php/prog/002054EC?bcast=121853514 (Accessed 28 August 2022).

West, T. (1959) *This Gun That I Have in My Right Hand is Loaded*, *clyp* available online at: https://clyp.it/fif3lyin, (Accessed 31 Aug 2022).

White, Graham (17 October 2010) *The Unfortunates*, dramatisation of BS Johnson's 1960s 'novel in a box', BBC R3, Available at: https://learningonscreen.ac.uk/ondemand/index.php/prog/016C1AFC?bcast=127975129, (Accessed 21 August 2022).

Wishengrad, M. (12 December 1943) *The Battle of the Warsaw Ghetto*, NBC network, available online at: https://collections.ushmm.org/search/catalog/irn702472 (Acccessed 31st Aug 2022).

Woods, A. (1976) *Maigret Sets A Trap*, in *George Simenon Maigret Collected Cases*, 5 CD pack, BBC Worldwide Ltd, 2017.

Archives

Collingwood, F. & Honess-Martin, J (2010) 'Auricular – Fresh Audio Drama Live' leaflet published by Theatre503, personal papers Tim Crook.

Entertainment, Drama Department 1924–1948, BBC Written Archives Centre, Caversham, R19/276 This includes articles by R E Jeffrey. The first manuscript has a handwritten note '1924?' under the title 'Wireless Drama: Published with slight exertions in the "Radio Times."' It has 3 numbered pages and will be referenced 'BBC Written Archives, Jeffrey, 1924a'. Another article referenced in the text is 'Notes on Technique of Playwriting for

Wireless Broadcast', numbered with 5 pages and may also have been written in 1924. This will be referenced 'BBC Written Archives, Jeffrey, 1924b'.

Writing Plays For Radio, BBC Radio Drama, BBC, Broadcasting House, circa 1989, personal papers Tim Crook.

Sandford, J. (26 Nov 1972) *Oluwale*, Script written for BBC Radio 3 production 'specially commissioned by BBC Radio Brighton in association with the 1972 Festival. This is a dramatisation of the story of David Oluwale, a Nigerian who came to Britain in 1949 full of hope. and who died tragically in 1969 in the river Aire in Leeds', BBC Written Archives Caversham.

Street, George S., *Waiting for the Bus*, Lord Chamberlain license Number: 1016, Gertrude E. Jennings, British Library Reference: LCP1917/13, 19 Jun 1917.

Films and Television Drama referenced in the text

Beau Travail (1999) directed by Claire Denis, screenplay by Claire Denis and Jean-Pol Fargeau, produced by Patrick Grandperret for Pathé TV/SM Films.

Blue (1992) written and directed by Derek Jarman, a Basalisk Communications/Uplink production for Channel 4 in association with the Arts Council of Great Britain, Opal and BBC Radio 3. Produced by James Mackay and Takashi Asai; composer: Simon Fisher Turner, associate director: David Lewis; sound design: Marvin Black.

Cathy Come Home (1966) written by Jeremy Sandford, directed by Ken Loach and produced by Tony Garnett for BBC Television.

Citizen Kane (1941) directed by Orson Welles, screenplay by Herman J. Mankiewicz and Orson Welles.

Dad's Army (2007) 'The Christmas Specials', written by produced by David Croft and Jimmy Perry. DVD produced by BBC Worldwide contains the television sketch 'Broadcast to the Empire' on *Christmas Night with the Stars* broadcast on BBC One 25 December 1972.

Heat (1995) directed and written by Michael Mann, and co-produced by Michael Mann and Art Linson.

Leaving Las Vegas (1995) directed and written by Mike Figgis and produced by Lila Cazès and Annie Stewart for Lumiere Pictures,

Shawshank Redemption (1994) directed by Frank Darabont, screenplay by Frank Darabont based on the short novel *Rita Hayworth and Shawshank Redemption* by Stephen King.

Sorry Wrong Number (1948) directed by Anatole Litvak, screenplay by Lucille Fletcher, and co-produced by Hal B. Wallis and Anatole Litvak.

The English Patient (1996) directed by Anthony Minghella from his own script based on the 1992 novel of the same name by Michael Ondaatje and produced by Saul Zaentz. Sound design by Walter Murch.

The Bridges of Madison County (1995) directed by Clint Eastwood, screenplay by Richard LaGravenese based on the novel *The Bridges of Madison County* by Robert James Waller, and produced by Clint Eastwood and Kathleen Kennedy for Warner Bros.

The Monocled Mutineer (1986) BBC Television Drama series directed by Jim O'Brien and produced by John Broke. Dramatisation by Alan Bleasdale of William Allison and John Fairley's 1978 book *The Monocled Mutineer.*

The Thirty Nine Steps (1935) directed by Alfred Hitchcock, produced for Gaumont British Film Corporation by Michael Balcon, screenplay by Charles Bennett & Ian Hay, based on the novel by John Buchan *The Thirty-Nine Steps* (1915).

When Trumpets Fade (1998) directed by John Irvin, written by W.W. Vought and produced by John Kemeny for HBO NYC Productions.

Internet Sites and recommended radio and online listening

The BBC is the leading and only major sustained producer and broadcaster of radio drama in the UK. You can hear the output live and every production is normally online for 'listen again' periods. Production resources and output is now often shared between the online 'BBC Sounds' and legacy broadcast networks such as BBC 4, 3 and BBC 4 Extra.

The independently developed online site originated and managed by Nigel Deacon *Radio Plays & Radio Drama* is, in my opinion, one of the most important publicly accessible online resources recording the history and appreciation of British audio drama in the world. http://www.suttonelms.org.uk/RADIO1.HTML

Recommended strands

BBC Radio 4

Afternoon play. Weekdays 2.15–3 p.m. (the main market for new writers)

The Saturday play. Saturdays at 2.30–3.30 p.m. (sometimes one and a half hours–4 p.m.)

The Classic Serial. Sundays 3–4 p.m., repeated Saturday nights at 9 p.m.

BBC Radio 3

The Sunday play. Usually Sunday nights from 8.30 p.m. to 10 p.m.

The Wire. Showcase for works that push the boundaries of drama and narrative. Usually Saturday nights at 9 p.m. for 45–50 minutes.

It is also worth listening to the digital station BBC R4 Extra that outputs a considerable amount of radio drama archive and comedy.

Recommended summary of audio play-writing advice from BBC World Service competition page (last updated 2012 and archived): https://www.bbc.co.uk/worldservice/arts/2010/10/100728_playcomp_writingtips.shtml

The International Radio Playwriting Competition 2020. BBC World Service. Ten tips for writing a play for radio. https://www.bbc.co.uk/programmes/profiles/tnkQgSgPJVWM4ZpZ3hHbjv/ten-tips-for-writing-a-play-for-radio

BBC Writers' Room Online 2022

Scriptwriting essentials https://www.bbc.co.uk/writersroom/resources/scriptwriting-essentials/

1. **Developing Your Idea**

All ideas are only as good as the characters that drive them, and all good ideas need to be dramatic. https://www.bbc.co.uk/writersroom/resources/scriptwriting-essentials/1-developing-your-idea/

2. **Know What You Want to Write**

Strong scripts know what they are and what they are trying to do. https://www.bbc.co.uk/writersroom/resources/scriptwriting-essentials/2-know-what-you-want-to-write/

3. **Beginnings (and Endings)**
Knowing where to start with the story that you tell is inextricably linked to the ending you are trying to reach. https://www.bbc.co.uk/writersroom/resources/scriptwriting-essentials/3-beginnings-and-endings/

4. **The Muddle in the Middle**
The difficulty with many scripts and stories is the middle – the stretch that connects the beginning with the end. https://www.bbc.co.uk/writersroom/resources/scriptwriting-essentials/4-muddle-in-the-middle/

5. **Characters Bring Your Words to Life**
Characters are the thing that separate great scripts from only competent scripts – and great writers from only competent writers. https://www.bbc.co.uk/writersroom/resources/scriptwriting-essentials/5-characters/

6. **Scenes**
A scene is the combination of time, place and setting you use to frame and show a significant moment or event in the story. https://www.bbc.co.uk/writersroom/resources/scriptwriting-essentials/6-scenes/

7. **Dialogue**
Dialogue is not just about what characters say – it's about what they express by what they say. https://www.bbc.co.uk/writersroom/resources/scriptwriting-essentials/7-dialogue/

8. **Writing is Rewriting**
So you've developed your idea, worked out what kind of story and experience it is, created characters, structured the story, brought it to scenic life, and voiced the characters. You have a draft and it feels like an achievement. https://www.bbc.co.uk/writersroom/resources/scriptwriting-essentials/8-rewriting/

Paul Ashton's Perfect 10. Blog at BBC Writers Room

1. **Medium, Form and Format** https://www.bbc.co.uk/blogs/writersroom/entries/117b337c-52fd-35c5-bf84-1ca9a3299b16

2. **Get your story going!** https://www.bbc.co.uk/blogs/writersroom/entries/2c2fdbe4-00e0-3a6c-85d8-9d6eb20de866

3. **Coherence** https://www.bbc.co.uk/blogs/writersroom/entries/2f228300-0fca-3bed-92e7-befe768d92cb

4. **Character is Everything** https://www.bbc.co.uk/blogs/writersroom/entries/1e2f143d-9356-396f-a745-246b99644025

5. **Emotion** https://www.bbc.co.uk/blogs/writersroom/entries/32ca8225-c334-384a-a205-d63cc1c94b17

6. **Surprise!** https://www.bbc.co.uk/blogs/writersroom/entries/8f99f831-cc42-3fe2-8141-e94176fcddcc

7. **Structure** https://www.bbc.co.uk/blogs/writersroom/entries/4ff33083-4a96-385a-b5f5-b20489845627

8. **Exposition and Expression** https://www.bbc.co.uk/blogs/writersroom/entries/7c325f56-3029-3539-868a-e73ae1d6541c

9. **Passion** https://www.bbc.co.uk/blogs/writersroom/entries/4fa734a4-07ed-314d-8e9f-f1db48c028aa

10. **Be Yourself** https://www.bbc.co.uk/blogs/writersroom/entries/62d634ad-9f00-3a60-b09b-7f1ee28074c7

Script Room latest: radio drama

By Paul Ashton Tuesday 14 May 2013, 10:28 https://www.bbc.co.uk/blogs/writersroom/entries/ae298ad7-8489-30fe-a76d-a703fa463a63

John Yorke's 10 Questions

John Yorke's 10 Questions are used by top TV writers all over the UK to unlock and refine their stories: https://www.bbc.co.uk/writersroom/resources/10-questions

Writing Radio Drama

Radio drama is the most intimate relationship a scriptwriter can have with their audience, and yet it can also cheaply create anything that you can imagine. https://www.bbc.co.uk/writersroom/resources/tips-and-advice/writing-radio-drama/

Monday–Friday 10:45–11am Radio 4 (repeated at 19.45 weekdays)

https://www.bbc.co.uk/programmes/b006qy2s
15 Minute Drama – Short form (15min) commissioned in multiples of 5, ideally a series with individual stories in each episode or short term stories that mature over five or ten episodes.

Monday–Friday 2:15–3.00pm Radio 4

Afternoon Drama – Daily narrative drama strand. A complete story that is imaginative, accessible and entertaining.

Saturday 2:30–3:30pm Radio 4

https://www.bbc.co.uk/programmes/b006qgxs
Saturday Drama – Enjoyment and escapism. For example: love stories, thrillers, and extraordinary personal stories.

Sunday (time varies) Radio 3

https://www.bbc.co.uk/programmes/b006tnwj
Drama on 3 – Radical drama, classics and new theatre productions.

BBC Radio 4 Drama https://www.bbc.co.uk/programmes/b04xxp0g

BBC Radio Drama Podcast of the week https://www.bbc.co.uk/programmes/
    p02nrv5m/episodes/downloads

BBC Sounds produces podcast/online drama, which is also broadcast on BBC Radio 4.
Examples.

Doctor Who: Redacted When a terrifying phenomenon starts redacting the
    Doctor from reality, three queer women become the world's only hope.
    #DoctorWhoRedacted https://www.bbc.co.uk/sounds/brand/p0c0krqf

Lusus What happens when your neuroses come to life? What shape will they take?
    Lusus is a brand new psychological horror podcast starring Ncuti Gatwa, Morfydd
    Clark and Alistair Petrie. https://www.bbc.co.uk/programmes/m00176y7

Life Lines Podcast

Al Smith's award-winning series set in an ambulance control room. https://www.
bbc.co.uk/programmes/m000bcm4/episodes/downloads

BBC Radio Four Extra Podcasts and Podcast Radio Hour

https://www.bbc.co.uk/programmes/b09n14fm/episodes/downloads

Script Library – Radio Drama

Scripts from the BBC Radio Drama archive https://www.bbc.co.uk/writersroom/
scripts/radio-drama/

Making Radio Drama – the bad news and the good news

Friday 7 March 2014, 12:35 by Stephen Wyatt https://www.bbc.co.uk/blogs/
writersroom/entries/dc3dc934-4287-36da-8d9a-2f5def642772

Writing for Radio – Find Your 'Itch'

Thursday 28 August 2014, 10:50 by Al Smith https://www.bbc.co.uk/blogs/
writersroom/entries/fe9b30bc-d2a5-3210-ac05-fc2539258025

The Writer's Prize commission: Bang Up

Thursday 8 August 2013, 11:51 by Sarah Hehir https://www.bbc.co.uk/blogs/
writersroom/entries/d797ecd1-db18-349d-b39c-69e83c7eb8e6

Creating Home Front – Radio 4's epic new First World War drama

Friday 1 August 2014, 11:54 by Jessica Dromgoole https://www.bbc.co.uk/blogs/
writersroom/entries/dc24c0c6-74ec-3071-8265-4a8184713d9a

Red Velvet – Rediscovering Ira Aldridge

Thursday 17 July 2014, 14:40 by Lolita Chakrabarti https://www.bbc.co.uk/blogs/writersroom/entries/885fd420-c3a0-3aac-8fa5-4dd3adacce8b

Writing The Archers: From idea to airwaves

Monday 21 October 2013, 9:15 by Keri Davies https://www.bbc.co.uk/blogs/writersroom/entries/989184e1-10a1-3c2d-916e-cfbf67c7a334

Five things I know about writing The Archers

Tuesday 22 October 2013, 12:25 by Carole Salazzo https://www.bbc.co.uk/blogs/writersroom/entries/391bb749-0c9b-38e6-ac56-1f0f31f8ae27

Gordon House talking about key things when writing radio plays. 1 Nov 1996

Launch of the International Radio Playwriting Competition. BBC World Service. Spotlight https://www.bbc.co.uk/sounds/play/p02sfxvq
Technical presentation or sound design for radio drama. BBC World Service Spotlight. 21st July 1996. https://www.bbc.co.uk/sounds/play/p02sfxkh

Ten tips for writing a radio play. 2020 BBC World Service International Radio Playwriting Competition

https://www.bbc.co.uk/programmes/profiles/tnkQgSgPJVWM4ZpZ3hHbjv/ten-tips-for-writing-a-play-for-radio
My Shakespeare Radio Drama at 90. The first radio drama, a scene from Julius Caesar, was broadcast 90 years ago. Now performed by Harriet Walter and Jenny Jules from Phyllida Lloyd's all-female Donmar Warehouse production. Introduced by Jeremy Mortimer Published on February 16, 2013. https://soundcloud.com/my-own-shakespeare/radio-drama-at-90-julius

Companion website pages

Additions and updates for individual chapters

Additions and updates for Chapter 1 Radio Drama is Born and in its Cradle https://kulturapress.com/2022/08/12/updates-for-chapter-1-radio-drama-is-born-and-in-its-cradle/
Additions and updates for Chapter 2 The Psychology of Writing and Listening https://kulturapress.com/2022/08/12/updates-for-chapter-2-the-psychology-of-writing-and-listening/
Additions and updates for Chapter 3 Instrumental Utilitarianism in Radio Playwriting – the Evolving Thoughts of Val Gielgud https://kulturapress.com/2022/08/12/chapter-3-instrumental-utilitarianism-in-radio-playwriting-the-evolving-thoughts-of-val-gielgud/
Additions and updates for Chapter 4 Achieving the Long Form Audio Drama https://kulturapress.com/2022/08/12/chapter-4-achieving-the-long-form-audio-drama/

Additions and updates for Chapter 5 Beginning the Sound Story https://kulturapress. com/2022/08/12/updates-for-chapter-5-beginning-the-sound-story/

Additions and updates for Chapter 6 Characterising the Sound Story https://kulturapress. com/2022/08/12/updates-for-chapter-6-characterising-the-sound-story/

Additions and updates for Chapter 7 Dialogue and the Sound Story https://kulturapress. com/2022/08/12/updates-for-chapter-7-dialogue-and-the-sound-story/

Additions and updates for Chapter 8 Sustaining the Sound Story: Techniques and Devices https:// kulturapress.com/2022/08/12/updates-for-chapter-8-sustaining-the-sound-story/

Additions and updates for Chapter 9. Plotting the Sound Story: Techniques and Devices https://kulturapress.com/2022/08/12/updates-for-chapter-9-plotting-the-sound-story/

Additions and updates for Chapter 10 Ending the Sound Story https://kulturapress. com/2022/08/12/updates-for-chapter-10-ending-the-sound-story/

Additions and updates for Chapter 11 Film, Internet and Stage dimensions to Sound Story Telling https://kulturapress.com/2022/08/12/updates-for-chapter-11-film-internet-and-stage-dimensions-to-sound-story-telling/

Special subject pages

David Pownall – Radio Drama Plays https://kulturapress.com/2022/08/09/david-pownall-radio-drama-laureate/

BBC Audio Drama Teaching and Learning https://kulturapress.com/2022/08/10/bbc-audio-drama-teaching-and-learning/

Gertrude E Jennings – BBC's Pioneering One Act Playwright https://kulturapress. com/2022/08/10/gertrude-e-jennings-bbcs-pioneering-one-act-playwright/

Richard Hughes – Playwright and Novelist https://kulturapress.com/2022/08/10/richard-hughes-playwright-and-novelist/

Val Gielgud – Longest Serving BBC Radio Drama Editor 1929–1963 https://kulturapress. com/2022/08/29/val-gielgud-longest-serving-bbc-radio-drama-editor-1929-1963/

Drama on the Air USA – One Day in September 1939 https://kulturapress.com/2022/08/29/drama-on-the-air-usa-one-day-in-september-1939/

Gordon Lea – Directing and Writing About Radio Plays https://kulturapress. com/2022/08/09/gordon-lea-radio-drama-and-how-to-write-it-1926/

Life Lines – Radio Drama and Podcasting Drama by the BBC https://kulturapress. com/2022/08/30/bbc-life-lines-sound-drama-for-radio-and-podcasting/

The Radio Plays of Lawrence du Garde Peach https://kulturapress.com/2022/08/18/the-radio-plays-of-lawrence-du-garde-peach/

Tyrone Guthrie – Pioneering Radio Playwright https://kulturapress.com/2022/08/29/tyrone-guthrie-and-radio-plays/

The Radio Plays of Reginald Berkeley https://kulturapress.com/2022/08/17/the-radio-plays-of-reginald-berkeley/

The Radio Plays of Caryl Phillips https://kulturapress.com/2022/08/13/the-radio-plays-of-caryl-phillips/

The Radio Plays of Susan Hill https://kulturapress.com/2022/08/18/the-radio-plays-of-susan-hill/

The Radio Plays by Angela Carter https://kulturapress.com/2022/08/18/radio-plays-by-angela-carter/

The Radio Plays of Lucille Fletcher https://kulturapress.com/2022/08/18/the-radio-plays-of-lucille-fletcher/

Short Story Radio Drama – Broken Porcelain by Tim Crook https://kulturapress. com/2022/08/23/short-story-radio-drama-broken-porcelain-by-tim-crook/

Anthony Minghella and Radio Drama https://kulturapress.com/2022/08/27/anthony-minghella-and-radio-drama/

Audio and Drama-Documentary Otherwise Known as the Feature in Britain https://kulturapress.com/2022/08/28/audio-and-drama-documentary-otherwise-known-as-the-feature-in-britain/

Arch Oboler and Radio Drama https://kulturapress.com/2022/08/28/arch-oboler-and-radio-drama/

Archibald MacLeish and Radio Drama https://kulturapress.com/2022/08/28/archibald-macleish-and-radio-drama/

Audio and Radio Drama Science Fiction https://kulturapress.com/2022/08/28/audio-and-radio-drama-science-fiction/

Giles Cooper Award Winning Scripts https://kulturapress.com/2022/08/09/giles-cooper-award-winning-scripts/

Audio/Radio Drama Soap Operas https://kulturapress.com/2022/08/30/audio-radio-drama-soap-operas/

BBC Life Lines Sound Drama for Radio and Podcasting https://kulturapress.com/2022/08/30/bbc-life-lines-sound-drama-for-radio-and-podcasting/

BBC Radio Drama History https://kulturapress.com/2022/08/30/bbc-radio-drama-history/

BBC Radio Drama of the 1950s https://kulturapress.com/2022/08/30/bbc-radio-drama-of-the-1950s/

BBC Radio Drama of the 1960s https://kulturapress.com/2022/08/30/bbc-radio-drama-of-the-1960s/

BBC Radio Great Play Series of 1928 & 1929 https://kulturapress.com/2022/08/30/bbc-radio-great-play-series-of-1928-1929/

BBC World Service Radio Drama – Play Publications https://kulturapress.com/2022/08/30/bbc-world-service-radio-drama-play-publications/

Benjamin Zephaniah Radio Plays https://kulturapress.com/2022/08/30/benjamin-zephaniah-radio-plays/

Cecil Lewis and Radio Plays https://kulturapress.com/2022/08/30/cecil-lewis-and-radio-plays/

Caryl Churchill and Radio Plays https://kulturapress.com/2022/08/30/caryl-churchill-and-radio-plays/

Cinema Television and Audio Drama https://kulturapress.com/2022/08/30/cinema-television-and-audio-drama/

Columbia Workshop and Radio Drama https://kulturapress.com/2022/08/30/columbia-workshop-and-radio-drama/

D G Bridson and Radio Plays https://kulturapress.com/2022/08/30/d-g-bridson-and-radio-plays/

Dylan Thomas Under Milk Wood and Radio Drama https://kulturapress.com/2022/08/30/dylan-thomas-under-milk-wood-and-radio-drama/

European Radio Drama https://kulturapress.com/2022/08/30/european-radio-drama/

German Radio Plays Hörspiel and the Avant Garde https://kulturapress.com/2022/08/30/german-radio-plays-ho%cc%88rspiel-and-the-avant-garde/

Giles Cooper and Radio Plays https://kulturapress.com/2022/08/30/giles-cooper-and-radio-plays/

Glossary of Audio and Radio Drama Terms and Vocabulary https://kulturapress.com/2022/08/30/glossary-of-audio-and-radio-drama-terms-and-vocabulary/

Harold Pinter and Radio plays https://kulturapress.com/2022/08/30/harold-pinter-and-radio-plays/

Independent Radio Drama Productions IRDP https://kulturapress.com/2022/08/29/independent-radio-drama-productions-irdp/

Kwame Kwei-Armah and Radio Drama https://kulturapress.com/2022/08/29/kwame-kwei-armah-and-radio-drama/

Lance Sieveking and Radio Drama https://kulturapress.com/2022/08/29/lance-sieveking-and-radio-drama/

Lee Hall and Radio Drama https://kulturapress.com/2022/08/29/lee-hall-and-radio-drama/

Louis MacNeice and Radio Plays https://kulturapress.com/2022/08/29/louis-macneice-and-radio-plays/

Mabel Constanduros and Radio Drama https://kulturapress.com/2022/08/29/mabel-constanduros-and-radio-drama/

Martin Esslin Radio Drama and National Theatre of the Air https://kulturapress.com/2022/08/29/martin-esslin-radio-drama-and-national-theatre-of-the-air/

Norman Corwin and Radio Drama https://kulturapress.com/2022/08/29/norman-corwin-and-radio-drama/

Oluwale Jeremy Sandford and Radio Drama https://kulturapress.com/2022/08/29/oluwale-jeremy-sandford-and-radio-drama/

One Act Plays and Radio Drama https://kulturapress.com/2022/08/29/one-act-plays-and-radio-drama/

Orson Welles and Radio Plays https://kulturapress.com/2022/08/29/orson-welles-and-radio-plays/

R C Scriven Radio Playwright https://kulturapress.com/2022/08/29/r-c-scriven-radio-playwright/

R E Jeffrey Pioneer Science Fiction Audio Playwright https://kulturapress.com/2022/08/29/r-e-jeffrey-pioneer-science-fiction-audio-playwright/

Radio Drama and Representation of the Holocaust and Final Solution https://kulturapress.com/2022/08/29/radio-drama-and-representation-of-the-holocaust-and-final-solution/

Radio and Audio Drama Academic Studies https://kulturapress.com/2022/08/29/radio-and-audio-drama-academic-studies/

Roy Williams and Radio Drama https://kulturapress.com/2022/08/29/roy-williams-and-radio-drama/

Sir Lenny Henry and Radio Drama https://kulturapress.com/2022/08/29/sir-lenny-henry-and-radio-drama/

Tanika Gupta and Radio Plays https://kulturapress.com/2022/08/29/tanika-gupta-and-radio-plays/

Winsome Pinnock and Radio Drama https://kulturapress.com/2022/08/29/winsome-pinnock-and-radio-drama/

Radio Drama and Dramatising Classical and Modern Literature https://kulturapress.com/2022/08/29/radio-drama-and-dramatising-classical-and-modern-literature/

Richard Durham and Radio Drama https://kulturapress.com/2022/08/29/richard-durham-and-radio-drama/

Samuel Beckett and Radio Drama https://kulturapress.com/2022/08/29/samuel-beckett-and-radio-drama/

Tom Stoppard and Radio Plays https://kulturapress.com/2022/08/29/tom-stoppard-and-radio-plays/

Tyrone Guthrie and Radio Plays https://kulturapress.com/2022/08/29/tyrone-guthrie-and-radio-plays/

US Radio Drama History https://kulturapress.com/2022/08/29/us-radio-drama-history/

Writing and Making Audio/Radio Drama Books https://kulturapress.com/2022/08/29/writing-and-making-radio-drama-books/

Podcasting and Audio Drama https://kulturapress.com/2022/08/30/podcast-and-audio-drama/

BBC World Service African Plays 1973 https://kulturapress.com/2022/08/30/bbc-world-service-african-plays-1973-2/

Audio Crime Drama and Radio Detectives https://kulturapress.com/2022/08/30/audio-crime-drama-and-radio-detectives/

Radio Drama and Stage Theatre https://kulturapress.com/2022/08/30/radio-drama-and-stage-theatre/

Phyllis M Twigg – the BBC's first original radio dramatist https://kulturapress.com/2022/09/24/phyllis-m-twigg-the-bbcs-first-original-radio-dramatist/

Kathleen Baker aka John Overton – a prolific BBC radio playwright lost to history https://kulturapress.com/2022/12/28/kathleen-baker-aka-john-overton-a-prolific-bbc-radio-playwright-lost-to-history/

Eric Fraser – Radio Drama Artist and Illustrator https://kulturapress.com/2022/09/24/eric-fraser-radio-drama-artist-and-illustrator/

INDEX

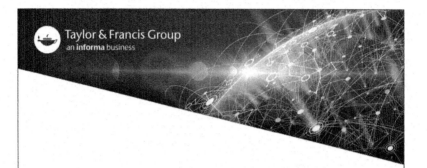